T0268148

A
HISTORY
OF THE
NETS

FROM TEANECK
TO BROOKLYN

RICK LAUGHLAND

THE
History
PRESS

Published by The History Press
Charleston, SC
www.historypress.com

Copyright © 2022 by Rick Laughland
All rights reserved

Front cover, clockwise from top left: Rick Laughland/NetsInsider.com; Steven Lipofsky/LipofskyPhoto.com; photo credit to Arthur Hundhause/ RememberTheABA.com; Steven Lipofsky/LipofskyPhoto.com; Steven Lipofsky/LipofskyPhoto.com.
Back cover, top left: Steven Lipofsky/LipofskyPhoto.com; *top center*: photo credit to Arthur Hundhausen/RememberTheABA.com; *top right*: Steven Lipofsky/ LipofskyPhoto.com; *bottom*: Steven Lipofsky/LipofskyPhoto.com.

First published 2022

Manufactured in the United States

ISBN 9781467147835

Library of Congress Control Number: 2022935409

Notice: The information in this book is true and complete to the best of our knowledge. It is offered without guarantee on the part of the author or The History Press. The author and The History Press disclaim all liability in connection with the use of this book.

All rights reserved. No part of this book may be reproduced or transmitted in any form whatsoever without prior written permission from the publisher except in the case of brief quotations embodied in critical articles and reviews.

This book is dedicated to my parents, my loving wife, Kristen, and our Mini Goldendoodle, Theo, for supporting me throughout this project and in all of life's endeavors. Additionally, I'd like to dedicate this to my entire family for sharing in many wonderful and not-so-wonderful Nets moments with me over the years while instilling in me a love for the game of basketball.

CONTENTS

CONTENTS

FOREWORD

On October 23, 1967, I went to the Teaneck Armory to watch my neighborhood friend and basketball hero, Tony Jackson, play for the New Jersey Americans in their first game in the newly established American Basketball Association. I had no idea this game would change my life forever.

When I walked into the gym, I noticed, standing in the corner, speaking with the team, head coach and General Manager, Max Zaslofsky. I knew Max quite well, having helped him out the previous season, when he organized a semi-pro AAU team, the ABC Freighters, financed by millionaire Arthur Brown and his ABC Freight Forwarding Company.

A native hoopster from our Brownsville neighborhood in Brooklyn who had played at Jefferson High School and St. John's University, as Tony also had done, Max went with familiar local players to fill out his new team's roster.

Instinctively, he signed up local collegiate players, starting with my very good friends from St. John's NIT and Holiday Festival Champs, All-American Bobby McIntyre, guards Bobby Duerr (my part-time housemate) and Dan Mascia (my best friend through high school and college) and forward Hank Cluess. Then, he added forward Joe Martini and center Albie Grant, classmates of mine at Brooklyn's Long Island University, as well as Harlem's Dexter Westbrook, a center from Providence College. The Freighters practiced and played their home games at nearby Xavier

Turetzky family collection.

Turetzky family collection.

Turetzky family collection.

Turetzky family collection.

Turetzky family collection.

High School on Manhattan's West Sixteenth Street. Max added in a few local players, including me, at almost every practice. It was a lot of fun for me, a gym rat.

This background came greatly into play when I met Tony and Max at the Teaneck Armory before the Americans' historic opening night game.

—Herb Turetzky

In memoriam of Herb Turetzky (December 19, 1945–April 4, 2022) for his fifty-four years as the Nets' official scorekeeper. Turetzky's career spanned over 2,200 games. (That is a certified record for professional basketball games scored in the *Guinness Book of World Records*.)

FOREWORD

In our 1975–76 championship season, it took every ounce of courage, willpower and fine play for us to beat the team with the best regular-season record. The Denver Nuggets' impressive 60-24 record did not intimidate us, despite the fact that we were 5 games back with a record of 55-29. What made us a bit nervous was the fact that the Nuggets had the home-court advantage and that we had lost 7 games during the season at the 18,000-seat McNichols Arena in Denver. In the first game of the championship finals, we showed up with a healthy and confident team, including the "Doctor," Julius Erving, who was ready to operate. We took a 9-point lead in the third quarter. Denver came back by the end of the fourth quarter and had a chance to win. Breathing in the 5,280-feet altitude in the "Mile High City" was a challenge. We fixed that by bringing oxygen tanks. During breaks, we put on oxygen masks and took in a little extra air to revitalize our lungs.

But the secret was not the tanks, but the Doctor, who scored several clutch baskets, including the final-second jumper from the right corner at the buzzer to seal the victory. We mobbed him and danced into the locker room with great joy. Doc scored 45 points, and we got our first win in Denver and the most important victory of the year. We lost the next game at Denver, then won 2 at home and traveled back to Denver up 3-1 in an attempt to clinch the series in Game 5. Not only did we lose a tough Game 5 to narrow the series lead to 3-2, we also found ourselves down 22 in the third quarter in our last home game of the series. The man of the hour in Game 6 was the late "Super John" Williamson. John came through when we needed his offense the most. He scored a crucial 16 points in the fourth quarter and totaled 24 in the second half. Our pressing defense and determination to win were just as important as the clutch baskets that Super John made. Lots of champagne, hooting and hollering in the locker room remain fresh in my mind. It was a glorious celebration.

Many people believe our 1973–74 team was the better of the New York Nets championship squads. Before the 1975–76 season, management traded away two of the team's All-Stars, Billy Paultz and Larry Kenon. That decision called for a great discussion, which continues today. Which of the two championship teams was the best? As to the answer, I leave that to our wonderful fans. Both teams were great. I was a lucky guy to be on both. I'm eager to tell you more, but this great book will do that for the fortunate readers.

—Brian Taylor

ACKNOWLEDGEMENTS

This book would not have been possible without the love and support of my family. Many thanks to Randy Zellea, a former member of the Nets' public relations team and founder of BackSportsPage.com, for coordinating scores of key interviews that appear throughout the work. All interviews within the book were conducted by the author unless otherwise noted. Reflections on the early ABA years and interviews from the Nets' ABA glory years are courtesy of Scott Tarter, cofounder of the Dropping Dimes Foundation. Nets photos spanning the final seasons in New Jersey are courtesy of Andrew Bernstein. Nets images upon the team's move to Brooklyn are courtesy of Dexter Henry. Photos that brought the Nets' ABA era to life are credited to Arthur Hundhausen, founder of RememberTheABA.com. Finally, I greatly appreciate the contributions of Steve Lipofsky of Lipofsky Photography for his stunning Nets photos that span his twenty-three-year career as an official NBA photographer.

INTRODUCTION

This story chronicles the nomadic history of the Nets—including the eight different arenas the franchise called home spanning nearly fifty-five years since its inception. Previously known as the New Jersey Americans, New York Nets, New Jersey Nets and (almost) New Jersey Swamp Dragons, the team has never had a shortage of new branding ideas or home courts to play on throughout the decades. The organization has endured its share of quirky marketing efforts and periods of prolonged financial and ownership instability but has managed to deliver many seminal moments during its ABA and NBA eras. This book uncovers the franchise's key highlights and lowlights along its circuitous journey from Teaneck to Brooklyn. Nets fans of all ages will gain a deeper appreciation of the team's roots and the improbable voyage that brought a professional sports franchise to the borough of Brooklyn for the first time since 1957.

no·mad·ic
/nōˈmadik/

adjective
roaming about from place to place aimlessly, frequently or without a fixed pattern of movement, wandering.

1

HUMBLE BEGINNINGS

1967–68 through 1969–70

A team nickname quickly abandoned, an endless search for a home arena and a one-game playoff forfeited—those are just a few of the many bizarre moments that marked the inaugural season of the franchise currently known as the Brooklyn Nets.

The team's initial campaign was indicative of the next five decades to follow, which saw the organization roam from arena to arena and city to city before eventually calling Brooklyn its now permanent home. The team's existence has been plagued by odd, unusual and even downright strange happenings, with several notable occurrences unfolding during its formative years as a charter member of the American Basketball Association (ABA), its rocky transitional period upon merging with the National Basketball Association (NBA) and the better part of the team's final few seasons playing as the New Jersey Nets.

The story of the Nets franchise started in 1967, when trucking magnate Arthur Brown envisioned turning the Amateur Athletic Union (AAU) team he was running, the ABC Freighters—unmistakably modeled on his trucking company, the ABC Freight Forwarding Corporation—into an expansion team that joined the ABA when it officially launched later that year.

Naturally, Brown sought to name his team the New York Freighters but later filed for a name change to the New York Americans. He aimed to play at Manhattan's 69th Regiment Armory. That deal fell through just three months before the ABA's opening day, due in large part to pressure from the New York Knicks on the Armory to back out over concerns related to territorial rights. The Knicks obstructing their crosstown rival's path reflected a theme throughout the Nets' continued pursuit to gain acceptance into the ABA and its eventual admission into the NBA nearly a decade later.

Brown was turned away at every possible attempt to find a suitable replacement to the 69th Regiment Armory for his team to play its home games. Nearly all potential venues in New York were either fully booked or simply unwilling to ruffle the feathers of the mighty New York Knicks by allowing a professional team, albeit an ABA squad, to play in the same city as the proud NBA franchise.

Still searching far and wide for a proper venue, Brown was quickly running out of time with the ABA season fast approaching, so he shifted his focus outside the confines of New York City and expanded his quest into New Jersey. In the back of his mind, Brown knew the clock was ticking.

The ABA published its schedule, and the Americans were slated to host the Pittsburgh Pipers on October 23, 1967, at a venue still to be determined. With just over a month until the season opener, Brown finally reached an agreement for the Americans to play their home games at the Teaneck Armory in New Jersey. Upon the landing in the Garden State, Brown filed for a name change, to the New Jersey Americans, and with that the first iteration of the current professional basketball franchise was born.

The Teaneck Armory was hardly a building designed to showcase the game of basketball, but it had served a historical significance before the Americans called it home in 1967. Built on thirteen acres as part of the New Deal, it was funded by the Works Progress Administration. Initially designed to hold the 104th Engineer Battalion of the National Guard, the sense of civic pride and national relevance it held was palpable, but transforming it into an adequate site to accommodate a professional basketball team was an entirely new and daunting challenge. While the Teaneck Armory drew an average of 2,054 fans per home game, the Americans were barely a blip on the radar in a market dominated by the Knicks.

One of Brown's first orders of business was to hire a head coach with name recognition in the New York metropolitan area and with an impressive enough résumé that he would garner the trust and respect of his players and staff. That man, former Knicks standout and St. Johns star Max Zaslofsky, became the first head coach and General Manager of the franchise.

Before attending college, Zaslofsky served in the U.S. Navy for two years during World War II. He played just one season of college basketball at St. Johns, leading the Red Storm to a 17-5 record and an appearance in the National Invitation Tournament (NIT). The Brooklyn native left college to join the Chicago Stags of the Basketball Association of America (BAA), the predecessor of the NBA.

At the age of twenty-one, Zaslofsky became the youngest player to receive All-NBA honors for the 1946–47 campaign, a record that remained intact until 2005, when it was broken by LeBron James. The very next season, at just twenty-two years and 121 days old, Zaslofsky became the youngest player to lead the league in scoring until Kevin Durant set a new mark in 2010.

A four-time All-NBA first-teamer, NBA All-Star and league scoring champion, Zaslofsky established a remarkable playing career throughout the 1940s and 1950s and became the obvious choice for Brown to appoint head coach.

For an entry fee of $30,000, an ABA franchise was awarded to Brown and partner Mark Binstein, while Mel Basel served as the team's Executive Director of Operations. The New Jersey Americans joined the Anaheim Amigos, Dallas Chaparrals, Denver Rockets, Houston Mavericks, Indiana Pacers, Kentucky Colonels, Minnesota Muskies, New Orleans Buccaneers, Oakland Oaks and Pittsburgh Pipers as the eleven teams comprising the upstart league. Each team played a 78-game schedule, and the ABA adopted a thirty-second shot clock, implemented the 3-point shot and used the signature red-white-and-blue basketball.

Viewed by many as the outlaw of the two leagues, the ABA established many innovative game rules, creative marketing ideas (some more hairbrained than others) and acrobatic players with a sense of pizzazz and style that mirrored the modern-day NBA game.

Scott Tarter, cofounder of the Dropping Dimes Foundation, a not-for-profit organization that aims to help former ABA players and their families who are experiencing financial or medical difficulties, shared his earliest recollections of the league and its contribution to the history of the game of basketball.

> *When the league was formed, there were no television contracts in the ABA. They had to figure out a way to compete, so they went out and got George Mikan, who was kind of the seminal representative of NBA greatness, to be the commissioner. Then they decided to have the iconic red, white and blue ball, which was Mikan's idea. One of the things he was quoted as saying is that he chose the red, white and blue ball because of the marketing potential. You could see the rotation on the ball better and all the players and coaches always said they needed to fill the arenas.*

The 1967–68 New Jersey Americans Inaugural Season Program Guide. *Photo credit to Arthur Hundhausen/RememberTheABA.com.*

They had goofy promotions and I think the ABA got a bad rap for that, but what they primarily did was open up the floor. They instituted the 3-point line, they had a much faster style of play, they allowed Afros, which weren't allowed in the NBA, they allowed beards, which weren't allowed in the NBA. The NBA, at that time, a lot of people don't understand this, but in the early days of the ABA, 1967–1971, the NBA was the slow league. They were all white-owned. They were all primarily white players. Their main focus was to get it in to the big guy, getting it in to Wilt Chamberlain, getting it in to Bill Russell, so it was a motion offense with lots of passing. Walking it up the floor in a slower, more conservative style of play. The ABA completely turned that on its head and that was very intentional. Where the ABA said, "We're going to take guys who love to play and who love to play athletically and we're just going to let them play." That's kind of what they did. The 3-point shot opened up the floor. It was a run and gun style. You would see some of those games being played in the 110s, 120s and 130s. In fact, the Indiana Pacers had a game where they scored 177 points in a single game. That was the record for the league. It wasn't that defense wasn't being played, it was that the offense was just a crazy, up-tempo style of play.

With virtually no local or national media coverage and sparsely attended games, the ABA faced an uphill climb to find a place in the minds and hearts of basketball fans across the country. The Wild West reputation that the league earned in its first few seasons cultivated a die-hard fan base, and the camaraderie between players and coaches became an unbreakable bond that lasted throughout the four-plus decades after the league ultimately folded.

On October 23, 1967, the New Jersey Americans opened their inaugural ABA season at the Teaneck Armory in front of a crowd of 3,089 against the Pittsburgh Pipers. Herb Turetzky, who served as official scorer in that game for the New Jersey Americans, remarkably served in that same capacity for the next fifty-four seasons. The Brooklyn native hardly knew at the time that a simple favor he did for a friend would evolve into a lifelong passion and create a legacy that made his name synonymous with the franchise's historic figures.

> *I went specifically to watch my neighborhood friend Tony Jackson, who I had followed straight through college in every one of his home games at the Garden for St. John's. Tony was the best coming out of Brownsville in Brooklyn that we had ever seen. After St. John's he got involved in that "scandal" and blackballed by the NBA. He bounced around in the ABL and anywhere else he could play in the Eastern League, and then the ABA came to life, and he was the Americans' first draft choice. I went there to see Tony play against Connie Hawkins, who I had seen play in high school and probably the best ever out of Brooklyn, really. My goal was to see those guys play against each other. When I walked in and saw Max and Tony and the three of us got together—all of us from the same neighborhood in Brownsville—we all went to Jefferson High School and knew each other. Max, I knew from the previous year from when he was coaching the AAU team, the ABC Freighters, and I was keeping score of their home games and helped him out at practices and worked out with the guys; they were friends of mine.*
>
> *We knew each other. Max knew what I was able to do. We started talking about the game and he said to me, "Herb, can you do us a favor? We need some help at the scorer's table, would you please score the game for us tonight?" So, I went and sat down at center court, and I was the official scorer that night and I never left that position. 2,200 some odd games that I've done and hopefully I'll be able to do it a long time more.*

Legendary hooper Connie Hawkins led the way for the Steel City in that game by dropping 34 points, while Dan Anderson paced New Jersey with an astonishing 41 points, a career high and still a franchise record for the most points scored by a center, during the 110–107 Americans loss. A former Augsburg College standout, Anderson made a terrific first impression on his teammates in the opener but wound up as the team's fourth-leading scorer that season behind Tony Jackson, Levern Tart (acquired via an in-season trade with Oakland) and Hank Whitney (signed midseason). St. John's product Bob McIntyre and Rutgers' standout Bobby Lloyd completed the rotation of impact players. The Americans featured a well-balanced lineup, with eight players averaging double digits in scoring during that first-year campaign.

New Jersey Americans' Tony Jackson contesting a layup against the Oakland Oaks during the ABA's inaugural 1967–68 season. *Photo credit to Arthur Hundhausen/ RememberTheABA.com.*

Tony Jackson, a St. Johns product and Brooklyn native, eventually had his number retired by St. Johns and was named an ABA All-Star in 1968. Just six years prior to his arrival with the Americans, Jackson, Doug Moe of UNC, Roger Brown of the University of Dayton as well students from NYU, North Carolina State and the University of Connecticut were implicated in the 1961 NCAA men's basketball point-shaving scandal. The major gambling scandal involved twenty-two different colleges and led to thirty-seven arrests. Hawkins, a New York City playground legend nicknamed the "Hawk," was never arrested or indicted but was expelled from Iowa and effectively blacklisted from the college ranks while acting NBA commissioner J. Walter Kennedy refused his entry into the league.

Early in the season, the Americans were barely staying afloat with a record of 4-7 and entered a home contest against the league-leading and eventual Western Division champion New Orleans Buccaneers, a squad coached by Babe McCarthy. New Orleans featured an even more perfectly assembled lineup than that of the Americans. The team fashioned six players averaging at least 13.4 points per contest, with its sixth-leading scorer, Larry Brown, dishing out a team high 6.5 assists per game. One of the team's captains, Brown evolved into a legendary collegiate and professional coach, was named a three-time ABA All-Star and was a 1969 ABA champion during his playing days. He pulled back the curtain and detailed his unusual first experience at the Teaneck Armory.

> *We played in Teaneck my first year and Max Zaslofsky was the coach. I remember the first game we played, I was the captain, and we went to half court and one of the referees was a guy named Monk Moyers, who was a roller derby referee. The other referee had an IZOD shirt on because one of the referees didn't show up. Max Zaslofsky called Babe McCarthy out with the captains and said, "This guy has basketball experience, don't worry about it. He'll be alright."*

In an upstart league, referee no-shows and double-booked arenas was the norm, but Brown's earliest memories of playing at the Teaneck Armory ranks near the top of his list of bizarre ABA moments. "You could never imagine that happening: a roller derby referee and Max Zaslofsky's best friend," remarked Brown. "I remember they had a girl that was Ms. Jersey Americans and I remember one of my teammates said, 'you know that girl ought to be so big that she could put the patch of all fifty states on.'"

BY ALL ACCOUNTS, THE Teaneck Armory was a less than stellar venue, and the pregame pageantry and in-game entertainment left a lot to be desired. Still, the strangest bit of Larry Brown's recounting involved being eventually ejected from the game. "I think I got in a fight with Bob Lloyd and we both got tossed and we were in the same shower room. That was an interesting first experience in the ABA. I loved that league."

The Americans, an inconsistent squad, reached the low-water mark of the year at 16-24 following a 107–104 defeat at the hands of the Houston Mavericks to make it nine losses in eleven contests. Zaslofsky rallied his crew to seven straight wins to pull to within a game of the .500 mark after the midseason rough patch. The final 29 games of the year were littered with hot and cold streaks: a 4-game losing skid, two 3-game winning streaks and two 3-game losing streaks mixed in with alternating wins and losses.

The Americans' lone season playing in Teaneck was full of challenges, and Arthur Brown spent much of the year searching for a permanent venue for the team to call home in New York. The final straw came when the Americans found themselves tied with the Kentucky Colonels for fourth place in the five-team Eastern Division at a record of 36-42 at the end of the regular season.

The Americans were scheduled to host a 1-game playoff, with the winning team advancing to the Eastern Division Semifinals. However, the Armory was already booked, with the circus being in town.

Arthur Brown, stuck between a rock and a hard place, was forced to find an alternate location. Luckily, he was able to book into the Commack Arena in Long Island to play host to the Colonels. When both teams arrived at the arena, it was discovered that the court was in unplayable condition, with missing floorboards and bolts, while the basket stanchions had no padding on them. The court was full of condensation from a Long Island Ducks hockey game that had been played the night before. It was also reported that one of the baskets was not at regulation height and thus provided a competitive disadvantage. The Colonels refused to play under those conditions, and ABA Commissioner George Mikan was left with no other choice but to declare a forfeit, awarding a 2–0 win to Kentucky. The Americans' season ended in even more bizarre fashion than it started.

1968–69

It became abundantly clear to Arthur Brown that the Teaneck Armory was not fit to be the long-term home of the New Jersey Americans, and thus he began forging a path to find a building adequately equipped to host a professional basketball game and in a city with enough fan support to fill the stands. Why on earth Brown decided to make the subpar Commack Arena—the same venue that caused the franchise to forfeit its first 1-game playoff—is still a mystery to many, including Turetzky.

I know he [Arthur Brown] was desperate to get the words "New York" accompanying our team's name. That was the franchise we were originally given. We were supposed to be the New York Americans. The Knicks really had almost total control of almost any venue within the five boroughs that their strength was such that anybody that Arthur Brown or his designees approached just flatly turned them down. They couldn't take a chance on getting the Knicks and MSG angry with them and they stretched out into Suffolk County, the closest you could get to New York City, and I don't know how or why they settled on the Commack Arena. For people in the city, it was an hour to an hour and a half to get out there. There really wasn't any suitable public transportation to get out there, it was really, really, out in the boondocks, but that's where he wound up.

Frustration mounted for Brown in the Garden State and precipitated his decision to pick up his franchise and head some fifty miles east, to Commack, New York. Long Island Arena (commonly known as the Commack Arena) opened in 1959 and served as the home to the Eastern Hockey League's (EHL) Long Island Ducks, as well as the New York Tapers of the National Alliance of Basketball Leagues (NABL), an eight-team league that lasted just one season and became known as the first league to adopt the 3-point shot. Brown took comfort in the fact that Long Island Arena had been home to a professional basketball team, albeit for the league's only complete season in 1962.

The 1968–69 New York Nets Media Guide. *Photo credit to Arthur Hundhausen / RememberTheABA.com.*

Along with a change in venue, a move across state borders from New Jersey to New York resulted in Brown ultimately rebranding the team with "New York" as the home state and adopting a new nickname. While "Americans" invoked a sense of civic pride in fans, Brown looked to take the marketability of his team to the next level on a regional basis. To that end, the franchise played off the popularity of the New York Jets and New York Mets in the metropolitan market and selected a name that rhymes with both. "Nets" became the new moniker for Brown's squad. The name capitalized on the likeness to "Mets" and "Jets" and incorporated a basketball-specific term into the team's name.

With a new nickname, home court and host city, the first iteration of many rebrandings to come was completed in the summer of 1968. Brown, who felt that his franchise could not sustain success in New Jersey, ultimately returned to the place he had originally set his sights on, New York.

Right after the Americans departed the Teaneck Armory, the venue was deemed unsafe due to lack of fire exits and was temporarily closed.

The move to Commack Arena in Long Island presented a sizeable opportunity for the newly minted Nets to carve out a place in the minds of basketball fans in the New York market. Long Island (or Commack) Arena had a capacity of 6,500 for basketball, nearly twice what Teaneck Armory could hold. A top media and fan market to go along with a substantially roomier arena were major advancements, but conditions were less than ideal during the Nets' one-year stay in Commack.

Larry Brown shared his recollections of the arena and the dangers the court setup posed to players. "It was an ice arena. They used to lay the floor right on ice. You did that in the NBA all the time, but they just had these cardboard slabs. I remember going out of bounds and if you hit one of those cardboard slabs you could slide into the boards and that could be a forty-foot slide. Guys were wearing overcoats on the bench, and that's where Rick [Barry] tore his ACL."

Suffice it to say that Arthur Brown and the Nets were hoodwinked into playing at a hockey-centric arena, and the forfeited playoff game against Kentucky was a bad omen of things to come.

The Nets' three leading scorers from the previous season—Tart (traded to Houston in January), Jackson (traded to Minnesota in November) and Anderson—played in just 63 games combined as the team finished dead last with a record of 17-61 in the eleven-team league. Barely treading water at 9-13 after a 112–107 victory over the Mavericks on December 13, the team would go on to lose 48 of its next 56 games. To make matters worse, attendance in Long Island paled in comparison to what the team was drawing in New Jersey. The Nets drew only 384 people on October 29 against the Rockets when they fashioned a 1-1 record early in the season. On December 25—granted, the Christmas holiday and a 10-17 record were factors—only 249 people came out to see the Nets take on the Rockets.

This scenario could not have been what Arthur Brown envisioned when he had big-city dreams of stealing some of the spotlight away from the Knicks in the metropolitan market.

One of the lone bright spots during a lost season for the franchise was the play of Duquesne product Willie Somerset. A former seventh-round pick of the Baltimore Bullets in the 1965 NBA Draft, the Farrell, Pennsylvania native struggled in his only NBA season. Undersized by both NBA and ABA standards, Somerset stood at just five feet, eight inches and weighed a mere 170 pounds.

With playing time and opportunities in the NBA dwindling, Somerset returned to his home state and joined the Scranton Miners for two seasons in the American Basketball League (ABL). After one year with Scranton, he joined the Houston Mavericks of the ABA and immediately made his presence felt in the scoring department, averaging 21.7 points per contest. After one and a half seasons littered with losses in Houston, Somerset was traded to the Nets with 31 games remaining in the 1968–69 season. The newly acquired point guard posted a team-high 24.1 points per game, but the real story was that New York finished 4-27 with him in the lineup, including 14 straight defeats to end the year. Somerset's shiny stat sheet proved to be nothing more than empty numbers for a pitiful team.

THE SILVER LINING IN the Nets' dead-last finish of 1968–69 meant that they were slated to hold the no. 1 overall pick in the 1969 ABA draft. Meanwhile, in the NBA, the Milwaukee Bucks held the top draft spot. The highly coveted college prospect Lew Alcindor, later known as Kareem Abdul-Jabbar, was the consensus choice to go to the highest bidder.

Both the Bucks and Nets were informed by Alcindor's representative, Sam Gilbert, that his client wanted to meet and listen to offers from each team before making his final decision.

According to Terry Pluto's book *Loose Balls* and referenced by NetsDaily, Pacers General Manager Mike Storen indicated that a $1 million certified check in addition to another $1 million over four years would be enough to get a deal done to make Alcindor a Net.

When Arthur Brown and Mikan went to meet with Alcindor and his agent, Mikan had the check with him but allegedly never took it out of his pocket.

According to Storen's account of Brown's heated exchange with Mikan in *Loose Balls*:

> Mikan said, "We decided that it wasn't necessary to give him our best offer. We figure when he comes back to us, then we'll use the check for the second round of talks."
> I screamed, "You did what?"

Mikan said, "Don't panic, we know that he's coming back. He's going to get the NBA's offer and he'll come back to us."

I said, "Is that what he said he would do?"

Mikan said, "Not exactly. The kid did say that he would make the decision."

I was really screaming. "You dumb SOBs, why did we spend all that money to find out all this information if you're not going to use it? How could you guys not give him the check?"'

The Nets eventually made a second offer of $3.2 million to Alcindor, but he declined, having already verbally committed to the Bucks. Just three months after the 1969 ABA draft was held in April, sans Alcindor officially in the player pool, Mikan announced his resignation as league commissioner. The former NBA great said that he was returning to Minneapolis to resume his law practice, but it is widely believed that the players, coaches, and executives ousted him for his mishandling of the Alcindor situation.

Alas, ABA fans and the Nets were cheated of their first chance of seeing a superstar don a Nets uniform.

Alcindor would evolve into arguably one of the NBA's greatest players by earning Rookie of the Year honors, garnering nineteen All-Star Game invitations, winning six MVP awards, being named a two-time NBA Finals MVP and becoming a two-time NBA scoring champion and four-time blocks champion.

The New York City native and former UCLA standout enjoyed an illustrious twenty-year NBA career, spending his first six seasons with the Bucks and final fourteen with the Lakers, winning five championships in Los Angeles and one in Milwaukee.

Mikan withholding his ace in the hole at the negotiating table with Alcindor impacted not only his own future, but it shifted the course of the Nets' franchise and the ABA's trajectory as well.

2

AN ABA DYNASTY IS BORN

1969–70 through 1975–76

The 1969–70 season ushered in many changes to the franchise, including a new owner, a new head coach, a new arena and a new cornerstone piece that would be an integral part of the 1974 and 1976 ABA Finals teams.

In May 1969, Arthur Brown agreed to sell the team to a group led by Roy Boe, founder of Boe Jests, a multimillion-dollar garment industry firm, for $988,000. Brown was never able to attract a marquee superstar to the franchise capable of generating enough buzz and excitement to fill an arena. His legacy was somewhat tainted by this fact, along with his inability to find a suitable, long-term arena for the team. As the club entered the third season of its existence, it was moving on to its second owner, second coach and second arena, further illustrating the franchise's penchant for acting like a rudderless ship navigating through rough seas.

Following a 17-61 campaign, Zasflosky officially announced his resignation from the team. The organization brought in UNC product York Larese to lead the coaching efforts.

Boe devised an unconventional agreement whereby Larese would serve as the team's coach for just the 1969–70 season and treasured collegiate head coach at St. Johns Lou Carnesecca would finish the final year of his contract and then join the Nets in 1970–71. Charles Theokas was hired by Boe as the team's General Manager. His tenure lasted only one season, but he would go on to have a second stint with the team in that very same role nearly a decade later.

Zaslofsky, at forty-one, was considered a young coach when his Nets' tenure started back in 1967, but Larese was just thirty-one when he took the reins of the franchise. Having been drafted by the NBA's St. Louis Hawks in 1960 and Chicago Packers in 1961, the newly hired leader had played just one total season in the NBA.

Larese was most remembered for being a part of Wilt Chamberlain's 100-point game after he was released by Chicago and signed by Philadelphia during the 1961–62 season. An accomplished collegiate guard at UNC, Larese was a sharpshooter who set the ACC record for free-throw percentage (86.8) in 1959–60. It was also a school record that stood for twenty-five years.

After bouncing around the ABL, and with things not panning out for him in the NBA, Larese entered the coaching ranks and inherited a Nets team with seven players aged twenty-three years or younger. An exuberant and youthful roster, along with a neophyte head coach, infused new energy into a franchise that had hit rock bottom the year before.

Along with new leadership and new blood, Island Garden Arena became the Nets' new home. Located in West Hempstead, New York, the facility was built by Arnold "Whitey" Carlson. It hosted professional boxing and wrestling matches, circuses, rodeos, boat shows, concerts and a bevy of other events. The Nets were fed up with being second-class citizens in their own building to the Long Island Ducks at Commack Arena.

Island Garden could expand its 5,200-seat capacity by adding additional seating for any potential playoff games or marquee regular-season matchups. The arena's layout was more akin to a high school gymnasium, but the flexibility to add seating and the fact that fans were right on top of the action made it a much more attractive option for Boe's franchise. The court was branded with a Nets logo at the tipoff circle to provide a sense of brand identity that had been missing during the franchise's first two seasons. Finally, fans and players could shed the overcoats they wore on the bench at chilly Commack Arena, and gone were the days when players suffered injuries slamming into the hockey boards.

The hope was that the move to Island Garden, a stay that spanned October 1969 to February 1972, would help stabilize the franchise and establish a loyal fan base in Long Island. This endeavor was an improvement over the one-year debacles in Teaneck and Commack, but it was not met without challenges. During the 1971 ABA Eastern Division Semifinals, the Nets faced yet another predicament, as they were unable to play any home games due to the arena being fully booked by other events. While the venue provided a more desirable and accessible location—being almost

Bill Melchionni won a pair of ABA Championships with the Nets in 1974 and 1976. *Photo credit to Arthur Hundhausen / RememberTheABA.com.*

thirty miles closer to New York City than Commack Arena was—it was still merely a stepping-stone on the way to the Nets becoming one of the marquee franchises in the ABA.

The course of the franchise began to gain upward momentum with the arrival of 76ers 1966 second-round draft choice Bill Melchionni. A local star at Villanova, the Pennsauken, New Jersey native enjoyed a distinguished collegiate career. In Melchionni's sophomore year, the Wildcats posted a record of 24-4 and reached the Eastern Regional of the NCAA Tournament before bowing out to Duke. In his junior year, Melchionni's club reached the finals of the NIT before falling to St. John's. In his final season at Villanova, he was named the MVP of the NIT by averaging over 30 points. He became the first player to receive MVP honors for a nonwinning team, as the Wildcats were ousted by NYU in the semifinals.

Melchionni's road to the NBA was a bit more tenuous than his decorated career at Villanova. It became immediately apparent to him that if he was to carve out a spot on the roster, he needed to develop his game. And that's exactly what he did. Melchionni spent his first summer with the AAU Phillips 66ers and took part in a world tour sponsored by the State Department of Pennsylvania. Melchionni, always a forward-thinker, planned to play abroad in Italy if he ultimately did not find a spot with the 76ers.

As luck would have it, Melchionni secured a spot on Philadelphia's bench, averaging ten minutes per game during the 1966–67 record-setting 68-win campaign. Just at the start of the 1967 NBA playoffs, Melchionni was called into military service and found himself in basic training when Philadelphia won the NBA finals. Philadelphia failed to repeat in 1967–68, and Melchionni took his talents to the Eastern Professional Basketball League and the Trenton Colonials for the 1968–69 season. The following year, Melchionni found a home in the ABA with the Nets and, upon signing with the team, had an immense impact.

Right out of the gate, Melchionni earned the starting point guard role and dished out a team-high 5.7 assists per contest while finishing third on the team in scoring average (15.2). The Nets enjoyed a 22-game improvement from the dismal 17-61 1968–69 campaign, to a 39-45 mark and a playoff berth.

Another key factor in the quick turnaround was Tart returning for a second stint with the club, as he was traded to the Houston Mavericks in exchange for Somerset the year before. Tart finished the 1968–69 season with Denver and was ultimately dealt back to the Nets for cash in an advantageous deal for New York. Tart was not only a clutch player but also embraced his role as the face of the team, always amenable to signing autographs with fans who flocked to him. With the floor general role filled, the Nets needed to rebuild their front lines and fortify their interior presence. Boe and company accomplished this with two trades, acquiring center Ed Johnson from the Los Angeles Stars for cash and, in a separate deal, receiving All-Star veteran power forward Les Hunter from the Miami Floridians for cash.

The 1970 ABA New York Nets Playoff Program. *Photo credit to Arthur Hundhausen / RememberTheABA.com.*

Boe's willingness to infuse capital into the team and actively pursue trades to improve the roster paid off tremendously in his first year at the helm. As expected for a young team with new players, there were early growing pains for New York. The team did not jell immediately, as it suffered an 8-game losing streak, only to follow with a 7-game winning streak and then a 7-game losing streak to produce a 14-23 record after 37 games. The squad fell to the low-water mark of the year at 21-31 following a loss to Kentucky on January 28. The Nets rounded out the regular season with a solid 18-14 stretch and clinched their first playoff berth in the three-year history of the team.

New York would engage in an epic 7-game series with Kentucky, and the more experienced Colonels squad outlasted the Nets. Louie Dampier led the charge, with the Colonels storming back to win the series after Melchionni's 39-point effort in Game 5 gave New York a 3–2 series edge. Kentucky was ousted by the eventual 1970 ABA champions, the Indiana Pacers, in the Eastern Division Finals. Despite the loss, the Nets were proving they were a young team on the rise and finding their way.

1970–71

While the 1969–70 campaign can be characterized as a crossroads moment that turned a rudderless franchise into a potentially powerful vessel, the 1970–71 season brought with it another major push into uncharted waters.

It was none other than another New Jersey native who helped the team reach new heights. That man, Rick Barry, changed the culture and perception of the team. The no. 2 overall pick in the 1965 NBA Draft, Barry was an instant star with the San Francisco Warriors, helping the team more than double its win total (from 17 to 35) en route to Rookie of the Year honors by posting 25.7 points and 10.6 rebounds per contest.

Barry propelled the Warriors to the 1967 NBA Finals, only to fall to Chamberlain and Philadelphia in 6 games. The sharpshooter averaged an astounding 40.8 point per contest in the finals, eclipsed by Michael Jordan twenty-six years later when he averaged 41 points per game against the Suns in 1993.

Following the season, Barry had a dispute with San Francisco's owner, Frankline Mieuli, over unpaid incentives in his contract. Considering his rift with ownership, Barry took a leap of faith and decided to accept a lucrative three-year, $500,000 contract with the Oakland Oaks to play for his former coach at Miami and father-in-law, Bruce Hale. Barry became one of the sport's highest-paid players. Included with the deal was a 15 percent stake in the franchise. A court dispute over his contractual obligation to San Francisco forced Barry to sit out the 1967–68 season, and he received a great deal of public backlash for jumping leagues. He was perceived by the fans as possessing selfish, greedy interests, despite many other professional players taking their talents from the NBA to the ABA.

Ironically, by the time Barry suited up for the Oaks, Hale had departed, and Alex Hannum was hired as the team's head coach. The 1968–69 season would be a Cinderella campaign, as the Oaks went on to win the ABA championship and Barry finished as league MVP runner-up despite being limited to just 35 games

Rick Barry facing the Pacers during the 1970–71 season. *Photo credit to Arthur Hundhausen / RememberTheABA.com.*

and missing the end of the year due to a knee injury. Ironically, Barry's injury came against the Nets at Commack Arena when he collided with Ken Wilburn and spilled into the cardboard slabs covering the hockey boards.

Hannum was named ABA Coach of the Year after defeating the Pacers, 4 games to 1, in the ABA Finals.

Despite all this success, the Oaks' home attendance was fledgling, averaging just 2,800 fans per game. Following the season, the team was sold by owner Pat Boone and announced its intentions to relocate to Washington, D.C., starting in the 1969–70 season. Barry was not keen on the move and attempted to return to the Warriors in the NBA but was ultimately barred in the courts again, as he had to fulfill and honor his contract, this time in the ABA.

After Barry sat out the first 32 games, the ABA forced him to join the team for the remainder of the season. The newly formed Washington Caps were defeated, 4 games to 3, in the Western Division Semifinals by the Rockets. Barry, who poured in a whopping 52 points in Game 7, was ejected in the closing seconds for fighting with Rockets players. It marked the last time he would play for the franchise.

Nets coach Lou Carnesecca organizing his club during a timeout during the 1970–71 campaign. *Photo credit to Arthur Hundhausen / RememberTheABA.com.*

Following the season, the Caps became the Virginia Squires, and Barry was even less enthusiastic about this latest relocation compared to the last move, from Oakland to Washington, D.C.

Barry denounced the NBA amid his dispute and drew a line in the sand between him and the Squires. Virginia sought trade partners to find the disgruntled star a new home, and on September 1, 1970, it traded Barry to the Nets in exchange for a draft pick and $200,000.

Barry's tumultuous seesawing between the two leagues finally saw him land with the Nets for a two-year stretch that was marked by deep playoff runs and the franchise's first ever trip to the ABA Finals.

After fulfilling the final year of his contract at St. Johns, Carnesecca, a future Hall of Famer, took the reins of the Nets with Barry as his cornerstone player. Boe entrusted Carnesecca with leading the coaching efforts while also doubling as the team's General Manager, a role he would fill for the next three years.

With a keen eye for talent, Carnesecca set his sights on his former player while at St. Johns, Billy Paultz. Paultz, a six-foot, eleven-inch scoring and rebounding machine, was originally drafted by San Diego in the seventh round of the 1970 NBA Draft and Virginia in the 1970 ABA draft. Paultz signed with the Squires, who ultimately traded his rights to the Nets in exchange for a draft choice and cash. Paultz evolved into a key member of the 1974 championship team and earned the nickname "Whopper" for his husky frame and unorthodox playing style.

With Carnesecca leading the charge, Barry filling the role as star player, Paultz cleaning the glass and Tart and Melchionni just starting to approach the prime of their careers, the makings of a special collection of talent started to form.

Surprisingly, the Nets somewhat underachieved, hovering below .500 for the majority of the 1970–71 campaign while compiling just three winning streaks of 4 games or more. Barry was limited to 59 regular-season games with lingering knee issues but returned to near full health in time for the playoff run. He set an ABA Nets record with 53 points on January 15 in a loss to Pittsburgh. The Nets finished 40-44 to cling on to third place in the ABA's Eastern Division.

The playoffs pitted the Nets against the Squires, Barry's former squad and now nemesis. Barry went on a scoring rampage, averaging 33.7 points per contest in the series to lead all scorers, including two separate 40-plus-point outings in Games 3 and 6. Despite both Melchionni and Paultz adding over

The New York Nets' 1971 ABA Playoff Guide. *Photo credit to Arthur Hundhausen / RememberTheABA.com.*

20 points per game apiece, the Nets fell in 6 games to the 50-win Squires, who would eventually be upset in the Eastern Divison Finals by Kentucky.

The Nets were forced to play Games 3 and 4 at Hofstra Physical Fitness Center and Game 6 at Felt Forum, a theater that was part of Madison Square Garden, due to Island Garden Arena being booked by other events.

For the second consecutive year, New York made the playoffs but failed to advance, even with the addition of a star player and proven coach. Things would change for the better, and the Nets would soon exorcise their playoff demons.

1971–72

The 1971–72 campaign marked the first time the Nets finished the ABA's regular season with a winning record. The team advanced deep into the playoffs and reached a new plateau: the ABA Finals. The nucleus of the team remained intact, but two major additions to the roster proved to be critical in helping elevate the squad into championship contention.

Enter John Roche, a six-foot, three-inch point guard out of the University of South Carolina, originally drafted by the Suns in the NBA and the Colonels in the ABA in 1971. The Nets ultimately obtained his rights from Kentucky. Not only was Roche an integral part of the ABA Finals qualifying team that year, but he also received ABA All-Rookie First Team honors. Roche's signature mop-top hairstyle drew comparisons to the NBA's Pete Maravich and captured the imagination of fans.

Roche's physical resemblance to a member of The Beatles was in stark contrast to his hard-nosed playing style and indominable will. He was never known to back down from a fight. In fact, the ballhandler was a notorious instigator and was right in the thick of several brawls throughout the course of his pro career. Born on the East Side of Manhattan, where he attended LaSalle Academy High School, he then graduated from the University of South Carolina. Roche was prepared to join the NBA's Phoenix Suns before Carnesecca convinced him to join the Nets, instead.

Additionally, a former ABA champion with the 1968 Pipers made all the difference for the Nets that season in controlling the paint and dominating the boards. Thomas "Trooper" Washington came over from the Floridians and emerged as the team's fifth-leading scorer, averaging 11.0 points, and finished the regular season second on the team in rebounds behind Paultz's 12.5 at 9.4 per contest. Paultz set a franchise record with 33 rebounds on December 17 against Dallas in a noteworthy moment at Island Garden Arena.

In the fifth year of the franchise's existence, the Nets were in the process of moving to their fourth different city and fourth different home arena. The traveling circus—otherwise known as the Nets—moved to Nassau Veterans Memorial Coliseum in Uniondale, New York, during the second half of the 1971–72 season. Opened in 1972 as part of Mitchel Field, a former U.S. Army Air Force base, the sixty-three-acre complex held its first event when the Nets took on the Pittsburgh Condors on February 11, 1972. The capacity of the arena reached 13,000 to 15,000 fans, depending on the event, and the 44,000-square foot arena served as the team's home from 1972 to 1977.

Brian Taylor, originally selected in the second round of the 1972 NBA Draft by the Seattle, joined the Nets after they made him their second-round pick in the 1972 ABA draft. The point guard eventually served as the maestro to the franchise's two ABA championship teams. The former Princeton star followed New York from afar throughout the 1971–72 season prior to joining the team that summer and shared his earliest recollection of the Nets' first two seasons at Nassau Coliseum.

They're coming off the previous year where they lost in the finals. I went to a couple of those games, so after making the decision whether I was going to stay at Princeton or leave, I thought man I'm going to have the opportunity to play in front of all those crazy fans and they had good attendance during that championship series. I'm anticipating that we would have that type of enthusiasm coming into my rookie year, but it just seemed like there were a lot of empty seats compared to what it was. It seemed so humongous. I'm coming from playing in the Jadwin Gym, a couple thousand capacity, which I played in big arenas in college, but nothing like the Nassau Coliseum. With it not being filled, maybe half with 12,000–13,000 capacity back then, can you imagine walking in to 5,000–6,000 people very excited and being like, "Wow where are the fans?" It seemed to me it was always a challenge even at Nassau Coliseum. They filled it up for hockey, but we had our challenges, I don't think they ever had a year where there were 1,000 season-ticket holders or things like that. Maybe you get a couple special games where Kentucky would come in or David Thompson during his rookie year, but I was just surprised with how many people were not there. It was a big arena and it was only half-filled, but I was still nervous. I was coming off the bench and I wasn't a starter back then. I'm sitting on the bench nervous, and saying maybe I'm happy it wasn't packed because what would I do if it there were 12,000–13,000 people there and I make a mistake? Then, I'm nervous. Fans were overly critical. They'd be yelling and screaming at me.

The Nets were 27-31 prior to their first home game in Uniondale against Pittsburgh on February 11 and finished the final 26 games with a mark of 17-9, going 12-4 in their new building.

New York was pitted against the heavily favored and top-seeded 68-win Colonels in the ABA's Eastern Division Semifinals. The Nets stole Games 1 and 2 in Kentucky as Barry went off for 50 and 35, respectively, while Roche dumped in 31 in each contest. The ABA's top flight offense—the

John Roche led the Nets to an upset win over the Colonels in the 1972 ABA Playoffs. *Photo credit to Arthur Hundhausen / RememberTheABA.com.*

Colonels—scored 100-plus points in just 3 of the 6 games in the series, and New York closed out Kentucky in Game 6 in front of a raucous home crowd of 11,533. The playoff series win was the first in the history of the franchise and a seminal moment for a team that had more embarrassing incidents than proud ones at that point. With a first-ever winning regular-season record, a playoff-round win and a bustling home crowd, optimism was swirling around Long Island's club. It was clear that a winning culture was being established, with even more exciting times still ahead.

The Nets finally ousted a Kentucky team that had bested them in the 1970 playoffs and next faced a Virginia squad that had sent them home packing during the 1971 playoff run. Virginia was led by none other than eventual ABA poster child Julius Erving.

Erving's place in the Mount Rushmore of ABA and NBA stars is unquestioned, yet his role as the Nets' nemesis during the early stages of his pro career is often overlooked.

Despite being featured in a Squires uniform through the ABA's marketing efforts, Barry never suited up for a game with the team in Virginia, yet his trade to the Nets continued to link him and Erving. Barry's arrival served as the impetus for the Nets' ascension in the ABA's power rankings, and Erving's eventual landing in New York ushered in a pair of league championships.

It did not take long for Erving to make a name for himself in the ABA, where he developed a reputation as a ferocious dunker with freakish athletic ability. The former University of Massachusetts star left after his junior year to join Virginia and scored 27.3 points per game, made the All-ABA Second Team and the ABA All-Rookie Team, led the league in offensive rebounds and finished just behind Artis Gilmore for the ABA Rookie of the Year Award.

While the Nets were a hot team that knocked off the ABA's best team record-wise in the opening round of the 1972 playoffs, the overwhelming feeling was that Virginia would make quick work of New York. The first two games of the series fit that narrative, as the Nets were blown out by 47 points in Game 1 and defeated by 9 points in Game 2. Erving posted game highs of 26 and 38, respectively.

Back in Long Island, the Nets edged the Squires, 119–117 in Game 3 and 118–107 in Game 4, with Barry and Roche shouldering the scoring load. Virginia held serve at Hampton Coliseum by capturing a 116–107 victory, with Erving leading the way with 24 points, 8 assists and an astonishing 32 rebounds. A return trip to Uniondale for Game 6 saw the Nets win a 146–136 shootout to force Game 7 with Barry, Roche and Paultz combining to score 113 points. New York then needed to win its first road game of the series if it hoped to clinch the franchise's first trip to the ABA Finals.

Three days after the frenetic pace of Game 6, Game 7 was the lowest-scoring game of the series, as the Squires shot 37.4 percent from the field to the Nets' 43.2 percent clip. Despite Erving scoring a game-high 35 and grabbing 20 rebounds, the Nets pulled off yet another shocking upset to take Game 7, 94–88, setting up a meeting with the Indiana Pacers in the 1972 ABA Finals.

At that time, the Pacers were the crown jewel of the ABA, making their third appearance in the finals and seeking to win their second ABA championship in the brief five-season existence of the league. Tarter of ABA's Dropping Dimes Foundation recalled the 1972 ABA Finals and the Nets-Pacers rivalry:

The Colonels beat the Pacers in the 1975 ABA finals, but the Nets and the Pacers had that epic ABA final in 1972, and the reason it was such a huge series to the Pacers is because Rick Barry was on the team. Barry was playing for the Oakland Oaks when the Pacers played in their very first ABA championship series in 1969 and they lost. When the Pacers played the Nets in the 1971–1972 season, that was just a crazy series.

Led by Mel Daniels and head coach Slick Leonard, Indiana finished the regular season 47-37 and outlasted the Rockets and Stars each in grueling 7-game series, with the final games of each series being decided by two points and four points, respectively. Daniels, Roger Brown and the eventual 1972 playoffs MVP, Freddie Lewis, headlined a team littered with tenacious defenders. The Pacers and Nets alternated wins and losses in the first 5 games of the series as Indiana's championship pedigree and experience proved to be the difference in a nail-biting 100–99 victory in Game 5 to put New York on the brink of elimination.

In the closing seconds of Game 5, a shrewd Pacers defensive play followed by a Nets' offensive gaffe ended up costing New York a chance to take a stranglehold on the series. Roche left the game with an injury, and backup floor general Oliver Taylor had the ball stolen by Lewis with the Nets holding a 1-point lead with under thirty seconds remaining. Taylor was forced to foul Lewis to prevent an uncontested go-ahead layup. Lewis hit both free throws to give the Pacers a 100–99 lead with nine seconds left. With one last gasp, Washington inbounded the ball to Barry, who had an open midrange jumper, but the sharpshooter started his motion before he secured the ball and it slipped through his hands and trickled out of bounds for a turnover.

Just like that, the Nets let a golden opportunity go by the wayside. That became an iconic moment in Pacers history and a regrettable one for the Nets and their fans. Deflated after the loss and without Roche in the lineup due to injury, the Nets fell, 108–105, in Game 6 as the Pacers captured their second ABA championship.

That game marked Barry's last with the Nets franchise. On June 23, 1972, a United States District Court judge issued a preliminary injunction to forbid the star from playing for any other team than Golden State after his contract ended with the Nets. On October 6, Barry was subsequently released by the Nets and rejoined the NBA ranks to play with the Warriors. While Barry's two-year tenure with the franchise failed to produce a championship, his presence elevated the franchise to unprecedented heights. Melchionni, and Paultz were named to the All-ABA First Team and Roche, the All-ABA Rookie First Team that season, setting the stage for the Nets to evolve into a powerhouse team even with Barry gone.

1972–73

Other than Barry's departure, there were few significant changes to the roster heading into the 1972–73 campaign, but drafting Taylor (ABA Rookie of the Year, 1973) out of Princeton proved to be a decision that Carnesecca and Boe would not soon regret. The rookie hit the ground running, averaging 15.3 points, 2.8 assists and 3.2 rebounds per game. ABA veteran and former 1970–71 ABA All-Star George Carter was acquired from Carolina for a draft choice and cash and transitioned seamlessly into the role as the team's leading scorer at 19.0 points per game.

Coming off a berth in the 1972 ABA Finals, New York collectively plummeted to a fourth-place finish in the ABA's Eastern Division without Barry's playmaking and leadership. After 20 games, New York earned 10 wins but posted a 20-44 mark thereafter. The Nets rounded out the year with a record of 30-54 and were easily ousted by Carolina, 4 games to 1, in the Eastern Division Semifinals. Taylor gained some much-needed playoff experience. Carter led all Nets scorers with 21.2 points per game in the playoff round loss. Taylor and Jim Chones were named to the ABA All-Rookie Team.

1973–74

Following the 1972–73 season, Carnesecca returned for a second stint at St. Johns and Boe assumed General Manager duties. The Nets had yet to fully replenish the talent in their player pool after Barry left for the NBA and were in dire need of a cornerstone piece to lead them back to ABA prominence. Ironically, that man was the same adversary the Nets had bested in the 1972 playoff run, when he was with the Squires.

Before Erving ultimately landed with New York, it appeared the Nets were going to watch another prized player head for greener pastures in the NBA. In 1969, the Nets famously lost out on the chance to draft Alcindor when Mikan refused to offer the lucrative deal it required to bring him to the ABA. Now, a contract dispute almost saw Erving land with Alcindor and Oscar Robertson with the Bucks in the NBA. Thankfully for the Nets, history did not repeat itself.

Following the 1972 playoff loss to the Nets, Erving, under NBA rules, became eligible for the 1972 NBA Draft and was selected twelfth overall by Milwaukee. Before the draft took place, Erving actually signed a $1 million contract with the Hawks that included a $250,000 signing bonus.

Dr. J glides to the rim during the 1974 ABA Finals win over the Stars. *Photo credit to Arthur Hundhausen / RememberTheABA.com.*

The Hawks, Bucks and Squires became embroiled in a messy legal dispute. NBA Commissioner J. Walter Kennedy contended that the Bucks owned Erving's rights and fined Atlanta $25,000 per game. The Hawks appealed the commissioner's ruling, but the owners upheld his decision. On October 2, 1972, Judge Edward Neaher issued an injunction that prohibited Erving from playing with any team other than the Squires in the ABA. This was not the outcome that Kennedy, Erving, the Hawks or the Bucks were expecting, but it ended up being a critical step in keeping the ABA's poster child within the league and paved the way for his golden years with the Nets.

Despite Erving going on to average a career-best 31.9 points per game in 1972–73, the fledging Squires franchise elected to sell Erving's contract rights to the Nets. Only a handful of athletes have left an indelible impact on a league and team the way Dr. J. did in the ABA and with the Nets. Erving was a basketball legend, a cultural icon and a trendsetter all wrapped into one. The Long Island native's agility and fluidity on the court, along with his suave persona and glamorous style in the public sphere, transformed him into a sports and fashion icon. So, when Erving signed an eight-year, $2.8 million deal to join New York, the sense of excitement and enthusiasm was palpable. Turetzky depicts a debonaire and gracious player whose game and personality were truly infectious.

> *I'm just sitting here smiling ear to ear. That's the feeling I get every time Doc comes into my mind. He was the greatest as a player, as a person, as a personality. He had no flaws. He wore a white Adidas warm-up suit that he traveled to some games in, and I've never seen anything like that in all the years I've watched guys travel in and out of arenas. Doc, in a white warm-up suit, so long and so slender, with bellbottom pants on was just magnificent. Then, he would get into his white Avanti Studebaker sports car with a wing on it which was beautiful. That was his personality, he was just smooth.*

The deal to bring Erving to the Nets was far from straightforward, as the Nets had to send $750,000, George Carter and the rights to Kermit

"Super John" Williamson was a clutch performer during the Nets 1973–74 ABA championship season. *Photo credit to Arthur Hundhausen / RememberTheABA.com.*

Washington to the Squires with Willie Sojourner heading to New York. Not only was New York sending a boatload of cash to Virginia, but it was also responsible for reimbursing the Hawks for the fines that had accumulated for having Erving on their roster during the contract dispute. Atlanta ultimately received $450,000 and the rights to draft compensation if the rumored ABA-NBA merger came to be. It was a hefty price to pay for one player, but the Nets' brass knew what kind of a game-changer Erving would be for the franchise. His presence on the team proved to be the tipping point in a process that culminated in the team's first championship season.

While Erving is looked upon fondly and with great admiration in Nets' lore, it was a twenty-two-year-old New Haven, Connecticut native who made a world of difference in catapulting the squad to new heights. John Williamson—"Super John," as most fans knew him—earned his moniker with outstanding play as a rookie. The New Mexico State product was eligible for the 1973 NBA Draft and was selected by the Hawks in the sixth round at no. 96 overall. Williamson was then cut by Atlanta and signed a free-agent deal to join New York prior to the start of the 1973–74 campaign. The rookie's feathery touch from the outside saw him shoot just under 50 percent from the field to help him earn a place on the ABA's All-Rookie First Team alongside Larry Kenon, who was acquired from Memphis in exchange for Jim Ard and Johnny Baum.

KENON AND WILLIAMSON WERE key cogs in New York's championship machine. Just one year prior to his arrival in Long Island, Kenon led the Cinderella-story Memphis Tigers men's basketball team all the way to the NCAA finals, where it fell to legendary coach John Wooden's undefeated UCLA team, 87–66. Kenon was the school's leading scorer and was selected by the Detroit Pistons in the 1973 NBA Draft and by the Memphis Tams in the ABA, but the Alabama native's draft rights were ultimately secured by the Nets in the trade with Memphis on September 20.

Following Carnesecca's departure from the ABA to return to his post with the Red Storm, Kevin Loughery became the fourth coach in the seventh year of the team's existence. A Brooklyn, New York native, Loughery had spent nine seasons with the Baltimore Bullets, two with the Philadelphia 76ers and two with the Detroit Pistons during his playing career. Loughery joined the coaching ranks in 1972–73 with Philadelphia and presided over the final 31 games of the season after Roy Rubin was fired with a 4-47 record. That Sixers team holds the distinction as the worst team ever record-wise in NBA history at 9-73.

In exhibition games against their NBA counterparts in 1973–74, Loughery's Nets exacted a small measure of revenge by defeating the Sixers twice, the Bullets and the Knicks before losing to Boston for a 4-1 preseason mark.

Despite success against NBA clubs, Loughery's transition to the ABA hit a major snag in the regular season. The Nets endured a whopping 9-game losing skid amid a 4-10 start. New York started clicking on all cylinders to the tune of 51-19 to wrap up regular-season play and finished an ABA-best 55-29.

Fan interest in the team was at an all-time high, with attendance rising over 30 percent from the year prior. Not coincidentally, the Nets games were heard on WIIN radio and televised on WOR, as the broadcast partners helped increase the team's visibility and notoriety in the New York market.

Erving was the team's leading scorer, shot blocker and assist man. He also led the team in steals and field goal percentage. Not only had a player who fans idolized finally landed with the Nets, but Erving's MVP-caliber play also left little doubt that he was the league's best all-around talent. After 50 games, Roche was traded back to the team that had drafted him, Kentucky, for Mike Gale and Wendell Ladner.

Erving led the way in scoring at 27.4 per contest, followed by Paultz's 16.4, Kenon's 15.9, Williamson's 14.5 and Taylor's 11.1. New York was a well-oiled machine and primed for a first-round matchup with Erving's former club, the Squires.

The Nets made quick work of Virginia, ousting them in 5 games with an average margin of victory of almost 18 points. Erving and company's high-flying offense met little resistance in the semifinal round. Many predicted that New York would face a tougher battle against the ABA runners-up from a season ago in Kentucky. To the contrary, the Nets breezed through to the conference championship round with a clean four-game sweep to the tune of a nearly 12-point-per-game margin of victory.

It was on to the ABA Finals, the second such appearance for New York in three seasons. Taylor, the team's floor general and fiery leader, reflected on the 1974 ABA Finals matchup with the Utah Stars and an altercation that helped shift the tenor of the series in his team's favor.

We were playing Utah my first championship year, and my job was to slow down Ron Boone. My former teammate Coop Washington used to tell me, "You have to protect yourself." He was a mentor and a veteran. He would always tell me things to do. I didn't realize what he was saying until I frustrated Ron so much that he wound up and threw a right-hand jab and knocked two of my teeth out. Then I tried to get back at him, but they held me back. He got the worst of it because he got an infection in his right hand right above his knuckle. So, the next morning I'm at the dentist getting my teeth fixed and I think we played the day game after, so we fly out to Utah and I'm still playing but he's got an infection in his shooting hand. So, the next year when the two

Brian Taylor was the Nets' starting point guard for both ABA championships in 1974 and 1976. *Photo credit to Arthur Hundhausen/RememberTheABA.com.*

leagues merge, I'm offered this contract to go to Kansas City and they draft Ron [Boone] *in the dispersal draft. We ended up being roommates the next year in Kansas City.*

Even the core of Jimmy Jones, Willie Wise and Ron Boone could not derail the Nets' championship run. Erving set the early tone for the series with a virtuoso Game 1 performance by dropping 47 points. Kenon grabbed 20 rebounds to pace New York

In Games 2 and 5, Nassau Veterans Memorial Coliseum reached maximum fan capacity at 15,934 as the Nets were developing a core fan base. Despite the team's success, the ABA's future was uncertain, and many basketball fans in New York were still riding high off the Knicks' pair of titles in 1970 and 1973.

The Nets had come a long way from forfeiting home playoff games, flip-flopping team nicknames and fashioning a rotating carousel of coaches and

Nets coach Kevin Loughery celebrates with fans after winning the 1974 ABA title. *Photo credit to Arthur Hundhausen/RememberTheABA.com.*

front-office executives. New York ousted Utah in Game 5, 111–100, to take its first league title, officially validating a groundbreaking campaign.

All the hard labor was finally bearing fruit, and the trajectory of the Nets during their ABA era shifted from a mere sideshow to the league's main attraction. Every young basketball fan wanted to be like Erving, and while a championship parade fit for a king was well deserved for the hometown Nets, the title was not exactly met with all the pomp and circumstance akin to the Knicks' ticker-tape parades down the Canyon of Heroes just a few years earlier.

Nevertheless, the Nets were a seven-year-old franchise just beginning to establish their roots in Long Island and starting to cultivate a loyal fan base that was steadily growing in concert with the team's success.

1974–75

The nucleus of the Nets' championship team returned in 1974–75 and was primed to defend its title. While the cast of characters remained largely the same, a tangible feeling of discord festered during that season and came to a head at the end of the campaign. Dave DeBusschere joined the front office to assist Boe prior to the title run and was promoted to General Manager ahead of the 1974–75 campaign.

Heading into the year, prognosticators predicted that the Nets would capture a 61-23 record to finish first in the league. Things looked to be trending in that direction as New York strung together ten straight wins to reach 22-9 following a dismantling of the Pacers on December 21.

Erving was part of a historic contest against San Diego on February 14. He tallied 63 points in a quadruple-overtime, 176–166 loss that held the distinction as the highest-scoring game in ABA history. Eight days later, Erving torched the Conquistadors again for 51, including 19 of 23 from the field and 13 of 15 from the line and grabbed 19 rebounds.

The team had all the makings of a candidate to repeat, toppling some of the ABA's elite teams along the way, including Kentucky, which finished with an identical mark of 58-26 at the end of regular season play.

The Nets and Colonels played a tiebreaker to determine the winner of the Eastern Division. Kentucky outdueled the Nets, 108–99, behind Gilmore's 33 rebounds and 28 points in front of nearly fourteen thousand fans at Freedom Hall in Louisville.

Led by legendary coach and basketball lifer Hubie Brown, the Colonels took the momentum from the tiebreaker and breezed through Memphis in 5 games in the Eastern Division Semifinals, the Spirits of St. Louis in 5 games in the Eastern Division Finals and the Pacers in 5 games in the ABA Finals to capture the franchise's first—and last—title.

The 1974–75 New York Nets Yearbook. *Photo credit to Arthur Hundhausen/RememberTheABA.com.*

The Nets, by contrast, went into a tailspin and were ousted by a St. Louis squad they went 11-0 against in the regular season and who had won just 32 games led by Marvin Barnes, Freddie Lewis and Maurice Lucas and coached by Bob MacKinnon. The Nets won Game 1 with a fourth-quarter rally and appeared to be on their way to the eventual clash with Kentucky in the Eastern Division Finals. The Spirits had other plans, capturing the next 4 games to take the series, including a dramatic come-from-behind victory in Game 5 as they turned a 10-point fourth-quarter deficit into a thrilling 1-point victory. Taylor reflected on what went awry during the playoff run and the problems behind the scenes with team chemistry that facilitated an off-season roster shake-up.

> *Going into the next year we were just as good, but something happened going toward the last quarter of the year, the final home stretch there was a little bit of discord in terms of who was the man. Doc was the man. Everyone had a hard time accepting that because there's only one ball and some guys began to think they should get more shots and we didn't play as well as we could have. We felt we could get back-to-back. We had the talent and we had what was necessary for us to win, but you've got to be willing to sacrifice and play together. St. Louis slipped in on us and got us that second year and that's why there were changes. I think a big part of being a championship team is you must have people willing to accept their roles.*

For his efforts, Erving was named co-winner with Indiana's George McGinnis of the ABA's MVP Award.

In the aftermath of the season, a tragic event took place involving Nets forward Wendell Ladner. On June 24, Ladner was among 133 passengers who perished aboard Eastern Air Lines Flight 66 as a microburst created windshear, causing the plane to crash on approach to John F. Kennedy International Airport. At the time, the crash was the deadliest in U.S. history. To honor his memory, New York's longtime trainer, Fritz Massmann, ensured that Ladner's no. 4 jersey was not issued to another Nets' player for the next seventeen years.

1975–76

It's not often that trading three of your team's top six players improves your chemistry drastically, but that was exactly the impact that unloading Kenon, Paultz and Gale to San Antonio had during the Nets' off-season.

In the first transaction, involving Kenon, the Nets received Swen Nater, who was eventually traded midseason with Bill Schaeffer to Virginia for Jim Eakins. The Nets then traded Gale to San Antonio for cash. He went on to have an illustrious career in San Antonio.

The Nets acquired power forward Rich Jones in exchange for Paultz in a separate five-player deal involving Chuck Terry, Kim Hughes and Rob

Warren joining from the Spurs. ABA journeyman Ted McClain (joined midseason) rounded out the revamped complementary players added to the core of Erving, Taylor, Williamson, Melchionni and now Jones.

Many of these off-season moves were facilitated by Boe, as DeBusschere accepted a post as the commissioner of the ABA in the league's final season before the merger.

Tarter paints a dreary picture of the ABA's curtain call, with the Nets' championship season serving as the backdrop to the impending merger with the all-powerful NBA.

> *That year a couple of other teams had folded just before the season started or in the early stages of the season. The NBA had the ABA where it wanted it. The ABA had run its course. It had done everything it could do to stay alive. The Memphis Sounds from 1974–1975 were purchased by a Baltimore owner, and they called themselves the Baltimore Claws. They played three preseason games then folded. That was the first ABA team to fold, then you had the Stars fold and then the Virginia Squires folded, [San Diego folds], so now you're down to six teams. The NBA only wanted the teams with the most visibility and the most fan support. With the Nets, Nuggets, Pacers and Spurs, you've got the best teams with the best fan support.*

On September 24, the Nets and Nuggets formally applied for membership into the NBA, leaving little doubt that the ABA's run had reached its final stages. Both franchises subjected themselves to a potential $2 million fine for trying to join the mighty NBA.

While it was clear to everyone, from ABA ownership all the way down to the fans, that the future of the league was in serious jeopardy, the Nets had unfinished business and became a tight-knit group. What they lost in the talent department they gained with improved chemistry and camaraderie.

During the exhibition period, the Nets went 5-2 against NBA teams, including Erving hitting a buzzer beater against the Knicks at Madison Square Garden on October 18 to secure a thrilling 103–101 triumph. During their ABA tenure, the Nets compiled a 15-9 record opposing NBA squads in preseason play.

The Nets suffered just one 3-game losing streak in the entire 1975–76 campaign, and while the 55-29 record failed to measure up to the regular-season success of the year before, the team stayed relatively healthy except for Taylor and Melchionni, who were sidelined due to injuries for a combined 47 games.

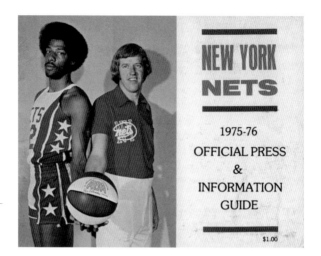

The New York Nets' 1975–1976 Media Guide. *Photo credit to Arthur Hundhausen/RememberTheABA.com.*

Erving appeared in all 84 games, but he was fresh in time for the playoffs, as he averaged a then–career low of 38.6 minutes per contest. On January 27, Dr. J won the ABA's first-ever Slam Dunk Contest held during halftime at the league's final All-Star Game in Denver. During the contest, Erving's iconic flight from the free throw line to the rim is still regarded as one of the best dunks of all time.

The Nets finished five games behind the top-seeded Nuggets at the conclusion of the regular season and geared up for what would be a grueling 7-game opening-round series with the very same Spurs squad that they had engaged with for a blockbuster trade prior to the start of the season.

The clash in the ABA Semifinals with San Antonio was littered with former Nets looking to exact revenge. Kenon, Paultz and Gale made life awfully difficult for New York. The Spurs stole Game 2 of the series behind a rousing 30-point performance from Kenon and defended home court in Game 3 to take a 2–1 series lead. Games 4, 5 and 6 were decided by a combined 5 points, with the Nets winning the first two and San Antonio salvaging Game 6, with the legendary Gervin splashing in 37 to force Game 7. Despite the imminent merger, 15,934 boisterous fans packed Nassau Veterans Memorial Coliseum to watch the Nets punch their third ticket to the ABA Finals. The Nets outlasted the Spurs, 121–114, as Erving, Williamson, Jones and Taylor all poured in 20-plus points to help the club advance.

New York needed every bit of a weeklong recovery period before taking on the ABA's top-ranked squad at McNichols Sports Arena in Denver, a venue they went 0-7 at in the regular season. A squad coached by Larry Brown with Dan Issel, David Thompson, Bobby Jones, Ralph Simpson

Left: Julius Erving lifted the Nets to a Game 5 win with 32 points in the 1976 ABA Playoffs Semifinal Round against the Spurs. *Photo credit to Arthur Hundhausen/RememberTheABA.com.*

Right: Julius Erving was an unstoppable force with the Nets during their ABA days. *Photo credit to Arthur Hundhausen/RememberTheABA.com.*

and Marvin Webster leading the way, was going to be New York's stiffest challenge yet, but they were up to the task.

The Nets and Nuggets were two of the four ABA teams included in the eventual merger, and it was more than fitting to have two of the league's premier franchises squaring off in the ABA's swan song.

Game 1's late-game dramatics set the tone for what is widely considered as a classic series, as Erving's last-second, eighteen-foot baseline jumper over Bobby Jones boosted the Nets to a 1–0 series lead by virtue of a 120–118 final. Dr. J finished the night with 45 points and, incredibly, topped that spectacular showing with a 48-point effort in Game 2, but the Nuggets roared back to even the series, 1–1. New York held serve at home, winning the next two contests to capture a commanding 3–1 series lead. Despite 37 from Erving, the Nuggets staved off elimination to force Game 6 back in Uniondale, New York.

All the pieces looked to be in place for the Nets to close out the series, but Denver came storming out of the gates with a 58–45 halftime lead. After three quarters of play, New York was down, 92–78, as the series appeared to be destined to return to The Mile High City in a winner-take-all Game 7. The Nets showed the true grit and resolve of a champion by outscoring the Nuggets 34–14 in a furious fourth-quarter run behind Williamson's 16 points in the period and 28 total. The Doctor led all Nets' scorers with 31. Al Skinner dribbled out the last few seconds before passing the ball over to Rich Jones for an easy layup and the final points in ABA history. Fans stormed the court in droves, swarming their beloved Nets as the celebration spilled into the locker room with teammates dousing each other in champagne. The Nets had reached the pinnacle of the sport by clinching their second ABA championship in three years.

Larry Brown recalled the battle that year with the Nets and the nine-year run the league had, with legends Thompson and Erving squaring off for one final hurrah. "Looking back, I don't know if I remembered in my heart that this would be the end of the league. But what I do remember, and it never changed, and it was always something that stood out to me, was the camaraderie in the league between the players and the coaches. Everybody was appreciative of playing and felt so loyal to that league. It was really unique."

3

COLLATERAL DAMAGE OF THE POST-ABA-NBA MERGER

1976–77 through 1980–81

Following a championship celebration that was largely tempered by the impending merger, the Nets joined the Nuggets, Pacers and Spurs in making the jump to the NBA. New York's success was short-lived. The move to the NBA brought with it the potential of gaining nationwide notoriety, but it was not without early obstacles and financial penalties that all but forced the championship squad to diffuse from the inside out.

Under the terms of the merger, ABA teams were required to pay a $3.2 million expansion fee to the NBA and would forgo any revenues from the league's television contracts for the first three years after joining.

During its nine-year existence, the ABA made a slew of poor business decisions, most notably failing to copyright its red, white and blue ball, which was a fan favorite throughout the 1970s. Only the Nets were in a top twenty U.S. media market, and as the years went on, it became clear that the league's cashflow problems were going to force owners to agree to a merger.

On June 17, the merger was made public. There were plans for two of the remaining six ABA teams to be dissolved, with their rosters dismantled and the players drafted into the NBA. The two ABA teams not absorbed into the NBA received a negotiated lump-sum payment. Kentucky Colonels owner John Y. Brown Jr. agreed to a $3.3 million payout, which he used to buy the NBA's Buffalo Braves, but it was Ozzie Silna and his brother Daniel who made one of the shrewdest business deals in American sports history.

The Silna brothers received a $2.2 million lump-sum payment in exchange for the Spirits of St. Louis players being drafted into the NBA, along with a one-seventh share of television rights in perpetuity for each of the four remaining ABA teams: Nuggets, Nets, Spurs and Pacers. The deal, consummated by the Silna brothers and their attorney, amounted to roughly $300 million from 1976 to 2014. In an ironic twist of fate, the Silvas lost a portion of their fortune in the Bernie Madoff Ponzi scheme in 2011. After nearly four decades of the now-NBA teams offering cash buyouts to the Silna brothers, in January 2014, the former ABA teams agreed to pay a $500 million cash buyout option for the four former ABA teams to regain control of television revenue, bringing the total amount earned from that deal to $800 million. As part of the settlement, the Silna brothers agreed to drop their lawsuit against the league that had sought to gain additional shares of media revenue streams.

While the Silna brothers made out like bandits during the merger, the Nets, on the other hand, were forced by the NBA to take a poison pill that decimated the once-iconic ABA franchise.

The first step that led the ABA's darling franchise to the brink of bankruptcy was the unreasonable demand from the Knicks for the Nets to pay $4.8 million for invading their territorial rights. Boe, backed into a corner, also faced a contract standoff with Erving. Erving earned and was entitled to a financially lucrative deal with the team he won two ABA titles with, but the Nets could not deliver the financial goods. Erving elected to sit out training camp, unsatisfied with his contract situation. This left Boe with no choice but to look for a trading partner. The Nets offered Erving to the Knicks in a deliberate effort to get the $4.8 million fee waived, but the offer was declined.

Eventually, Boe was forced to turn to other clubs to consummate a deal. Erving landed in Philadelphia, with $3 million going to the Nets to help offset the territorial rights fee and $3 million going to Erving to pay his salary in Philadelphia. The Nets were still responsible for footing a $3.2 million bill to satisfy the NBA's entry fee.

Thus, in a power move by the NBA and the Knicks, Erving was yanked off the Nets just months after delivering a second championship. Dr. J left an indelible mark on the franchise in his three seasons with the team, winning three straight ABA MVP awards spanning 1974–76, two ABA scoring titles and two ABA playoff MVPs. Erving's illustrious basketball career would climb to new heights in the NBA as he led Philadelphia to four finals appearances, including a title in 1983 with a clean sweep over the Lakers.

Few athletes transformed the culture, vibe and trajectory of a team the way Erving did when he landed with the Nets in 1973. His no. 32 rightfully

The Nets were forced to part with their superstar player, Julius Erving, upon the merger. *Photo credit to Arthur Hundhausen / RememberTheABA.com.*

hangs in the team's rafters alongside those of ABA greats Melchionni (no. 25) and Williamson (no. 23).

Erving's departure marked the end of an era. Following the merger, Williamson was the only one of the three franchise legends to find himself on the roster at the start of the 1976–77 season.

In fact, from the 1976 championship team, only Rich Jones, Skinner, Bassett and Williamson played significant minutes in the Nets' inaugural season in the NBA. Taylor shared his perspective on what transpired during the merger, particularly the trade that sent him and Eakins along with draft picks in 1977 and 1978 to Kansas City for Nate "Tiny" Archibald and cash.

I was not in the draft because I was a free agent. I had signed a four-year deal with the Nets, and my contract expired. Of course, you had the right of first refusal, which meant if you signed with anybody, they still owned your rights, so you had to compensate them. I was free as you could be back then. I knew I was going to be traded, since the Nets said since you're a free agent we're willing to sweeten the pot knowing you're willing to sign a contract with us knowing you're going to be traded to Kansas City for Nate "Tiny" Archibald. I knew they didn't have the money to sign me and Doc, and as it turned out they didn't have the money to sign either one of us. The reason they were attracted to Tiny, of course he was a great player and a Hall of Famer, is because he had a contract where he had a lot of deferred hours coming. They said we can handle this because we don't have to pay him for a while.

Another key cog in the Nets' championship puzzle was dealt away, and it was a not-so-subtle plunge from the top of the ABA world to mere bottom-feeders in the NBA's hierarchy. New York selected Jan van Breda Kolff in the dispersal draft from the defunct Colonels squad and signed free agents "Bubbles" Hawkins and Mel Daniels, with all the additions of little consequence to the win-loss department. But the team stockpiled multiple draft picks by disassembling its roster.

Archibald spent just one injury-riddled season with the Nets, appearing in just 34 games. Williamson, the team's leading scorer at 20.8 points per game, was traded on February 1 to Indiana for Darnell Hillman and a 1977 first-rounder, while Rich Jones was waived the following day. The Nets' talent deficit, coupled with starting players sidelined, became too much to overcome. Unsurprisingly, New York finished last in offensive efficiency in the league and with the worst regular season record (22-60).

1977–78

Loughery returned for his fifth season with the club, and his NBA years were in stark contrast to the Nets' ABA glory days, when the club reached at least 55 regular season wins, three playoff berths and two titles in each of his first three seasons. Presiding over a Nets team that won consecutive games just three times in the entire 1976–77 campaign proved to be a character-building moment for Loughery.

By virtue of their miserable 22-win campaign, the Nets held the no. 2 overall pick in the 1977 NBA Draft. (The current NBA Draft Lottery system did not go into effect until May 12, 1985.)

The Nets' 1977 top draft pick was sent to the Royals in the Archibald deal, as Kansas City selected a future four-time NBA All-Star, Otis Birdsong.

The pressure was on the Nets to draft a game-changer, and the player they ended up drafting via the Pacers trade involving "Super John" became a future NBA scoring champion, a four-time NBA All-Star and an eventual inductee into the Naismith Basketball Hall of Fame. Bernard King, a six-foot, seven-inch small forward out of the University of Tennessee, was an electrifying athlete who scored 1,909 points and averaged 24.2 points per game on his way to earning NBA All-Rookie First Team honors.

Bernard King's arrival was reason for optimism, as the Nets were floundering in their first season following the ABA-NBA merger. Boe's franchise was under financial distress, as its former biggest draw, Dr. J, was playing in Philadelphia. With woeful attendance at Nassau Veterans Memorial Coliseum, Boe began the process of initializing yet another move, this time a return to New Jersey.

The move was met with strong opposition from the Knicks yet again, as they sued the Nets, alleging this time that Boe's team was infringing on their territorial rights in New Jersey. Boe refused to back down, countersuing the Knicks, claiming that their actions violated antitrust laws and essentially aimed to create a monopoly in the New York market.

Ultimately, the NBA and the State of New Jersey intervened. The Nets once again had to pay the Knicks for the right to move back to New Jersey, this time $4 million. Exasperated from legal battles with his crosstown rivals and disenfranchised with the terms of the merger, Boe settled on an arena at the State University of New Jersey, Rutgers.

From Teaneck to Commack to West Hempstead to Uniondale and now Piscataway, the Nets completed an entire circuit, having crossed back and forth between the Garden State and the Empire State. The Rutgers Athletic Center, nicknamed the "RAC," opened on November 30, 1977. The eight-thousand-seat arena was a significant downgrade in size for Boe, and the renamed New Jersey Nets drew an average of just 4,856 fans per game in 1977–78, which was the fewest in the entire NBA.

Turetzky echoed the notion of the nomadic Nets and recounted the team's turbulent stopover in Piscataway.

The phrase that comes to mind is "Thataway to Piscataway." No one had any idea where Piscataway was. Rutgers was in the boondocks, there was nothing but grass out there. There were no highways, no trains, no buses, you had to get off Route 287 at Felton Road and drive past a strip club and a high school and a greenhouse, then you'd go another few miles and you'd find this big building with nothing else around it, and that was the Rutgers Athletic Center. It was still under construction, and all of a sudden that was home. "Thataway to Piscataway."

Theokas rejoined Boe as a front-office executive to help manage roster decisions. Boe focused on the team's long-term plans, including the eventual planned move to the Meadowlands. On September 1, the Nets unloaded Archibald to Buffalo for George Johnson and first-round draft picks in 1978 and 1979 to continue building for the future. Kevin Porter, acquired from Detroit in November, set the NBA record for assists in a game with 29 versus Houston on February 24, 1978, a feat that survived for twelve seasons.

Despite Bernard King's prolific scoring and show-stopping turnaround jumper, the Nets managed just a 2-win improvement over the season before and started the year with a 3-22 record. On January 27, Williamson was traded back to the Nets from Indiana for the final 34 games of the year. The team went 9-39 prior to acquiring him and a respectable 15-19 with him in the lineup. Williamson notched a career-high 50 points in the Nets' 129–121 win on April 4 against Indiana. Former Rutgers star Eddie Jordan, the Cavaliers' second-round pick in the 1977 draft, was claimed off waivers by the Nets 22 games into his rookie year. The ex–Scarlet Knight's homecoming was a feel-good story that year. While the slight improvement might be overlooked by some, the subtle nudge in the right direction helped New Jersey escape out of NBA purgatory.

1978–79

The Nets were treading water after the financial burdens levied following the ABA-NBA merger, territorial rights fees paid to the Knicks not once but twice and a reported accrual of $19 million in debt along the way. Boe had reached his wits' end trying to dig the team out of an endless financial abyss and, in 1978, finally resorted to selling the team to a syndicate, later known as the "Secaucus Seven."

The group of investors ultimately carried the team through its eventual move from Piscataway to the Meadowlands, with the most prominent co-owner being Joseph Taub. A Paterson, New Jersey native, Taub's lucrative business career hit the ground running when he and his brother Henry founded Automatic Payroll in 1949, later known as Automatic

Data Processing Company (ADP). Henry was also a member of the Secaucus Seven, but Joe was the most actively involved owner in terms of the team's day-to-day operations, in addition to being a charitable figure in the tristate community.

The Nets held the no. 4 overall pick in the 1978 draft, but Theokas dealt that pick and a 1979 NBA first-round pick to the Knicks, who selected Micheal Ray Richardson (1978 draft pick) and sent Phil Jackson and their 1978 first-round pick to New Jersey. Jackson, who won a pair of rings on the 1970 (did not play due to injury) and 1973 championship Knicks teams, was on his last legs, but his defensive acumen and championship pedigree were among the reasons the Nets climbed up the standings and toward respectability that season. Prior to the start of the regular season, Theokas traded Kevin Porter to the Pistons in exchange for Eric Money.

Theokas also signed Skinner that off-season to stabilize a roster that featured five players with limited to no experience at the NBA level. The Nets were the biggest surprise in the league that year, jumping out to a 17-12 mark. As the trade deadline drew near, Theokas then flipped Money and Skinner to Philadelphia for Harvey Catchings, Ralph Simpson and cash considerations. Simpson was a shell of his former self and a far cry from his ABA glory years circa 1971 and 1972.

The Nets sat at a 33-33 mark before suffering a 5-game losing streak, closely followed by a 4-game losing streak, over the final 16 games. The team finished at 37-45 to barely secure a playoff berth. As luck would have it, New Jersey locked horns with franchise savior–turned area rival Erving and the 76ers. The Nets fought valiantly in Game 1 but fell, 122–114, with Williamson leading the way with 38 points. Bernard King added 25. In Game 2 of the best-of-three series, Philadelphia closed out New Jersey in Piscataway by virtue of a 111–101 victory to send the overachieving Nets home for good. The Nets' pitiful attendance directly correlated with their inadequate facility, situated in a college town that refused to embrace the team. This led Taub, partner Allan Cohen and company to take measures to stop the team from hemorrhaging money.

1979–80

Theokas shook up the roster in the off-season by dealing Catchings to Milwaukee for John Gianelli and a 1979 first-round draft pick.

Heading into the 1979 NBA Draft, the Nets held two first-round picks, the no. 8 and no. 11 overall selections. They opted to take power forward Calvin Natt out of Louisiana-Monroe and center Cliff Robinson out of the University of Southern California, respectively. On October 2, just ten days before the regular season was set to get underway, Theokas shipped out Bernard King, along with Gianelli and Jim Boylan, to Utah for seven-footer Rich Kelley and cash considerations.

King's phenomenal two-year run with New Jersey ended abruptly, and his four NBA All-Star selections came with future stints in New York and Washington. On October 12, New Jersey acquired Mike Newlin from Houston for a 1980 second round pick. Newlin recorded a career-high 52 points on December 16 against Boston and scored 40 points on two other occasions that season.

In February, Natt was traded 53 games into his rookie year to Portland for Maurice Lucas and first-rounders in 1980 and 1981, while all-time Nets great "Super John" Williamson was traded one last time, after appearing in just 28 games. The Nets were hoping to build on the playoff-clinching 1978–79 season, but that hope quickly faded as they managed just 34 wins, good enough for tenth in the Eastern Conference, effectively missing out on any opportunity for the postseason.

While the first four years following the ABA-NBA merger were the darkest in team history, there were plans already in the works for the Nets to find a permanent place to call home at the Meadowlands. The arena's construction started in 1979 at a cost of approximately $85 million. While the venue did not open its doors until July 2, 1981, the Nets had to endure four dismal seasons in the glorified college gym in Piscataway.

1980–81

The 1980–81 season served as the final campaign for the Nets in Piscataway. The team's attendance woes continued, as they drew an average of just 7,363 fans a game. New Jersey was twentieth of twenty-three teams in the NBA in attendance, despite being in the most densely populated state in the country and in a top media market. The imminent move to a supersized venue, the Meadowlands, was long overdue.

In the 1980 NBA Draft, New Jersey selected guard Mike O'Koren out of the University of North Carolina and center Mike Gminski out of Duke.

Both rookies had impactful seasons, with Gminski posting averages of 13.2 points and 7.5 rebounds and O'Koren adding 11.0 points and 6.1 rebounds per game. Even the ascension of Newlin to the role as team's leading scorer (21.4 points per contest) and twenty-year-old Robinson's promising evolution (19.5 points per contest) did not translate to team success. On July 17, Darwin Cook signed with the Nets and became a mainstay on the roster for the following six seasons.

Nevertheless, just 35 games into the season, sitting at a miserable 12-23 mark, the franchise's longest tenured and most successful coach, Loughery, resigned in his eighth season. Loughery had compiled an impressive 168-84 record in three ABA seasons, including two titles, while amassing a 129-234 mark with one lone playoff berth in parts of five losing seasons with the NBA Nets. Loughery went on to coach eleven more seasons in the NBA, with stops in Atlanta, Chicago, Washington and Miami.

Loughery's departure ushered in a new voice along the sidelines and the start of a fresh chapter for New Jersey as it bid farewell to Piscataway and its move to the Meadowlands right around the corner. It was a former adversary in the ABA, Bob MacKinnon—whose Spirits of St. Louis squad effectively ended the Erving-led Nets' bid for back-to-back titles—who rose to a prominent position with the team. MacKinnon joined New Jersey as an assistant on Loughery's staff in 1979–80 alongside Phil Jackson, and his role eventually evolved into two separate stints as the team's General Manager in the years ahead. Taub and the rest of the Nets' ownership group slapped the interim coaching tag on MacKinnon for the final 47 games of the regular season. The team went 12-35 under his watch to round out the year at 24-58. In March 1981, the Nets signed five-time NBA All-Star Bob McAdoo after he was released by the Pistons, but the former University of North Carolina standout appeared in just 10 games. Seven months later, McAdoo was traded to the Lakers, where he would go on to win two NBA championships. New Jersey's consolation prize was a 1983 second-round pick. The Nets' final season in Piscataway, like many seasons in the team's history, was both a regrettable and a forgettable one.

4
RISE TO NBA RESPECTABILITY

1981–82 through 1985–86

The Nets' first five seasons in the NBA resulted in losing records and lukewarm fan interest at a subpar home arena. Wholesale changes were on the way, none more significant than the Meadowland Sports Complex project finally coming to fruition.

The decades-long effort to erect the Meadowlands Sports Complex dated to the mid-1960s, when New Jersey civic leaders spearheaded efforts to construct a sports complex to entice the Jets and Giants to play home games in the Garden State. In 1971, Governor William T. Cahill approved the creation of a governing body for the state's sports development projects, duly named the New Jersey Sports and Exposition Authority (NJSEA). The organization's first chairman was none other than David "Sonny" Werblin. Werblin, a Rutgers alumnus, purchased the New York Titans of the American Football League (AFL) in 1963 and along with his partners eventually renamed them the Jets. Werblin was instrumental in signing former Alabama quarterback Joe Namath for $427,000 in 1965 but ultimately sold his ownership stake prior to the franchise winning the Super Bowl during the 1968–69 season. A true visionary, a shrewd businessman and a noted philanthropist, Werblin flexed his negotiating muscles by persuading the Giants to move out of Yankee Stadium in the Bronx with his construction underway for Giants Stadium and the Meadowlands Racetrack on November 30, 1972. The former was completed on October 10, 1976, and the latter opened over a month earlier, on September 1. In 1978, Werblin took over as head of Madison Square Garden Properties, a post he held until 1984.

The stage was set for the Meadowlands to be the shiny new epicenter for sports and entertainment in the metropolitan area. The General Manager of the Meadowlands Sports Complex (1987–95) and the future co-owner and President of the Nets (1995–2000), Michael Rowe, brought to light Werblin's vision for the project.

I've come at some particular reckoning to the understanding that I think the beauty that was the Meadowlands, which was invented by a man named Sonny Werblin, who ran Madison Square Garden many years ago, was to have a sports complex that was the opposite of what was in New York. He wanted a wide-open, clean surplus of parking with pristine white buildings in the middle of highways that could allow people to come from any particular direction, park conveniently, walk into a building and be able to enjoy themselves at a very leisurely pace. What works in the New York market was just the opposite. When the Meadowlands was new in 1976, it was an extraordinary place.

There was no crime in the streets. There were no smells of folks who were hanging around outside the building. There was no crime outside the ticket windows. There were no police cars streaming through the streets. It was a nice, comfortable, sit in the back of chair when you got in, fold up your legs and relax kind of place.

The arena was originally named for New Jersey Governor Brendan Byrne, who filled the state office from 1974 to 1982. Before the Nets christened their state-of-the-art arena in the fall of 1981, they had to refashion the roster, with their first order of business finding a head coach for the club. MacKinnon moved into the role as the team's front-office executive. On March 18, MacKinnon made his first major splash of the off-season by hiring Larry Brown, who had led the coaching efforts for the ABA's Carolina Cougars, Denver Nuggets in both the ABA and NBA and the UCLA Bruins before returning to the professional ranks and joining the Nets. Brown was a standout player at UNC under Hall of Fame coaches Frank McGuire and Dean Smith and developed a reputation during his ABA days as a pass-first, cerebral point guard. Coaching was his calling, and taking over a Nets team looking to embark on a new era of basketball in their new digs was appealing to the Brooklyn, New York native. MacKinnon tinkered with the roster by sending New Jersey's former top draft choice from 1979, Cliff Robinson, to Kansas City for Otis Birdsong and a 1981 second-round draft choice. The trade was completed just one day before the 1981 NBA Draft, and with the

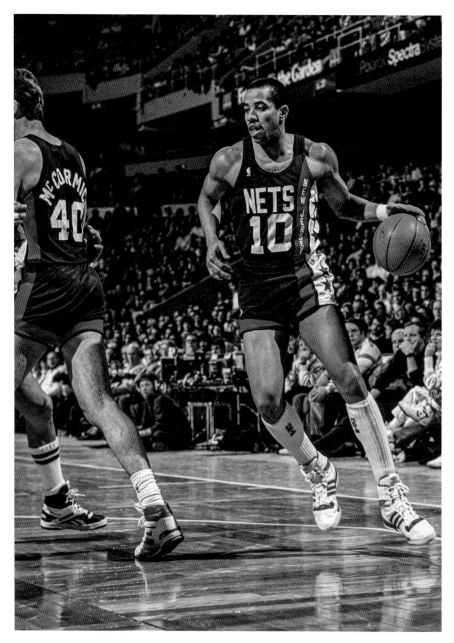

Otis Birdsong was a four-time NBA All-Star and earned the honor once during his Nets career. *Steven Lipofsky/LipofskyPhoto.com.*

Nets holding the no. 3 overall pick, there was anticipation that the draft choice could be a game-changer.

Brown reflected on his impressions of the Nets' organization prior to joining them and how the club's 1981 NBA Draft selection came to be.

I left UCLA because my athletic director, J.D. Morgan, and I got the Net job when they were playing in Piscataway. They had Cliff Robinson from Southern Cal and Maurice Lucas, Mike Newlin, Robert McAdoo, so they had a lot of talent. It was just kind of disjointed. I don't think any of the guys liked playing in Piscataway. I remember it was the hardest floor I ever felt. Then I go to New Jersey, and I had a phenomenal owner, Joe Taub, who was just wonderful, but he had a bunch of other guys that were investors and that was uncomfortable for me. I only wanted to deal with Joe. He loved the game, he loved his players, he allowed you to coach. Bob MacKinnon was an unbelievable GM, they had a guy, Fritz Massmann, who had been the trainer forever and he was a beautiful guy.

We drafted Buck [Williams] at three. We had the third pick, tenth pick and eighteenth pick when I got there. I had just been with the 1980 Olympic team that didn't get the gold and Buck was on that team. Isiah [Thomas] was on the team, [Mark] Aguirre was on the team, and they went before and I could tell you stories, but to make a long story short, Mr. Taub wanted us to draft [Kelly] Tripucka at three. Isiah was so special, but Aguirre went one and Isiah went two and I fought with Taub, and we ended up drafting Buck. Buck was like family to me. I thought he was sensational. When we got Buck we had Maurice Lucas on that team, I thought Maurice and Buck could play together. Maurice told me: "Coach me as a power forward, I got something on everybody like my intimidation factor. If I have to play against centers, I lose all that." We ended up trading him for Ray Ray Williams, who had a remarkable year for us. We signed Otis to the largest free-agent contract at the time, but he got hurt right away.

He didn't really play for us. Don Nelson gave me Len Elmore. He was like the third- or fourth-string center because Gminski wasn't 100 percent healthy. Then we had the tenth pick and Tripucka was still on the board. I had this big argument again, I said I loved Lefty Driesell's guys and Buck and I were so close, and he thought Albert [King] was so great. I had nothing against Tripucka, but I just thought the way that I coached and the relationship that Buck and Albert had, I finally talked them into drafting Albert. We were going to draft Larry Nance with our other pick, and I remember getting a call from Colangelo and anybody who asks me who I was drafting generally I was really honest because I thought if you're honest half of them don't believe you anyway. So, I told him I loved Larry Nance because when I was at UCLA, we beat Clemson to go to the Final Four and I just thought this guy was sensational.

I didn't even know why we didn't draft him sooner. Shame on me. But I got a call from Bill Musselman right after Colangelo's call and Bill and I were close, and he was in Cleveland. He said, "Larry, Phoenix is trying to trade up and get in front of you guys and do you know of any player they might want?" And lo and behold it was Larry Nance. So now we get to the eighteenth pick and Mike Shuler, who I hired because Bill Blair said you have to hire my friend Mike Shuler, jumped up and said, "Oh this guy Ray Tolbert is the greatest and Mike had worked for Bobby Knight and I have so much respect for Bobby."

The owners were so pissed at me. They said, "Alright, we're drafting Ray Tolbert." Larry Nance goes to Phoenix and the rest is history.

Buck Williams was the no. 3 overall pick, Albert King was chosen at no. 10 (coincidentally, both were teammates at the University of Maryland) and Maurice Lucas was traded on October 25 to the Knicks for Ray Williams. The Nets' pair of rookies and Ray Williams were the team's leading scorers that upcoming season and helped transform a fragmented but talented roster into a cohesive unit with the perfect blend of youthful exuberance and veteran leadership.

Birdsong posted an impressive 14.2 points per game but managed to play in just 37 games due to injury. Ray Williams' lone season in the Garden State saw him hang up 20.4 points per game and 6 assists, including a career-high 52 points on April 17 against Detroit. Before the personal accolades and winning basketball came, it took time for Larry Brown to build team cohesion.

Growing pains were apparent from the start. The Nets fell, 103–99, to the reviled Knicks in their home debut at their newly opened venue, Brendan Byrne Arena. In fact, New Jersey faltered to a 2-10 start and fell to a season-worst 6-16 following an overtime loss to the Bulls on December 16. From there on out, Larry Brown's crew went 38-22, amassing five separate winning streaks of 4 games or more to capture the fourth seed in the conference. On January 31, the Nets hosted the 1982 All-Star Game, with Buck Williams making his debut in the glorified exhibition contest. Larry Bird was named the game's MVP for his clutch play down the stretch as 20,149 fans filled

Brendan Byrne Arena to the hilt. The East topped the West, 120–118, in an instant classic.

The furious stretch run set up a first-round playoff meeting with the Washington Bullets. The Meadowlands hosted its first NBA playoff game, with over fourteen thousand fans taking in the action. In Game 1, the veteran-laden Bullets lineup featuring balanced scoring and hard-nosed defense overwhelmed a Nets squad that shot a paltry 16.7 percent from 3-point range, shot 36.4 percent from the field, and converted just 60 percent of their foul shots.

While the shooting numbers improved for the Nets in Game 2, the result was the same, as they fell at the Capital Centre in Landover, Maryland, 103–92. New Jersey failed to crack the century mark in scoring in both games and lost to a more seasoned and physical group. Nonetheless, early returns of Larry Brown's coaching tenure

Buck Williams finished no. 1 in Nets' history in free throw attempts with 3,818. *Photo credit to Steven Lipofsky / LipofskyPhoto.com.*

were promising. The hiring of Brown and a well-crafted roster, along with a spacious, modern arena, saw the Nets draw over 560,734 fans, remarkably catapulting them to no. 4 overall in the NBA in team attendance that year. "We just had unbelievable chemistry," noted Brown. "The older players like Lenny were so supportive of the young guys. Losing a player like Maurice Lucas is ridiculous, but Ray Ray Williams for our team was phenomenal, and because Otis got hurt, he became even more important. I fell into a group of young, overachieving kids that believed in each other, and it was almost like a college team with some seniors that helped me coach."

The exciting core featured Buck Williams as the team's next franchise-caliber player. He won the NBA's Rookie of the Year Award. That marked the first time a Net received that honor since Brian Taylor garnered that distinction following the 1972–73 season.

1982–83

The 1982 NBA Draft saw Larry Brown and company select Georgetown product Sleepy Floyd with their first-round pick, no. 13 overall, and Eddie

Phillips at no. 21 out of Alabama. Coming off a career year, the Nets surprisingly shipped out Ray Williams in a draft-day trade to Kansas City in exchange for former 1979 Rookie of the Year and 1979 All-NBA Second Team point guard Phil Ford, a pass-first floor general.

Ironically, just four months and barely seven games into his Nets tenure, Ford, along with a 1983 second-rounder, was traded to Milwaukee for forward Mickey Johnson and Fred Roberts. Ford spoke openly after his retirement about battling drug and alcohol addiction. The twenty-six-year-old's once-promising NBA career ended disappointingly in Houston just two years later. While Ford's tragic story was a major setback for New Jersey, another trade brought splendid results on August 27. Darryl Dawkins, nicknamed "Chocolate Thunder," among other monikers, spent the previous seven seasons in Philadelphia before landing in New Jersey in exchange for a first-round pick in the 1983 NBA Draft. The best years of Dawkins' career came with the Nets. Uncoincidentally, the team's most successful NBA years to that point came with the high-flying slam-dunk specialist in the starting lineup.

New Jersey had seven players average double digits in scoring; Buck Williams and Albert King led the way, both with 17 per game. Many of the Nets' prolific scorers had to settle for fewer shot attempts for the betterment of the team, resulting in the best win-loss season for the franchise since joining the NBA. New Jersey defeated the Knicks in consecutive games on November 9 and 10—not a harbinger of things to come in the 1983 NBA playoffs. Larry Brown's crew won 11 consecutive games from December 23 to January 12. On February 6, the Nets traded Floyd and Mickey Johnson to Golden State for Micheal Ray Richardson. The Nets soared to 19 games over .500 with an April 1 win over Dr. J's 76ers to put New Jersey at 46-27. On the court, things were as peachy as they could be. But as the team prepared for the playoff push, rumors began to surface that Larry Brown was interviewing for the vacant coaching position with the University of Kansas. Rowe recounted what transpired once ownership got wind of this development.

Larry's issue, very publicly, was that he was interviewing for another job, Kansas. He was trying to get the team into a playoff mode, but when one of the Nets owners found out about it, he went down in his personal vehicle, went to the team charter, confronted Larry on the plane, and Larry admitted that he had interviewed for the job, and the owner replaced him on the tarmac. So, if that was a confused owner, I don't know what the definition would be of any other kind of an owner. This was an owner

Darryl Dawkins was an electrifying dunker with a larger-than-life personality. *Steven Lipofsky/LipofskyPhoto.com.*

who was interested in the team, he was interested in loyalty, and if he was paying someone to lead a group of 12 healthy players and 3 injured players on the road to win a basketball game, he expected that kind of loyalty. The nomadic Nets really bumped into a very nomadic coach, and the Nets won that disagreement. There are some who think the team would have been better if Larry had stayed, but Larry was going somewhere at some point anyway. He was a wanderlust. He's a great coach, but residency was not his strength.

Larry always had a change of residency/forward my email card in his wallet at all of his stops. If he were a stock, you could not go long on Larry Brown. You had to be happy with short-term results.

Larry Brown went on to coach thirty-one seasons in the NBA and ABA combined, making eleven different stops on his professional journey and three stints heading up college programs, at UCLA, Kansas and finally SMU.

Brown contends that he was upfront with Nets' ownership about his desire to return to the college game and compared his situation to that of a New York football Giants coach of that same era.

I missed the last six games. A lot of the owners were kind of a little intimidated by the fact that Joe had so much say in the team. There was a movement to try and limit his control. I remember I went to Coach MacKinnon, I came here for Mr. Taub and I think one of the guys involved was a major owner of Kinney Parking Company, Allan Cohen. I think they wanted to get control of the team from Joe, and I basically said I'm not going to work for anybody else. I'm not sure what transpired, but at the end of the year I heard from Kansas. I told Mr. Taub the year before that I always saw myself more as a college coach and there might be a time where I might want to go back to college. He never said anything, he never told me what to do, he was always just unbelievable to our players and our coaches. People don't remember that Ray Perkins was coaching the Giants, he left the Giants to go to Bama when Coach Bryant retired, and he was allowed to coach the playoffs and they lost. So, when I went to talk to Mr. Taub about going to Kansas after the year, he didn't let me coach the last six games. He was going to hire Bob MacKinnon to take over and Bill Blair came to me and begged me to talk to Joe, I said, "Bill, you don't have to beg me, you should be the next coach." I tried to beg Mr. Taub to let me finish, and he didn't think it was right, and I think it was based on what happened with the football Giants. We didn't finish that strong, and we got beat in the playoffs. I'll always regret that. You can have owners— and some were better than others—but this guy was great. We had gotten Darryl Dawkins, that team was due to win 50 games and make a run, you never know who you're going to play. That team was pretty good and only getting better, but we had to trade Ray Ray Williams, and that was a very difficult situation. The only reason Mr. Taub traded Ray was they had all this money invested into Otis and really they both played the same position. I tried to tell Mr. Taub we can try to figure out how to play those guys together since they're so good, but finances were different at that time. It gave me two of the best years of my life, but it was a little disappointing the way it ended, and I'm sure I was a big part of that because of me wanting to go and be a college coach.

As Brown so bluntly outlined, the conclusion of his coaching tenure with the Nets was far from pretty, and the team stumbled to a 2-4 record in the final six regular-season games under Bill Blair, rounding out the year just shy of the 50-win plateau. Despite holding the no. 4 seed and home court advantage over the crosstown rival Knicks in the postseason, former Net Bernard King went off for 40 to steal Game 1 at Brendan Byrne Arena. The Knicks swept the Nets out of the playoffs upon returning to MSG for Game 2 before Dr. J's eventual NBA champion Sixers swept New York out of the semifinal round. A season brimming with excitement culminated with a highly coveted coach leaving abruptly, an area rival pulling a playoff upset and a former franchise savior, Erving, winning his first NBA championship with a divisional foe.

1983–84

A new coach was signed in the immediate aftermath of the playoff loss to the Knicks. Stan Albeck, a man with twenty-seven years of head coaching experience spanning the collegiate and pro ranks to that point, was charged with helping the Nets advance further in the playoffs. MacKinnon's last move as acting General Manager was hiring Albeck with Lewis Schaffel, who led the front office efforts of the Utah Jazz and Atlanta Hawks for one year each, started calling the shots in New Jersey from that point on.

Albeck's unit did not improve on its NBA franchise-best 49 regular-season wins from the season before but managed 45 wins, with Birdsong being named an All-Star for his first time as a Net. On November 5, Dawkins set the franchise mark for blocks in a game with thirteen against Philadelphia. Despite winning 45 contests, New Jersey finished fourth in the division behind the powerhouse Celtics, Sixers and Knicks, respectively.

The Nets secured the sixth seed in what many anticipated would be a nightmare matchup for New Jersey against ABA hero turned NBA nemesis Dr. J. In 1984, the NBA expanded its playoffs from twelve to sixteen teams. In doing so, the league extended the first round from a best-of-three to a best-of-five series.

Much to Philadelphia's chagrin and the Nets' delight, a championship hangover saw New Jersey earn convincing 15-point and 14-point wins in Games 1 and 2, respectively. Erving scored just 30 points combined in the two contests, and the underdog Nets appeared to be on the verge of closing

Julius Erving gave New Jersey all it could handle in the 1984 NBA Playoffs. *Steven Lipofsky/ LipofskyPhoto.com.*

out a series for the first time in their NBA history. Erving erupted for 27 points in Game 3; Moses Malone added 21 and snatched 17 rebounds. Showing the true resolve of a defending champion, the Sixers returned to their home court for Game 4 and handed New Jersey a second straight 8-point defeat.

Albeck's Nets took advantage of Philadelphia's penchant for committing costly turnovers by forcing them into 22 miscues in Game 5 while holding Erving to just 12 points on 5-of-11 shooting. Richardson and Birdsong carried the day with 24 apiece, and Buck Williams snared 16 rebounds to go along with 17 points.

The youthful exuberance of the Nets outlasted the grit and resolve of Philadelphia as New Jersey earned its first NBA playoff-round win. In the conference semifinals, Albeck and company faced Don Nelson's Bucks and pulled a surprise win in the opening game. Milwaukee rebounded for back-to-back wins in Games 2 and 3 to capture a 2–1 series lead. New Jersey held serve at home in Game 4, turning a 9-point fourth-quarter deficit into a

7-point win by virtue of outscoring Milwaukee, 35–19, in the final frame. The Nets dropped Game 5 in Milwaukee, 94–82, and came within an eyelash of winning Game 6 back in New Jersey but fell, 98–97. All told, the 1983–84 campaign was a landmark moment for the franchise, as it completed its rise from obscurity and in doing so was mentioned in the same breath as the top teams in the Eastern Conference.

Albeck's series win validated the culture established by Taub and the rest of the ownership group as well as the framework that Larry Brown put into place. The Nets would not win another playoff round until the 2001–02 season.

1984–85

In 1984–85, a rash of injuries barred the Nets from making a deeper push into the conference playoffs. All told, Albert King, Dawkins, O'Koren, Birdsong and Cook missed a combined 172 games due to injury-related issues and rest. To put things in perspective, that amounted to over two full regular seasons of games missed for key starters and rotational players on the team. The Nets drafted Jeff Turner with their first-round pick in the 1984 NBA Draft but made virtually no notable free-agent signings ahead of the season. The Nets won a memorable Christmas Day contest, 120–114, over the Knicks at MSG, with Richardson scoring 36 and former Net Bernard King splashing through a whopping 60. Richardson represented the Nets in the 1985 NBA All-Star Game and led the league in steals with 3 per game.

The team clinched its fourth consecutive playoff berth, which was a much-needed departure from its initial five dismal seasons upon joining the NBA. For most of the regular season, the Nets stayed under the .500 mark, as injuries forced Albeck to mix and match lineups. New Jersey had six separate winning streaks longer than 3 games and by early March finished in the middle of the pack in offensive and defensive rankings. Despite a middling 42-40 record, the Nets managed the fifth seed, setting up a meeting with fourth-seeded Detroit.

The core of what would eventually become the infamous "Bad Boy" Pistons teams was starting to formulate its rough-and-tough identity. Isiah Thomas, Bill Laimbeer, Vinnie Johnson and Kelly Tripucka, under the tutelage of Chuck Daly, surprisingly dropped five of six regular-season meetings with the Nets, but things were vastly different come postseason time. The Pistons protected home court and secured double-digit wins by 20 and 10 points in Games 1 and 2, respectively. Despite Buck Williams' 28 points and 12 rebounds, New Jersey suffered a nail-biting 116–115 Game 3 home loss. This marked the first time the two franchises squared off in the playoffs and the last time they would until the 2002–03 season. While Detroit was building the foundation of what ultimately culminated in back-to-back championships, the Nets teams under Larry Brown and now Albeck that garnered widespread respect and admiration for their play over the early part of the decade started a precipitous freefall back into NBA oblivion.

1985–86

As the Nets entered the 1985–86 off-season, it was reported that there was mutual interest between Albeck and the Chicago Bulls to fill the team's coaching vacancy left behind after Loughery was fired. Chicago's GM, Jerry Krause, praised Albeck's handling of the injury-riddled Nets and began the process of courting him to come to the Windy City. Loughery, who was the longest-tenured coach in team history—spending eight seasons from the New York Americans to New York Nets to New Jersey Nets—was now set to be replaced by the Nets' veteran coach of the past two years. Loughery coached a player you may have heard of, Michael Jordan, during his rookie campaign, as the team reached the playoffs with a record of 38-44 before losing to Milwaukee in the first round. The man who was instrumental in drafting arguably the most decorated basketball player in history, Rod Thorn, was a front-office executive with Chicago who would later be a revered name in Nets' lore.

Albeck's departure had a domino effect on the franchise, as it would take until the start of the 1990s for it to return to perennial playoff status. As New Jersey turned its attention to its next coaching hire, Taub and company elected to hire a former Loughery assistant from 1978–79.

That man, Dave Wohl, an East Brunswick, New Jersey native and University of Pennsylvania alum, became the ninth coach in the team's nineteen-year existence. Besides Loughery's nearly decade-long tenure, the average shelf life of a Nets coach to that point was about two years. Wohl was a reserve point guard on the Nets starting from the 1976–77 through the 1977–78 seasons. MacKinnon returned to the Nets' bench as Wohl's assistant for the 1985–86 campaign to provide guidance and support for the first-time head coach. The Nets selected six-foot, eleven-inch center Yvon Joseph, nicknamed the "Haitian Sensation," out of Georgia Tech with their second-round pick in the 1985 NBA Draft. Suffice it to say, Joseph's career was far from sensational, as he played in just 1 NBA game, registering five minutes, scoring 2 points and committing one personal foul. Since the 1981 draft that brought Buck Williams and Albert King, New Jersey whiffed on virtually all draft picks in the next four seasons, and that trend would continue for the better part of the decade. This was a major factor in the franchise's five-year playoff drought following Wohl's first year at the helm.

The usual suspects—Birdsong, Cook, Dawkins, Buck Williams, Gminski, Richardson and Albert King—kept a cleaner bill of health than they had the season before. Near the midway point of the year, New Jersey was off to a stellar 23-14 pace but plummeted to 16-29 thereafter. Dawkins' ailing back forced him to miss 31 games, and Richardson played in just 47 games before receiving a lifetime ban by NBA Commissioner David Stern for repeatedly violating the league's substance-abuse policy. Richardson's lifetime ban was eventually lifted, but the thirty-year-old took his talents to the United States Basketball League (USBL), Continental Basketball Association (CBA), then eventually Europe, and never played in the NBA again. In parts of four seasons with New Jersey, Richardson was first in franchise history with 2.7 steals per game.

Coincidentally, the Nets sat at 30-29 with Richardson and went 9-14 after his abrupt banishment on February 25.

Wohl's crew stumbled its way to the regular-season finish line to latch on to the seventh seed and, for the second time in three seasons, had a playoff date with Nelson's Milwaukee Bucks. While the teams' prior matchup was a competitive bout, the second clash was literally a first-round knockout, as the Nets suffered double-digit lopsided defeats in both games in Milwaukee. Even Birdsong's 28 points in Game 3 was not enough to salvage New Jersey a single victory in the series. That loss marked the end of the Nets' most successful era of NBA basketball to that point—a stretch that featured five straight playoff berths and an upset series win over Dr. J and the reigning champion Sixers in the 1983–84 season, along with Buck Williams evolving into a perennial All-Star.

5

NBA DARK AGES

1986–87 through 1990–91

The second half of the 1980s was not a friendly part of the decade to the Nets and their fans. After spending the year on Wohl's staff, MacKinnon returned for a second season as assistant coach while also sharing a lead front-office role alongside former Cleveland Cavaliers executive Harry Weltman. New Jersey traded sixth-year point guard Cook to Washington for cash, and the Bullets agreed to not select Syracuse floor general Dwayne "Pearl" Washington with their first-round pick in 1986. New Jersey added Orlando Woolridge, originally drafted by Chicago, for a 1988 second-round pick, a 1989 first-round pick and a 1989 second-round pick as compensation. Woolridge would enjoy marvelous individual achievements in the upcoming season, leading the team in scoring at 20.7 a clip, but he failed to inspire overall team success. The six-foot, nine-inch NBA vet was a scoring force in the paint but hardly a defensive-minded player and a lightweight rebounder for his size. Woolridge's dominance of the paint forced Buck Williams to follow suit, yet the team lacked the outside shooting capabilities and floor spacing to create a cohesive offensive unit.

Dawkins was limited to just six games and Birdsong to seven due to injury, and Albert King averaged a then-career low 9.5 points while shooting just 42.6 percent from the field. With two of the Nets' most exciting players going down for the year only a handful of games into the regular season, the team would endure its second-worst record since joining the NBA and its worst in six seasons. Even more disconcerting, attendance was floundering in the six-year-old arena; the team plummeted from tenth in the NBA rankings the year before to sixteenth at year's end. Clearly, the on-court product was nearly unwatchable, and the novelty of the new arena was starting to wear off as newer and even grander facilities started popping up in several markets with the NBA's planned expansion. Over the course of the next twenty-plus seasons the Nets spent at the Meadowlands, they would never finish in the top ten in attendance.

Aside from the intrigue level with Pearl Washington, a Brooklyn, New York native and local playground and high school sensation, the Nets' lineup lacked pizzazz and flare. Unfortunately for Washington, his jaw-dropping moves at the Carrier Dome in Syracuse and at Boys and Girls High School in Brooklyn never materialized into an impactful career with the Nets. New Jersey played a historic four-overtime marathon with Golden State on February 1, with Buck Williams setting a franchise record with 27 rebounds in sixty minutes, but the Nets suffered their thirty-third loss in what turned out to be a 24-58 campaign.

1987–88

As MacKinnon, Weltman and Wohl turned their attention to the 1987 NBA Draft, New Jersey held its highest pick since selecting Buck Williams in the 1981 draft class. San Antonio sat atop the draft and selected David Robinson. The Phoenix Suns selected Net-to-be Armen Gilliam with the second pick. The Nets were on the clock, and the list of draft-eligible players available included Scottie Pippen, Kenny Smith, Kevin Johnson, Horace Grant, Reggie Miller and Mark Jackson—all players who would become All-Stars in the NBA. Pippen and Miller would be inducted into the Naismith Basketball Hall of Fame. New Jersey became enamored by Ohio State sharpshooter Dennis Hopson to replace the hole left in the backcourt following Richardson's league ban.

The Nets doubled down on their perimeter shooting needs in the second round of the draft by selecting Jamie Waller out of Virginia Union University. Waller's rookie year with the Nets would be his lone season in the NBA. New Jersey then made the difficult but prudent decision to trade fan favorite Dawkins, who missed 150 of a possible 246 games the previous three seasons, along with James Bailey to Cleveland for John Bagley and Keith Lee. A leg injury sidelined Lee for the entire 1987–88 season, while Bagley

Roy Hinson (*left*) and Buck Williams (*right*) wreaked havoc in the paint from 1987–88 through 1988–89. *Steven Lipofsky/LipofskyPhoto.com.*

averaged a career-high 12 points per game. As for Dawkins, he currently ranks as the Nets' second-all-time leader in field-goal percentage (60.1). The man nicknamed "Dr. Dunk" played in just 26 games over the next two NBA seasons with Utah and Detroit, but his infectious smile and comedic nature was a binding force in the Nets' locker room and endearing to his fans.

Expectations for the upcoming season were far from high, and the Nets failed to replenish talent through the draft or free agency and then felt the reverberations of those misfires. On November 24, Albert King signed with Philadelphia, with the Nets receiving a 1988 second round pick as compensation.

New Jersey floundered to a 2-13 record before it pulled the plug on Wohl, with MacKinnon taking over as the interim head coach. Things improved ever so slightly under MacKinnon's watch, with the team amassing 10 wins against 29 losses. Barely a month after taking over as coach, MacKinnon, along with Weltman, orchestrated a trade that sent Ben Coleman and Gminski to Philadelphia for Roy Hinson, Tim McCormick and a 1989 second-round draft pick. Hinson shined by producing 17.6 points per contest, including a franchise-best 13-of-13 from the field on March 22 against Philadelphia. Buck Williams led the team in scoring (18.3 points) and rebounds (11.9) on his way to NBA All-Defensive Second Team honors.

In an ill twist of fate, Woolridge, the team's leading scorer from the 1986–87 season, was suspended after 19 games by NBA Commissioner Stern for repeated violations of the league's drug policy and was ordered to undergo rehabilitation.

The Nets hired former two-time NBA champion and Knicks legendary center Willis Reed for the remaining 28 games. The decorated star was an integral part of New York's 1970 and 1973 championship squads and was named a two-time NBA Finals MVP. Reed was also selected to the NBA's fiftieth-anniversary team; he was a seven-time All-Star and a league MVP in 1970. His credentials place him in the pantheon of the league's all-time greats.

Reed's transition from his playing career to the coaching profession was not seamless to that point. He led the Knicks to a 43-39 record and a playoff berth during the 1977–78 campaign at the age of thirty-five before being relieved of his duties just 14 games into the next season at a 6-8 mark. After two seasons as a Hawks assistant, Reed's next opportunity came with New Jersey. He was set to become the third coach to attempt to guide the team through a bumpy 1987–88 season. New Jersey went 7-21 under Reed's watch to secure a 19-63 mark, the worst winning percentage since the team's second season in the ABA.

1988–89

Wins were few and far between during Reed's two seasons along the sidelines, but the move signified that the Nets—and in part Reed—were taking a not-so-subtle swipe at the big-brother Knicks by hiring one of their franchise's most beloved players.

Entering the 1988 NBA Draft, the Nets held the no. 4 position, so the fact that four out of the first six draftees would participate in multiple future All-Star Games bode well for Reed and company to select a cornerstone piece. Instead, New Jersey selected two-time All-SEC First-Team player Chris Morris out of Auburn. During his first year, Morris was selected to the NBA's All-Rookie Second Team, but much of his career was overshadowed by a talented pool in his same rookie draft class that included Danny Manning, Rik Smits, Mitch Richmond, Hersey Hawkins, Dan Majerle and Rod Strickland. Morris' rookie campaign was the second-most productive of his career, as the twenty-three-year-old averaged 14.1 points. Thereafter, Morris did not show vast improvement during his seven seasons in the Garden State. With the thirty-second overall pick in the second round, the Nets nabbed Charles Shackleford out of North Carolina State. He amounted to a reserve player in his two seasons with the team. The former Wolfpack star was infamous for telling a reporter: "I can shoot with my left hand, I can shoot with my right hand, I'm amphibious."

The misuse of the word in the interview has since been replayed throughout the years.

Prior to that year's draft, the Nets lost Pearl Washington to the Miami Heat in the NBA's expansion draft, and a roster that produced just 19 wins the season before saw minimal improvements that off-season. Woolridge signed a free-agent contract with the Lakers, and Birdsong was waived and would land in Boston for the final, uneventful year of his storied career. New Jersey opted to trade a 1991 second-round pick and 1996 second-rounder to Sacramento for Mike McGee, who averaged 13 points per game in his only season with the team.

Buck Williams was among the few veterans left on the squad, as eight players had less than three years of pro experience. The group of neophytes delighted Reed during the first 14 games of the season, posting a respectable .500 record. Hinson led the team in scoring at 16 per game while snatching 6.4 rebounds. The Nets' second-leading scorer, Joe Barry Carroll, was acquired at the start of the campaign along with Lester Conner from Houston. The Nets sent out Tony Brown, Frank Johnson, McCormick and Lorenzo Romar

Willis Reed coaching his club during the 1988–89 season. *Steven Lipofsky/LipofskyPhoto.com.*

as part of the package. Carroll was a former All-Star and a top pick in the 1980 NBA Draft, and the early returns on the trade for him were favorable for New Jersey. But that success was short-lived. After compiling 7 wins in 14 tries, the Nets went 19-49 the rest of the way with a roster littered with unproven and inexperienced players for a 26-56 finish.

1989–90

Just prior to the 1989 NBA Draft, all-time Net Buck Williams was traded to Portland for its 1989 first-round draft choice and Sam Bowie, who had been selected no. 2 overall in the 1984 draft—one pick ahead of Air Jordan.

With his eight seasons in New Jersey, Williams maintains the top spot in franchise history in several categories: games played (635), minutes played (23,100), 2-point field goals (3,979), free throws made (2,476), free throws attempted (3,818), offensive rebounds (2,588), defensive rebounds (4,988) and total rebounds (7,576). The three-time All-Star, Rookie of the Year Award winner and two-time All-Defensive NBA First Team selection holds claim to a laundry list of franchise records. Williams' longevity and star-caliber

Left: Sam Bowie enjoyed the best years of his NBA career in New Jersey. *Steven Lipofsky/ LipofskyPhoto.com.*

Right: Buck Williams' no. 52 is among the Nets' retired numbers currently hanging at Barclays Center. *Steven Lipofsky/LipofskyPhoto.com.*

play with the Nets throughout the 1980s has his no. 52 jersey hanging in its rightful place in the team's rafters. The Nets were already amid a pseudo-rebuild prior to trading Williams, but his departure spelled the official end to an era of perennial playoff teams in the 1980s.

New Jersey sent its 1989 first-round pick to Chicago in the trade involving Woolridge. The Bulls selected Stacey King with the no. 6 pick. The Nets held the twelfth spot and opted to take point guard Mookie Blaylock out of Oklahoma. The six-foot floor general was known for pushing the pace in the open court and was a lockdown defender who would lead the NBA in steals twice and was named to the NBA's All-Defensive First Team on two occasions in his decorated thirteen-year career. In August, Reed stepped down as head coach but remained with the team as the Senior Vice President of Basketball Operations under a new five-year contract agreement. Working alongside Weltman in the team's front office, Reed presided over roster decisions and eventually served as a key architect of the Nets' playoff teams of the early 1990s. Weltman and Reed led the coaching search and targeted Bill Fitch,

Rick Carlisle (*left*) and Bill Fitch (*right*) coaching along the Nets' bench. *Steven Lipofsky/ LipofskyPhoto.com.*

a two-time NBA Coach of the Year, NBA champion coach with the Celtics in 1981 and Western Conference champion with the Rockets in 1986. Throughout the course of his professional coaching career, Fitch developed a reputation for helping struggling teams gain respectability and ascend the NBA hierarchy of teams. He improved the Cavaliers win total from 15 in their inaugural year of 1970–71 to 49 in their sixth season. At his next stop, Fitch propelled Boston from a 29-win club in 1978–79 before his arrival into a 61-win club the next year.

Butch Beard stayed on as an assistant, now under coach Fitch, and thirty-year-old Rick Carlisle, who was signed by the team in October and was waived in December, made a transition to the coaching staff. The roster was hardly a spectacular collection of talent, but seven players averaged double figures. Hopson, Morris, Bowie and Purvis Short were former top-five NBA Draft picks.

Surprisingly, the Nets jumped out to a 2-0 start with wins over the Miami Heat and Orlando Magic, which had been added to the league via expansion the year before. The final 80 games of the year were nothing short of an unmitigated disaster, as the team posted a 15-65 mark the rest of the way.

In February, the Nets unloaded Carroll to Denver in exchange for Michael Cutright. Predictably, New Jersey drew the second-fewest fans that season, with 473,760 traveling to the Meadowlands to marvel at the opposing teams' star players. Fitch endured losing seasons during his first years rebuilding the programs in Cleveland and Houston, so, while the 17-win campaign was disconcerting to many, it was not exactly unforeseen. The franchise needed time to retool after hitting rock bottom.

1990–91

The 1990 NBA Draft set the stage for the Nets' teams that ultimately secured a run of three consecutive playoff berths in the early 1990s. Reed made two major trades two days before the draft. The first trade involved sending second-round picks in 1993 and 1995 to Orlando for the rights to thirty-three-year-old, two-time All-Star Reggie Theus.

The second transaction was a more intuitive move for a rebuilding team. New Jersey stockpiled draft picks by acquiring a 1990 first-rounder, a 1991 second-rounder and a 1992 second-rounder from Chicago for Hopson.

The Nets held the first overall pick in the 1990 draft and took power forward Derrick Coleman out of Syracuse. There was a great deal of trade talk between the front offices of the top teams on the draft board: Reed's Nets, Pat Williams' Magic and Bob Whitsitt's SuperSonics. Seattle held the second pick and desired Oregon State point guard Gary Payton, while Orlando had its sights set on shooting guard Dennis Scott of Georgia Tech. In the days leading up to the draft, Reed was vacillating between Scott and Coleman with the team's pick, and the three executives organized a conference call to ensure that Scott landed in Orlando. Williams offered two second-round picks as compensation in the deal. Jud Buechler, Seattle's second-round pick, was sent to the Nets as part of them agreeing not to take Scott.

As for Coleman, he drew comparisons to eventual Hall of Fame power forwards Charles Barkley and Karl Malone in the months leading up to the draft, but unlike those two legends, he had a knack for stretching the floor with accurate 3-point shooting. The Syracuse product won the NBA's Rookie of the Year Award by averaging 18.4 points, 10.3 rebounds and 1.2 blocks while shooting 34.2 percent from 3-point range. Coleman's rookie campaign was nothing short of sensational, but his NBA career plateaued during his five seasons in New Jersey, and he eventually regressed during what should have been the prime years of his career. Coleman, despite going down as an all-time Nets great, fell short of the lofty expectations of many analysts, who felt the Syracuse alum had the potential to be one of the NBA's best power forwards of all time. Talent-wise, Coleman had it all—Herculean strength, surprising bounce for a big man, nifty low-post moves, a soft shooting touch from short and long range and a nose for the ball. But by most estimates, he lacked the dogged work ethic and fiery passion of the game's greats.

Derrick Coleman won the 1990–91 NBA Rookie of the Year Award. *Photo credit to Steven Lipofsky/ LipofskyPhoto.com.*

Fitch opted for a veteran-laden lineup for the opening game of the 1990–91 season against the Indiana Pacers: Blaylock, Morris, Theus, Chris Dudley and Jack Haley. New Jersey's starting five would be reshuffled throughout the year until Fitch was satisfied with a consistent unit.

Despite a 2-9 record out of the gate, the Nets showed signs of improvement. Ten players were under twenty-six years old, and six of them were twenty-three or younger. New Jersey finished in the top ten in offensive pace, and Fitch maximized the youthful energy of his group to play at breakneck speed, but this did not translate to a winning formula. The Nets would lose 11 straight games spanning December 13 through January 15 and executed a three-team trade with Denver and Portland that brought one of the most memorable players in franchise history to the Garden State. Reed sent Greg Anderson and a 1992 first-round pick to the Nuggets for Terry Mills, while the Nuggets sent Walter Davis and a 1992 second-round pick to Portland, who then sent Dražen Petrović and a 1993 second-round pick to the Nets. None of the players or picks involved in the trade made anywhere near the impact that Petrović did at the Meadowlands.

The Croatian shooting guard had become frustrated with his lack of playing time under coach Rick Adelman in Portland, a team that would finish that year as the Western Conference runners-up and with a league-best 63-19 regular-season record. Petrović was an overlooked player in the 1986 NBA Draft as a third-round selection by the Trailblazers. The Croatian honed his talents overseas in the Yugoslavian pro league for two seasons, playing alongside his brother Aco in the backcourt, and he spent

Dražen Petrović was undoubtedly the purest shooter of his era. *Photo credit to Steven Lipofsky/ LipofskyPhoto.com.*

one season in a Spanish pro league before making his NBA debut during the 1989–90 season.

At the time of the Portland–New Jersey–Denver trade, the list of European players who transitioned to the NBA game was not long, but the list of European stars who turned into NBA stars was even shorter. Petrović was part of an elite club of late-1980s and early 1990s European-born players who gained fame and notoriety for their play in the NBA.

Over the final 43 games of the 1990–91 season, Petrović averaged 12.6 points on 50 percent shooting from the field. Less than two weeks after the trade, Petrović poured in a career-high 27 points against the Washington Bullets on February 7. He transformed from a malcontent with Adelman in Portland to an impactful player in Fitch's rotation, but the Nets managed just a 13-30 record with him in the lineup. Theus led the team in scoring (18.6) in his only season with the Nets and his last in the NBA before taking his talents to Greece for one season and then Italy before retiring. Coleman's stellar rookie campaign lives in the annals of Nets history. He tallied a career-high 42 points against Denver on February 15, while Blaylock added 4 points per game to his scoring year over year to reach 14.1 points per contest. Given Fitch's history, the 26-56 Nets were right on track to follow the Cleveland and Houston models of rebuilding under the experienced coach. New Jersey's 1991 NBA Draft pick was another driving force in ultimately bringing the franchise out of the doldrums.

6

RETURN TO PERENNIAL PLAYOFF CONTENTION

1991–92 through 1993–94

The Nets held the no. 2 overall pick in the 1991 NBA Draft, with Reed and company conducting due diligence on a loaded draft class. The only problem became evaluating one of the players the team had its sights set on, point guard Kenny Anderson out of Georgia Tech. Anderson admits he did not exactly take the customary route throughout the draft process.

> *I didn't have workouts. When I came out of school, I told all the NBA teams that I wasn't going to work out; accept me or don't. I did not even visit the Nets. So, I visit Sacramento, who was going no. 3 in the draft, so I thought they were going to pick me. I had no clue the New Jersey Nets were going to pick me. Joe Taub was on the decision-making on Kenny Anderson coming to the Nets, and Willis Reed was on that call.*

The Nets made Anderson their top choice despite no pre-draft workout and even with Blaylock coming into his own as the team's draft choice just two seasons earlier. On October 4, the Nets signed twenty-seven-year-old Jersey City native Rafael Addison, who spent the prior four seasons playing professionally in Italy after Phoenix drafted him in the second round of the 1986 NBA Draft. New Jersey was a team on the upswing but far from one of the NBA's elite clubs, and Anderson acknowledges he was not entirely sure what kind of situation he was walking into in New Jersey.

I really didn't know much about the NBA, but for some of the players. I'm coming from Oak City—Kenny Anderson—one of the best in high school and college, I just played and worked out on my own. I seldom watched NBA basketball. I really didn't know. I just thought the team was well-equipped with Mookie Blaylock, Derrick Coleman, Sam Bowie, all these college players that did very well. I just went in and did my part. I worked hard and waited for my chance to play.

Kenny Anderson thrived in his role as the Nets' franchise point guard of the 1990s. *Photo credit to Steven Lipofsky/LipofskyPhoto.com.*

The Nets posted a miserable 2-9 record in what had the makings of another lost season. New Jersey sunk to 7-18 before storming back with a 12-3 stretch. Anderson was incorporated into the lineup 47 games in to help the team find its footing. Just when the team was turning it around for Fitch and crew, things hit a snag. The Nets suffered an 8-game losing streak that spanned games before and after the All-Star break. Of New Jersey's losses, 4 came on a West Coast trip, while 7 of the 8 games overall were on the road. The Nets were showing classic signs of an untested team playing well in the friendly confines of their home arena and not so well in hostile road environments.

The Nets sat at 27-35 heading into a March 13 matchup with the Celtics. Sharpshooting Dražen Petrović would go off for a then-career-high 39 points as the Nets outscored Boston in the fourth, 34–20, for a dramatic 110–108 comeback win. Not only did Petrović establish himself as the Nets' leading scorer at 20.6 per contest, but he was also developing a leaguewide reputation as a lethal long-range threat and dynamic offensive force, something his backcourt mate Anderson took notice of.

Dražen Petrović was a great guy. He wasn't playing much in Portland, so he needed to get out of Portland so he could just play. He came to the New Jersey Nets, and he became that player. I watched his work ethic and it kind of rubbed off on me throughout my career. He was just a hard-nosed worker. He wanted to be known on the NBA pedestal, and he was. He had some big games for us. He could shoot the lights out, and he worked. I used to come into practice an hour before and he was just drenched with sweat, and he would stay after and get extra shots and worked extremely hard on his game. Other than that, he was a great friend, a great teammate, didn't say much, just did his work. That's what you want on a pro level.

The Croatian's tireless work ethic paid off, as he reached no. 17 on the NBA's leading scorer list that season. The Nets were climbing toward the .500 mark and into the Eastern Conference playoff picture. Despite Petrović emerging into a star and Coleman's progression from a rookie sensation into one of the most feared power forwards in the game, the top-heavy Nets did not have the requisite depth to compete with the NBA's upper-echelon franchises. Nonetheless, Fitch's crew was on pace to snap a five-year playoff drought. The 1991–92 campaign saw the team end up sixth in the conference at 40-42 for its best record in seven years. This set the stage for Fitch to square off with the team his NBA coaching career had started with, the Cavaliers.

A veteran club led by Brad Daugherty, Mark Price, Larry Nance, "Hot Rod" Williams and Craig Ehlo did exactly what many anticipated they would to an upstart Nets team that struggled on the road in hostile environments. The Cavs narrowly defeated New Jersey, 120–117, in the series opener, with Petrović tying Daugherty for a game-high 40 points. Coleman finished 1 assist shy of a triple-double. Clearly, the Nets had the Cavaliers' attention. Cleveland cruised to a 22-point Game 2 win, as it built a 16-point first-quarter lead and never looked back. The Nets returned home to an arena with the fifth-worst attendance in the league, but 15,258 boisterous fans packed the stands as Morris tied Nance for a game-high 28 points to stave off elimination. The Nets eyed an opportunity to send the series back to Cleveland for a do-or-die Game 5. The Nets held a 6-point advantage heading into the fourth quarter, but the experience of the Cavaliers prevailed, and they advanced to the semifinals with a 98–89 win. New Jersey persevered through some of the darkest moments of its rebuild and started to gain respectability across the NBA. Reed was pulling the right strings in the front office, and Fitch proved for the third time in his career that he could coach through a rebuild and come out the other side.

1992–93

While the team appeared to be trending up from the outside looking in, there was a clash between Fitch's old-school coaching style and his players, with two public incidents bringing this fact into the public eye. Coleman and Morris refused to check in during the Nets' late-season playoff run after a disagreement with Fitch, and Petrović pulled the exact same stunt during the team's Game 4 playoff elimination at the hands of the Cavaliers. Even though he didn't see eye to eye with Fitch, Petrović enjoyed a stellar season and finished second in the NBA in 3-point shooting percentage (44.4).

With tension filling the backdrop to a successful season, Fitch decided that his best course of action was to resign from his post with one year left on his contract and just two weeks after the Nets were ousted from the playoffs. In the span of three seasons, New Jersey more than doubled its win total, but Fitch's coaching and motivational philosophy was not resonating with his players. Reed commenced the search for a replacement in earnest, and several names were linked to the coaching vacancy, including former Hawks coach Mike Fratello and former Pistons coach Chuck Daly.

Chuck Daly brought championship experience and instant credibility to the Nets. *Photo credit to Steven Lipofsky/ LipofskyPhoto.com.*

On May 28, Daly was appointed the twelfth head coach in team history. His reputation preceded him as the director of the "Bad Boy" Pistons, winners of back-to-back titles in the 1988–89 and 1989–90 seasons. Like Fitch, Daly's coaching experience dated to the mid-1950s. Daly served under Duke head coach and future College Basketball Hall of Famer Vic Bubas starting in 1963. In six seasons as a college assistant, Daly was part of two NCAA Final Four teams and gained national notoriety and attention for being an integral part of the Blue Devils' successful run. From there, Daly was appointed head coach of Boston College. The independent Golden Eagles failed to qualify for the NCAA Tournament in either of Daly's two seasons at the helm. He returned to his home state to coach Penn of the Ivy League for six seasons and spurred the Quakers on to four NCAA

Tournament berths, surpassing 20 wins four times and reaching no. 2 in the AP Poll in his first year with the team. They ultimately lost in the regional finals to Dean Smith's Tarheels. As fate would have it, Daly would have his first opportunity in the NBA with none other than the same franchise with which Fitch had begun his coaching career, the Cavaliers. Fitch's public run-ins with his players were well chronicled, and Daly brought an entirely different philosophical approach, according to Anderson.

Chuck Daly was a great coach. We became good for each other. I really believe that. He let me do my thing. He was the type of coach where the point guard coached the team. I remember him from his Detroit days with Isiah Thomas, it was just a great feeling to have a great coach like that in your corner who is willing to better you not only as a player, but as a human being.

He really wasn't that attitude type of coach like if you didn't do this or do that you weren't going to play. It was just that somehow you wanted to do well for yourself. He told you the ins and outs and you went about doing it. He was a professional. He handled everything as a coach like a professional. That's what I learned. How to be a professional under Chuck Daly. How to take care of your own, and you had to do that when you are a professional. High school and college you have coaches telling you what to do, but in the pros your coach tells you, but if you don't get it done, they'll get somebody in to get it done. That's the kind of realm of a coach he was. He was a great coach.

On February 15, 1992, Daly was officially named the coach of the Men's Olympic Basketball Team, later nicknamed the "Dream Team." It featured an immensely talented roster littered with stars and larger-than-life personalities. Daly's team won all eight contests by an average margin of 43.8 points that summer and ran roughshod over all international competition, including a Petrović - and Kukoc-led Croatian team in the gold medal game, 117–85. The 32-point triumph in the gold medal game marked the narrowest win in the Dream Team's historic run, and Petrović tallied a game-high 24 points, topping American-born basketball legends Jordan, Pippen, Barkley, Patrick Ewing and his own teammate, Kukoc. As fate would have it, the Croatian star (Petrović) and the two-time NBA champion coach (Daly) saw their paths cross again—this time, fighting on the same team, the Nets.

Daly was consumed with Olympic duties in Barcelona, Spain, but back in the Garden State, Reed was preparing for a 1992 NBA Draft class that featured imposing big men: Shaquille O'Neal, Alonzo Mourning and Christian Laettner. The Nets' no. 12 overall selection was already packaged and sent to the Nuggets in the three-team deal between New Jersey, Denver and Portland that brought Petrović to the Nets. Astonishingly, outside of Latrell Sprewell, who was selected no. 24 overall by Golden State, not a single player beyond no. 6 Tom Gugliotta would receive a single All-Star nod. The top-heavy 1992 NBA Draft had virtually no quality depth in the player pool, but a handful of impact players were selected, and the Nets found a more than serviceable power forward in Louisiana Tech's P.J. Brown.

Instead of playing his rookie season in the NBA, New Jersey's second-round pick elected to play in the Greek Basket League (GBL). The decision ultimately proved to be the right one for Brown's career, which spanned fifteen meaningful seasons in the NBA, his first three with New Jersey.

With a renewed sense of buzz surrounding the team's new coaching hire and the progression of a talented young roster, Brendan Byrne Arena drew roughly 103,000 more fans in Daly's first year in New Jersey than in Fitch's last year.

Prior to the start of the regular season, the Nets swung a trade with Philadelphia that sent a pair of future second-round picks in the 1994

Maurice Cheeks played the final season of his storied sixteen-year NBA career with the Nets. *Photo credit to Steven Lipofsky/ LipofskyPhoto.com.*

and 1997 NBA Drafts in exchange for St. John's product Jayson Williams. The former no. 21 pick in 1990 by Phoenix was dealt to Philadelphia for a 1994 first-rounder before he ever played for the Suns. After two seasons in the City of Brotherly Love, averaging just over eleven minutes, Williams joined New Jersey. He would make a name for himself on the court by way of his ferocious rebounding and inside presence, but his off-the-court antics and legal problems created a distraction for the franchise and ultimately derailed his once-promising NBA career. Less than one month after acquiring Williams, the Nets sent Blaylock and Hinson to Atlanta for Rumeal Robinson, as it was clear that the mantle was being passed to the second-year floor general in Anderson to run the show. Less than a week after the Blaylock trade,

Daly was instrumental in signing free-agent forward and former Piston Rick Mahorn. After 11 games, the Nets sat at 4-7 before a 6-game win streak. Daly's crew failed to topple the teams ahead of them in the Eastern Conference pecking order: the Knicks, Bulls, Cavaliers and Hornets. At the conclusion of the campaign, the Nets picked up just 5 wins in 16 games against those upper-echelon clubs. Reed tried to make a pair of moves to solidify and add to the veteran leadership of the club, signing thirty-six-year-old point guard Maurice Cheeks in early January and teaming him up with an all-time Net in thirty-six-year-old Bernard King.

Leading up to and though the All-Star break, New Jersey was really hitting its stride and earned a rousing 102–76 home win over the Knicks (36-18) on February 28 to improve to 31-24. The win in a nationally televised game had dire consequences for the Nets on the injury front. Knicks guard John Starks committed a flagrant foul with 8:52 left in the third quarter on Anderson, who absorbed the contact to convert an acrobatic, fast-break layup. New Jersey's guard landed awkwardly on his left wrist attempting to break his fall. The foul was not out of character for Starks or the brawling Knicks teams of the era. Nonetheless, it infuriated Daly and ultimately rallied the Nets to a lopsided victory, recalled Anderson.

The injuries were devastating for the New Jersey Nets the year I got hurt and broke my wrist with the illegal foul when John Starks pushed me out of the air. It was frustrating for me and something I just had to learn from. Injuries, they happen. They brought in different point guards, Rumeal Robinson, he played pretty solid for us, they brought in Maurice Cheeks, some older, veteran guards, but we just couldn't keep up with the teams that were ahead of us. It was a trying time for me because I wanted to be out there playing, but I couldn't play. When this is brought up to me, if I wouldn't have got injured, what would have happened? You just have to continue to play on. Derrick had a great season. It was just crazy man. I wish I had that season back.

In the immediate aftermath, Daly inserted the newly acquired Rumeal Robinson to replace Anderson as the starting point guard, and the Nets pushed their record to 13 games over the .500 mark and capitalized on a forgiving schedule by knocking off bottom-feeding teams in the month of March.

As the calendar turned to April, the wheels fell off the wagon for New Jersey, as it faced a bevy of premier Eastern Conference clubs and lost seven in a row to go 1-10 to conclude the year. New Jersey sat in a virtual tie with

Boston for the no. 3 seed in the East prior to the late-season collapse and was suddenly in an eerily similar scenario to 1992—another playoff meeting with Cleveland. The Cavaliers again were the no. 3 seed, and the Nets sat at no. 6.

The core of Cleveland's roster that foiled the Nets in the 1992 playoffs was fully intact and even more battle-tested than the year before. New Jersey and Cleveland traded wins and losses, Cleveland claiming Games 1 and 3 and the Nets winning Games 2 and 4. In Game 5, Daughtery, Nance and Price combined for 60 points, while Coleman's 33 was not enough to stave off elimination. New Jersey's power forward put forth an otherworldly effort by posting series averages of 26.8 points, 13.4 rebounds, 2.6 blocks and 1.2 steals and shot 53.2 percent. While Coleman's output was nothing short of heroic, Petrović struggled from the field (45.5 percent) and from long range (33.3 percent), making just two of six 3-point attempts. At first glance, the Croatian's final numbers do not reflect a poor shooting performance, but when compared with his production in the 1992 playoffs against Cleveland (24.3 points on 53.9 percent shooting, including the 4-of-12 output from 3-point range), it becomes clear that Lenny Wilkens' plan to lock down the Nets' sharpshooter was effective. Petrović missed 12 games during the year with a partially torn ligament in his left knee, but he still led the team in scoring during the campaign. Morris was second in team scoring for the playoff series against Cleveland (17 points per contest) and converted a sizzling 55.7 percent of his shot attempts. Coleman and Petrović were named to the All-NBA Third Team, but the Nets suffered a second consecutive first-round exit at the hands of the Cavaliers.

Clearly, Anderson's season-ending injury was a dashing blow to the team's hopes of a deep playoff run, but while Anderson would return healthy in time for the start of the 1993–94 campaign, tragedy struck one of New Jersey's most beloved stars.

1993–94

On June 7, Dražen Petrović was tragically killed on the rain-soaked Autobahn 9 outside of Munich, Germany, when a Volkswagen Golf driven by his girlfriend, Klara Szalantzy, twenty-three, spun out of control and slammed into a truck that had skid across and blocked the roadway. According to the accident report, the truck driver exited his vehicle and

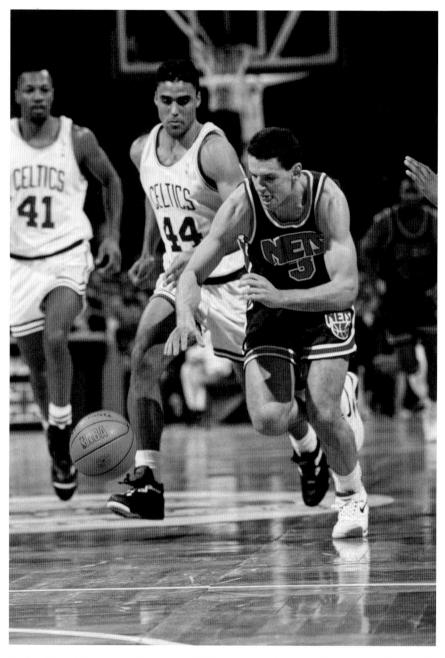

Dražen Petrović's tragic passing saw the NBA lose an all-time great far too soon. *Photo credit to Steven Lipofsky/LipofskyPhoto.com.*

tried to notify oncoming cars, but heavy rain and the high rate of speed of cars on the highway made it nearly impossible for Petrović's car to avoid the deadly crash. Szalantzy and Hilal Edebal, twenty-three, another passenger in the vehicle, were hospitalized with serious injuries. Petrović died at the scene. The Nets' shooting guard was participating in the 1993 EuroBasket qualifying tournament in Berlin with the Croatian national team and was departing Germany en route to his hometown in Croatia's capital city, Zagreb. Fatefully, Petrović reportedly opted to skip his return flight to Zagreb and decided to drive with Szalantzy and Edebal instead.

Thousands of people attended Petrović's funeral on June 11 in Zagreb, and millions of basketball fans worldwide paid their respects to one of the greatest European players to ever play on the NBA stage. At just twenty-eight years of age, the Nets' cultural icon and basketball sensation was gone in a flash. The Nets had to find a way to handle the heartbreak and spiritual toll that losing a leader on and off the court ultimately had on the franchise. As part of the healing process, the Nets paid homage to the basketball legend by retiring his no. 3 jersey during the upcoming season on November 11.

Anderson, a close friend and confidant of Petrović, shared his thoughts on that emotional night in November and how, in his mind, it spelled the beginning of the end for New Jersey's rise to basketball prominence.

> *It was just tough man. When his mother came back for the ceremony it was tough. Very emotional. Rex Walters tried to fit in and do what he did, but they couldn't get it done. They were good players, but they weren't Dražen Petrović. Myself, Derrick Coleman, Dražen Petrović, we had all the pieces together, the one, the two and the four or five with Derrick Coleman, so it was just tough to rebound from that. We tried, but I know that if we would have stayed together, Derrick would have re-signed, I would have re-signed, I think we would have been Eastern Conference champs one of those years. We would have won it. We would have. We were determined to if he would have lived.*

With a heavy heart and tears still in his eyes, Reed prepared for the 1993 NBA Draft facing a gargantuan void in the middle of the team's starting lineup. Two weeks prior to the 1993 rookie draft class being selected, Reed sent Bowie and the Nets' second-round pick in 1998 to the Lakers in exchange for center Benoit Benjamin, a ten-year vet. Bowie started 231 of 280 games he played in four seasons with the Nets and had the most successful run of his career at the Meadowlands, producing averages of

The Nets celebrated Dražen Petrović's life in a touching ceremony in the Meadowlands on November 11, 1993. *Steven Lipofsky/ LipofskyPhoto.com.*

12.8 points, 8.2 rebounds and 1.6 blocks. Unfortunately for Bowie, he would never shed the unfair label as a "draft bust," as he was selected behind top pick Hakeem Olajuwon and—even more notoriously—ahead of Jordan in the 1984 NBA Draft.

New Jersey was aiming to select a potential starter with the no. 16 pick, but the 1993 draft would be another top-heavy rookie class that featured only a handful of players with any NBA staying power. It was no secret that the Nets were hungry for a shooting guard, but identifying an adequate replacement for Petrović would prove a near impossible task. Much like Bowie's unfair "draft bust" label, the Nets' eventual pick at no. 16 overall, Kansas' left-handed sharpshooter Rex Walters, had huge shoes to fill.

The summer of 1993 was nothing short of brutal for the Nets, but that largely solemn period included a neat piece of basketball pop culture that unintentionally paid homage to Petrović and showcased another Nets starter in its marketing efforts.

In April 1993, just two weeks before the Nets' playoff elimination and less than two months prior to Petrović's passing, video game developer Midway released NBA Jam Arcade throughout North America. The cover art for the game featured several notable 1990s NBA superstars, including the Nets' Coleman attempting a chase-down block of Clyde Drexler on the arcade's cabinet art. NBA Jam became an instant nationwide and, eventually, worldwide phenomenon. Petrović appeared in the arcade version of the game posthumously.

Outside of the virtual world, the Nets' GM hunted for a starting-caliber two-guard for his playoff-ready team. Scouring the free-agent market, Reed identified five-year vet Kevin Edwards, twenty-eight, as a viable candidate. The combo guard signed a five-year, $9.6 million deal to join New Jersey. He would start all 82 games in that upcoming season and enjoyed a career year. The Nets added free-agent forward Armen Gilliam on a three-year, $4.68 million contract. Reed then signed David Wesley for depth behind Edwards in a chaotic off-season that required the team to make moves to stay relevant in a highly competitive Eastern Conference.

On the front-office side, Jon Spoelstra, father to future Heat head coach Erik, served as the team's president starting in 1993 and through 1995 following eleven years as Portland's GM. Jon Spoelstra was instrumental in growing New Jersey's local sponsorship sales from $400,000 to $7 million during his tenure, along with selling out the arena twenty-nine times compared to zero sellouts before his arrival. He successfully navigated the post-Petrović era. Spoelstra, along with members of the Secaucas Seven, collaborated to concoct unconventional marketing and branding campaigns in the years ahead, including trying to convince the City of East Rutherford to change its name to "Nike." The corporate sponsorship and change of the team's host city never gained much traction, but at one time Spoelstra and ownership initially approved a proposed name change from "Nets" to "Swamp Dragons," as the team ranked dead last in merchandise sales. When word got out about the proposed change days before the final vote by the team's board of governors, there was a great deal of public backlash, including most notably from NBA Commissioner David Stern and New Jersey governor Christine Whitman. The cartoonish renditions of the fictional Meadowlands beast remains a fun tidbit in the team's zany history, but this outlandish idea also died on the vine. The league voted on the proposed name change, with the Nets being the only team to vote against it. Once again, the Secaucus Seven couldn't reach a consensus and the quirky marketing ploy never came to fruition.

Derrick Coleman electrified the Meadowlands in five seasons with the Nets. *Steven Lipofsky/ LipofskyPhoto.com.*

On the hardwood, Anderson fully recovered from wrist surgery and compiled a career year, while his partner in crime, Coleman, also produced career-best numbers. The Nets extended a record eight-year, $69 million contract offer that would have made Coleman the NBA's highest-paid player per season. Coleman's representation rejected the offering, stating that the most lucrative years were backloaded while the Nets controlled the eighth-year option. In a way, Coleman wanted to bet on himself and see what the market would bear the next several years as he built his overall free-agent value.

Personal accolades were aplenty for Anderson, Coleman and Edwards, but a 7-13 record through the first 20 games of the year was hardly spectacular. New Jersey's early-season schedule was littered with Western Conference opponents; seven of those ten matchups were on the road. The unconventional early slate put the Nets in an early-season sub-.500 hole that they did not climb out of until the first two games following the All-Star break. Daly experimented with several starting lineups, including plugging in third-year seven-footer Dwayne Schintzius at center and Morris at small forward, a combination that was quickly abandoned after the first five games. Ron Anderson, who had signed a free-agent deal in November, was briefly inserted into the lineup to replace Morris but was waived just a month later. Relegated to bench duties after an off-season dedicated to replenishing the roster sans Petrović, Robinson was dealt to Charlotte in early December in exchange for Johnny Newman.

The Nets hit their stride, winning 5 consecutive games from January 14 through January 22, and they amassed a 13-4 record spanning before and after the All-Star break.

Remarkably, the 1993–94 campaign marked the eighteenth season since New Jersey joined the NBA. Anderson and Coleman started in the 1994 NBA All-Star Game, marking the first time any Net started in an NBA All-

Star Game. The game was held in Minneapolis, Minnesota. The Nets duo started alongside Chicago stars B.J. Armstrong and Pippen, with Shaquille O'Neal playing center.

Over the final 24 regular season games, Daly started Anderson, Edwards, Benjamin, P.J. Brown and Coleman, and this produced a 15-9 record for a 45-37 overall mark to peg them seventh in a stacked Eastern Conference. Anderson tallied a career-high 45 points in an overtime win against the Pistons on April 15. New Jersey was on a collision course with their crosstown rival, the no. 2 seeded Knicks—a team they beat four out of five times in the regular season.

Anderson's 1992–93 campaign was cut short by Starks' foul that resulted in the point guard suffering a season-ending wrist injury. New Jersey's hopes were high entering the playoff matchup, and for Anderson, no love was lost in the area rivalry. "I just thought we were going to beat them in the playoffs. We really handled them in the regular season. The playoffs with the Knicks and the Nets was awesome. I know the Garden was sold out, and I think the Meadowlands was sold out. I played for the New Jersey Nets. I just really didn't like the New York Knicks organization."

The two clubs would meet in the playoffs for the first time since 1982–83 season, when the Knicks swept the best-of-three first-round series, 2–0. New York finished with the top overall defense in the NBA this time, surrendering just 91.5 points per game. The Nets got a rude awakening at MSG for Games 1 and 2, with Ewing and company putting the clamps down and limiting New Jersey to just 13 first-quarter points in Game 1 on their way to a 91–80 win.

The story of the series became a combination of the Nets' scoring droughts coupled with the Knicks' tenacious defense. New Jersey shot 36.6 percent from the field in the Game 1 loss and a paltry 29.2 percent in the Game 2 defeat. In their return to Brendan Byrne Arena for Game 3, the Nets finally cracked the 90-point scoring plateau, and they shot over 40 percent from the field for the first time in the series. Despite holding an 11-point

Chuck Daly left the Nets after just two seasons as head coach. *Steven Lipofsky/LipofskyPhoto.com.*

lead entering the fourth quarter, the Nets were forced into overtime, as the Knicks' stingy defense held New Jersey to just 9 points in the fourth quarter in East Rutherford.

New Jersey ultimately prevailed in overtime, 93–92, to clinch its first ever playoff win over the Knicks and, in doing so, avoided a first-round sweep. The Nets' season ended in Game 4, as Ewing went off for 36 points and 14 rebounds. Coleman dropped in 31, and Anderson was the only other Net in double figures with 12. New Jersey's third consecutive playoff run ended in the same fashion as the first two, in a first-round exit.

Many fans could not help but think how the series outcome could have been different with Petrović's shooting prowess in the fold to open the floor and force the Knicks to extend their defense outside the paint.

Nonetheless, that off-season brought about another change for the organization, with Daly resigning from his post on May 26, amid reports that a lack of maturity from some of his players created frustration. The basketball lifer then entered the broadcasting realm with TNT throughout the mid-1990s. He coached Orlando for the final two seasons of the decade before closing the book on his storied coaching career.

7

THE LOST SEASONS

1994–95 through 1995–96

Daly's two seasons in New Jersey failed to deliver the deep playoff runs that many fans anticipated, but his hiring brought instant credibility to the franchise. Ironically, Daly's tenure mirrored Fitch's time with the team, as neither coach could propel the Nets beyond the opening round of the playoffs. Philosophical differences with star players prompted each to ultimately resign. New Jersey hardly knew at the time that it had a pair of assistant coaches on staff who would go on to have successful head-coaching careers in the NBA in Carlisle and Paul Silas. As is often the case in the NBA fraternity, familiarity and loyalty can trump qualifications and competence. To that end, Reed hired former Knicks teammate Butch Beard, who had spent four years as an assistant coach in New York on Reed's and then Red Holtzman's staff immediately following his retirement as a player. Beard joined the Nets as an assistant for two seasons starting in 1988–89, then coached Howard University for four years before taking the head job at the Meadowlands.

Even with Reed's comrade in the fold, the team's expectations were minimal. Prognosticators pegged the Nets as a 32-win club. With fan interest waning, Spoelstra unleashed a famous marketing campaign whereby he mailed rubber chickens to all Nets season-ticket holders who had not yet renewed their seats with the tagline, "Don't Fowl Out!"

Coleman and Anderson were unable to get on the same page, even with Daly there. Rumblings of discord between the Nets' two All-Stars casted doubt about the duo's future together. New Jersey's biggest draft need was clearly a man in the middle, as Benjamin was underwhelming in the starting lineup. The 1994 draft class featured Glenn Robinson and future co–Rookies of the Year and future Hall of Famers Grant Hill and Jason Kidd, who were immediately off the board within the top three picks.

The Nets sat at no. 14 overall, and while every NBA team in the first round selected an American-born player, the Nets went for an international phenomenon and an intriguing prospect in Nigerian Yinka Dare out of George Washington University. Dare spent just two years in college before declaring for the NBA Draft, but in his short time with the Colonials, he became the school's shot-blocking leader. As a freshman, he led the team to the NCAA Tournament Sweet 16 round for the first time ever. In his sophomore season, the team advanced to the Round of 32. Posting collegiate averages of 13.8 points and 10.7 rebounds was impressive enough for a mid-major standout, but skepticism centered on whether his game would translate to the NBA. Reed signed point guard Chris Childs, who had spent the previous five years in the Continental Basketball Association (CBA) after going undrafted in the 1989 NBA Draft out of Boise State. "Sleepy Floyd" returned to the Nets on a veteran's minimum deal to finish his playing career in New Jersey.

Injuries ravaged the Nets' fracturing roster. Coleman missed 26 games, Anderson 10, Edwards 68 and Childs 29. Dare appeared in 1 game, playing just three minutes before suffering a season-ending ACL tear. New Jersey sat at a middling 12-15 after winning its third straight on December 21, but as injuries piled up, Beard's crew went just 18-37 for the remaining two-thirds of the slate to finish with the league's seventh-worst record at 30-52.

1995–96

Prior to the 1994–95 campaign, the NBA announced that it would be expanding the league by two teams following the season, holding an expansion draft. Two Canadian-based franchises were established: the Vancouver Grizzlies and the Toronto Raptors.

As part of the expansion draft, the Nets left Benjamin and Dare unprotected, and so the Grizzlies selected Benjamin, leaving the Nets down a starting center. New Jersey saw future NBA all-time big men Rasheed Wallace and Kevin Garnett fly off the 1995 NBA Draft board at nos. 4 and 5, respectively, leaving behind a thin pool of centers still available at no. 9.

Fresh off an NCAA championship with UCLA, in a season during which he was named the tournament's most outstanding player, Ed O'Bannon became New Jersey's top draft choice. Accolades were aplenty for the Consensus First-Team All-American, but his wiry, six-foot, eight-inch, 220-pound frame raised doubts about his ability to endure the physical punishment of battling in the paint with bruising big men in the '90s NBA landscape. The South Los Angeles native tried to adjust to the East Coast climate and the faster-paced lifestyle, but the homesick twenty-three-year-old was not able to build on his decorated collegiate career after he joined the NBA.

Bobby Marks, who joined the Nets in the summer of 1995 as a seasonal intern and eventually ascended to a prominent role as the team's Assistant General Manager in 2010, shared his early recollections working under Reed during less than glamourous times in the Garden State.

> *My first impression of the Nets was how poor their facilities were. We had an office space at 405 Murray Parkway, it was the whole top level of an office building. From the business standpoint, it was great because there was a bullpen for ticket sales, but we also had basketball operations in there. It was a small department, there was Willis, there was no assistant GM, there were two scouts, and we had a secretary. I would say probably in total we had twelve people in all when you considered the trainers, and I don't think we even had a strength coach. We used A-P-A practice facility in North Bergen, which was a trucking facility that you basically shared. It was a watered-down, poor version of a YMCA and that is being kind to a YMCA. You basically were getting changed in the locker room with guys who were driving trucks cross-country, who were making a pitstop to drop off stuff in New York City.*

Marks joined the Nets during a transitional period in the franchise's history, amid rumblings that Coleman would test the open market when he became a free agent while dropping not-so-subtle hints that his future with the Nets was tenuous at best. Thus, an opportunity existed for O'Bannon, but it never panned out.

Playoffs were only a pipe dream with the Nets starting 5-8 and they promptly consummated a deal with Philadelphia to send Coleman, Walters and Sean Higgins in exchange for Shawn Bradley, Greg Graham and Tim Perry.

Rowe, who served as the Executive Vice-President and General Manager of the Meadowlands Sports Complex from 1987 to 1995, then joined the

Nets in November 1995 as a Co-owner, President and Alternative Governor, detailed how Coleman's trade to Philadelphia came to be.

> *When I first got to the team in November of 1995, I talked to everybody in the league office, I talked to a couple other general managers and scouts on other teams, and I relied very heavily on Willis Reed's great basketball mind. While he probably didn't enjoy the success off the court that he had on the court, he had a great basketball mind. When we looked through the roster my first couple of weeks, we realized that Derrick Coleman was a former All-Star and Kenny Anderson was a former All-Star, but we needed future All-Stars, and they were our two most marketable players. When I was at the Meadowlands, I had worked to try and build an arena in Camden for the Philadelphia 76ers, and I developed a relationship with the then-owner of the 76ers, a guy named Harold Katz. As luck would have it, within my first week of being with the Nets, Harold's team is playing against the Nets at the Meadowlands. I sat with him, and we began talking about the team and there was a player on his team, Jerry Stackhouse, who he loved, and we started talking about rosters, and I said, "Well, do you have anybody on your team that's not touchable?" And he said, "Stackhouse." I said, "What about the Big Guy?" I was talking about Shawn Bradley. And he said, "You can have him, who do you have?" At this point, I'm like playing fantasy basketball here. I'm at the game looking at my roster and his roster. Now, I know why I'm sitting down, I'm sitting down because Willis instructed me to trade Derrick Coleman. Willis had not been able to do it in the year before I got there but he knew Derrick would be on a different team. He knew the Nets would be better without Derrick Coleman. I had become friends with Derrick Coleman, I see him once a year from other business that I have in Detroit. I like him a lot, love his family, but the Nets got better without Derrick Coleman, and Willis was right. We wound up making the Shawn Bradley–Derrick Coleman trade the following week after that basketball game when I sat next to Harold.*

As Rowe illustrates, Coleman's trade was in the best interest of both the player and the team, but the former Syracuse standout left a lasting impact during his five seasons with New Jersey, holding claim to several top-ten all-time franchise records, including: tied at no. 7 in blocks per game (1.6), no. 6 in rebounds per game (10.6), tied at no. 5 in total triple-doubles (4), no. 7 in offensive rebounds (1,148), no. 4 in free-throw attempts (2,413), no. 10 in field goal attempts (5,368), no. 4 in defensive rebounds (2,542) and no. 9 in points (6,930).

Coleman's NBA career took a precipitous fall after his trade to Philadelphia, a squad with title aspirations hoping the former no. 1 overall pick could be the missing piece. Coleman played in just 11 games in his first season in the City of Brotherly Love, as ankle problems and issues with staying in game shape plagued him that season and really for the remainder of his NBA career. In his ten seasons after leaving New Jersey, Coleman never approached the 20-point-per-game scoring plateau and averaged double digits in rebounds just once. By comparison, Coleman achieved that scoring feat in three of his five seasons with the Nets and averaged double-digit rebounds in four of five seasons. What should have been the prime years of his career were squandered by a questionable

Standing at a towering seven feet, six inches, Shawn Bradley was one of the tallest players in NBA history. *Steven Lipofsky/ LipofskyPhoto.com.*

work ethic, off-the-court issues and injuries. The centerpiece of the trade from the Nets' perspective was a unique big man with an imposing height (seven feet, six inches) but a scrawny build (just 225 pounds). Bradley would go on to become the Nets' eventual franchise leader in blocked shots per game (3.8).

While things had run their course for Coleman in the Garden State, the Nets' regime was ready to make a change. Rowe needed to assure everyone in the organization that it was not going to be open season for trades and that things would stabilize once the dust settled. "The following week, the Nets' owners were a little concerned about the trade and thought we were breaking down the team. Some of the players were very concerned because within a week or two after that we then traded Kenny Anderson. I went down for one of my few team meetings, Willis asked me to come down and make the players a little more comfortable that I wasn't trying to get rid of everybody. I think I did an okay job. It was the first time I was ever the shortest guy in a group of fifteen people."

Anderson was the next domino to fall. He was dealt with Gerald Glass to Charlotte for Kendall Gill and Khalid Reeves. Gill, a twenty-seven-year-old shooting guard who spent two seasons in Seattle and three and a half with

Kendall Gill wanted to create his own legacy in New Jersey. *Steven Lipofsky/LipofskyPhoto.com*.

Charlotte before joining the Nets, became the poster child for the late 1990s and early-2000s Nets teams. Gill welcomed the trade to the Nets and recalled an unfortunate injury that curtailed his first season with the franchise. "I can tell you this, when I came to New Jersey, Butch Beard was the coach and I was so ecstatic because I got an opportunity to play my natural position at the two guard, and Chris Childs moved into the one position. Then you had P.J. Brown, Armen Gilliam and we actually started winning. We could feel that we could be a playoff team, now. Unfortunately, about 16, 17 games into my first year with the Nets, I broke my hand on Reggie Miller's elbow and our momentum stopped."

Even after Gill's setback, the Nets compiled a 5-game winning streak spanning February 13–21 to improve their record to 23-29 and get within striking distance of eighth-seeded Miami.

Gill recalls attempting a comeback from his injury over the final two months to make a late playoff run, but the Nets' GM would have none of it.

I can remember getting ready to come back and I'm out on the court warming up, and Willis Reed, who was the GM at the time, comes to me and says, "Kendall what are you doing?" I'm warming up because I wanted to play and was excited to get back since we still had an opportunity if we got on a winning streak to get in the playoffs. He was like, "No, we're going for the draft pick." So, he totally shut it down.

Even if we did make the playoffs, we probably wouldn't have gone very far, and the front office was looking toward the future. Still, I think when a team makes the playoffs, it still gives you momentum going into the next season. We make the playoffs, and we can build from there. That's the way I felt about it.

Formerly known as Brendan Byrne Arena, the newly branded Continental Airlines Arena hosted the NCAA Final Four in March 1996. The nationally televised event would draw considerable attention to the venue. Rowe details how the organization successfully landed a corporate naming-rights sponsorship deal just in time for the showcase event.

Our building was one of the earliest to do it, if not the first to have a naming rights partner that wasn't part of the construction of the building. It wasn't a concrete company that helped build the building, it was an independent brand that was looking to market itself. We had extraordinary relationships with Continental Airlines at the time. There were a number of people that both I knew and people who were on our board at the Meadowlands who knew a number of people who were doing marketing and public relations for Continental Airlines. They were looking to really make an impact. They were just growing and were a shell of what you now see at Newark Airport in terms of Terminal C and the hub that it's become. They were looking to brand themselves as something really big. I'd like to tell you there was a long chase and we came out bloodied from chasing them for years, but timing was perfect. They were looking to make an impact and a statement in the New York and New Jersey market because of their growing brand and we had a little event coming up in 1996, called the Final Four, which they thought was an extraordinary opportunity to have their brand advertised on the outside of that building. So as luck would have it, there was a lot of hard work by my marketing department of course, those two forces came together, and we actually had two bidders. We had another huge national brand which was located in New York who wanted it and Continental Airlines. Long story short, we got Continental in there just in time to get them up and running for the Final Four in 1996.

Even though it was a part of the greater New York metropolitan market, East Rutherford, New Jersey, became the smallest town at the time to host the event. The NCAA Final Four featured Rick Pitino's Kentucky Wildcats against John Calipari's Massachusetts Minutemen, followed by Jim Boeheim's Syracuse Orangemen taking on Richard Williams' Mississippi State Bulldogs. Kentucky advanced to the final round, ultimately defeating Syracuse for its sixth title in the program's storied history. Point guard Tony Delk won the tournament's Most Outstanding Player Award. Of more consequence to the Nets, the NCAA Executive Committee investigated Minutemen center Marcus Camby for allegedly receiving improper gifts from agents. This brought increased scrutiny to Calipari by the NCAA and made his future with the program doubtful. (On May 8, 1997, the school was eventually forced to vacate its Final Four appearance.)

These events coincided with New Jersey parting ways with Beard, as New Jersey went 2-12 over the final 14 games to finish 30-52 for the second straight season, missing the playoffs yet again.

8

TEAM IDENTITY REDEFINED

1996–97 through 1997–98

Before Calipari jumped on the Nets' radar, the team unsuccessfully courted another NCAA 1996 Final Four coach to take over at the Meadowlands: Rick Pitino. Unlike Calipari, Pitino had prior NBA coaching experience, having spent two years as an assistant with the Knicks in the mid-1980s. He then rejoined the organization as head coach in the late 1980s after a two-year stint as head coach of Providence. New York made the playoffs in both of Pitino's seasons at the helm, winning 52 games in his second season and pushing Jordan's Bulls to six games in the semifinals. In fact, Pitino, a UMass alum, endorsed Calipari when the school conducted a head-coach search in 1988. Now, the two legendary college coaches' paths would intersect, but it was Pitino who rejected a $25 million contract offer to become the franchise's next coach, General Manager and part-owner. Just one week after swinging and missing on Pitino, the Nets and Calipari agreed to a five-year, $15 million deal, with the former UMass coach gaining control of basketball operations. Reed ultimately became the team's senior vice-president of basketball operations, while Calipari served as the primary front-office executive. Reed was still very much in the picture in a senior-level advisory role, but the 1996 NBA Draft would be on Calipari's watch during a transformative period for the team.

Winds of change were swirling around the Meadowlands, and the ownership group, the Secaucus Seven—or, as Rowe clarifies, the Secaucus Eight—endured substantial challenges getting on the same page to share a unified vision for the club.

John Calipari wasted little time revamping the Nets' roster ahead of the 1996–97 season. *Steven Lipofsky/ LipofskyPhoto.com.*

The Nets owners were not the type of owners that you see now in sports with a very expensive asset which needed to be founded by very strong business principles. Certainly, they wanted to win, they wanted to not lose money, they wanted to enjoy the franchise. In those days, franchises were not worth 2-plus billion dollars, mostly thanks to Steve Ballmer for creating that level of asset price by his purchase of the Clippers. There were a lot of individual owners. I remember meeting David Stern several times, and he knew that the future of the league was going to be a league that was more expensive for owners to hang on to. The Madison Square Gardens of the world began to be corporately owned, the Knicks. He was happy when Ross Perot got involved with the Dallas team. David would never have any personal or professional issues about ownership structures. He knew going forward it was going to be long pants and long bank accounts. The Nets were to a great degree struggling in that regard. Each of them had individual wealth, but without there being a strong business foundation to it with ownership rules and regulations and operating agreements and things like that that govern their actions, they were allowed to participate in various functions. There was no shortage of folks that could come in on marketing ideas. There was no shortage of owners who would feel like they could talk about basketball trades. There were times I recall when we were getting film on high school players and college players from various owners, not just the basketball owners. Every one of the seven owners—the eighth owner was very silent—but every one of the seven owners had some responsibility, but the other six could jump in at any time. I think that might be what Larry Brown is talking about, but I didn't have any issues with that. The ownership was very good to me. If they had a bad idea, I would explain why it wouldn't work and we would work together to come up with a better idea. If they had a good idea, I didn't care who I got it from, and if it came from the basketball guy and it was about marketing, I was happy to have it.

Anderson provided the player's perspective to the unorthodox ownership situation and intimated that it accelerated his trade demand and closed the chapter of his Nets career back in January 1996. "If you don't have too much say-so, especially if star players don't have too much say-so, it's going to affect you. And it affected us down the road. Then Dražen Petrović, his passing affected us and then Derrick Coleman getting traded, then I was like, 'Wow, let me go.' Then I left. We were rebuilding then. That's what we saw. They weren't going to do well because of too many owners."

Calipari built a reputation as a coach with a keen eye for talent who was an unrivaled recruiter and wore many hats building UMass into a nationally relevant program. The 1996 NBA Draft was held at none other than the freshly rebranded Continental Airlines Arena, with New Jersey staking claim to the no. 8 overall selection. Georgetown star Allen Iverson went no. 1 overall, while Camby was selected no. 2 by the newly founded Toronto Raptors. On draft day, John Nash, who had served as the Sixers' General Manager (June 1986–June 1990) and the Washington Bullets' GM (June 1990–April 1996), signed on as the Nets' GM just in time to gear up for draft day. Nash was Calipari's right-hand man, yet the Nets' head coach had final say over all matters related to personnel. The 1996 rookie draft class featured an intriguing seventeen-year-old prospect from Lower Merion High School in Pennsylvania, Kobe Bryant.

New Jersey met with and worked out Bryant several times during the pre-draft process, but the teenager stayed on the board until the no. 13 pick, held by the Hornets, and was subsequently traded to the Lakers. In Los Angeles, Bryant spent twenty seasons building a Hall of Fame career with five NBA titles and seven finals appearances. There were a bevy of pre-draft reports and rumored reasons attributed to why the Nets, who appeared on the verge of drafting Bryant, went in a different direction. Bobby Marks gave a glimpse into what transpired barely twenty-four hours before the Nets were on the clock.

From the surface, from high school to the NBA, besides Kevin Garnett, it wasn't like it was a thing. Kevin was different, he was big, and he wasn't a wing, so there wasn't much of a track record. Cal [John Calipari] was coming into his rookie season, he was a 38-year-old coach, who was just coming from UMass and never coached in the NBA. As I said, we worked out Kobe a lot of times. The day before the draft, he was the No. 1 guy on our draft board, and there was a meeting between John Calipari, John Nash and Arn Tellem and Kobe Bryant's parents at the Radisson on Route 3 East in Secaucus, the night before the draft. It was there that the threat that Kobe would go play in Italy if the Nets drafted him was made. Looking back, do I believe he would have played in New Jersey? Yes, I do. I don't think Kobe Bryant would have gone to Italy and played. I think he said during the 2002 NBA Finals when we played him that he would have played in New Jersey.

The Nets-Bryant 1996 NBA Draft drama has been characterized as the player leaving the team at the altar, but while Nash and Calipari were supposedly fully on board the Kobe express, not all eight team owners were on the same page. Some had reservations about drafting the young phenom. Unfortunately for Nets fans, the full story of the courtship never truly surfaced. The player the Nets drafted would pale in comparison to the legendary career Bryant built. Kerry Kittles out of Villanova joined the club and was an integral starter on the Nets' back-to-back conference championship teams in the years ahead. In fact, at the time he was drafted, Kittles was the leading scorer and steals man in Villanova school history. New Jersey had an abundance of talent at guard, which caused Gill, as he recounts, to move from his natural position of shooting guard to small forward in order to open a starting spot for Kittles.

Kerry was one of the rare rookies that I had seen that was ready to play right away. A lot of that was due to him being in school for four years. Of course, kids don't stay in school that long now. They come out after their first year if they're any good. But Kerry was ready to play. If I can remember correctly, he had a 40-point game when he was a rookie. He didn't have any fear of anybody. He was highly skilled.

He surprised me. I didn't think he was going to be that good and ready to start and play significant minutes as rookie. The first time you see him, it looks like you could fax him because he's so skinny. So, you didn't think he was very strong, but he more than held his own.

The Nets were turning the page from the Coleman-Anderson era, with Gill and Bradley the only two veteran household names on the roster. Gill's prolific scoring and sharpshooting skills mimicked those of the late Petrović, but the Chicago native claims he never embraced the comparisons to the former European star and all-time Net.

Dražen and I went back and forth while we were playing when I was in Charlotte, and he was in New Jersey. I knew Dražen was popular when

Kerry Kittles' blazing speed in the open court made the Nets a nightmare to defend in transition. *Steven Lipofsky/ LipofskyPhoto.com*.

he was with the New Jersey Nets. I knew he was wildly popular. I always thought I was better than Dražen. Filling his shoes wasn't a big deal to me. All due respect to him, but I didn't think talent-wise that he was on my level.

Great, great shooter, great player, but I just thought that I was better. Moving into his slot did not bother me at all.

Gill wanted to etch out his own place in Nets history, and the upcoming campaign evolved into a magnificent individual season, but it amounted to another chapter in the rebuilding era for the team.

Prior to the 1996–97 campaign, the Nets released Gilliam and Mahorn and signed Tony Massenburg and Xavier McDaniel to veteran minimum deals. Calipari's crew endured a campaign in which wins were few and far between. After a lopsided season-opening night loss to Cleveland, the Nets traveled to Tokyo for a two-game international showcase against the Magic.

The league's fourth installment of the Japan Games saw the Nets drop both contests to a star duo of Shaquille O'Neal and Penny Hardaway. Losses piled up from there to the tune of 5-15 over the first 20 games of the season. To that end, the Nets were looking to shed payroll and compile assets, particularly team-friendly contracts for veteran players, draft picks or young players with untapped potential. Just prior to the 1997 NBA All-Star break, the Nets consummated a trade with Dallas to send Bradley and Robert Pack—two of the three highest-salaried players that year ($5.13 million and $2.7 million, respectively)—along with Khalid Reeves and O'Bannon, for Sam Cassell, Chris Gatling, Jim Jackson, George McCloud and Eric Montross. The Nets turned around three days later and sent McCloud to the Lakers for Joe Kleine, a 1997 first-round draft pick and a future conditional second-round draft pick that was not exercised.

From the Dallas–New Jersey mega trade, only Cassell and Gatling remained with the Nets beyond that season. Gill led the team with 21.8 points per contest, while the rookie standout Kittles made the All-NBA Rookie Second Team by averaging 16.4 points and knocking down 37.7 percent of his 3-point attempts. One of the under-the-radar storylines for that season was the emergence of seven-year vet Jayson Williams, who had spent the previous four seasons languishing on the Nets' bench. Williams got the starting nod in 40 games during the 1996–97 campaign and posted impressive numbers (13.4 points and 13.5 rebounds per game). Undersized by NBA center standards at six feet, nine inches, Williams had a nose for the basketball and developed into a menace on the offensive glass and one of the league's most feared rebounders. New Jersey finished with a familiar 26 wins for fifth place in the Atlantic Division.

As for the once-nomadic Nets, the 1996–97 campaign marked the twenty-first season since joining the NBA and the sixteenth playing at the Meadowlands. The two-decade span represented the franchise's most stable ownership period as well as its longest stay at one venue since its inception in 1967. The franchise was progressing, and Bobby Marks saw a marked improvement in the team's practice facility arrangement from the end of Beard's era as coach to the summer Calipari was hired.

Things got better when John Calipari came on in '96. Cal was never going to step foot in that place [A-P-A Transport Practice Facility in North Bergen]. *He would have rather practiced in the parking lot and put up a few hoops there. We then transitioned to Fairleigh Dickinson–Teaneck, which was an upgrade as a Division 1 college, and we used the*

Sam Cassell orchestrated the Nets' high-octane offense in parts of three seasons in New Jersey. *Steven Lipofsky/LipofskyPhoto.com.*

practice facility there. The problem was we were sharing it with three or four other sports, so you were behind men's basketball, women's basketball, and volleyball as far as when your practice was going to be. So, unlike today when you can pick 10-1, you might be going 3-5 on one day, 9-11 on another day, you were basically waiting for them to let you know when your facility time was going to be. So of course, that was not good. That's where the infamous Kobe Bryant workouts occurred before the draft in '96 when Kobe came through and we worked him out, I would say five times maybe even more. Back then, you were allowed to have draft prospects work out against NBA players, and he took it to Ed O'Bannon and Khalid Reeves in these workouts. I had seen Kobe play in high school, but my first Kobe Bryant experience was those draft workouts of '96. We then transitioned from Fairleigh Dickinson to Ramapo College because it was closer to Cal's home in Franklin Lakes. It was a fifteen-minute drive, and the facilities were better. It was a little bit easier for everyone, because we had a lot of players that lived up in Franklin Lakes and Saddle River, Keith Van Horn, Kerry Kittles and that group. Cal was the architect of building the practice facility that eventually was 390 Murray Hill Parkway, and we moved in there in the spring of 1998 before we played the Bulls. That was our home up until 2016, when the practice facility moved to Brooklyn.

1997–98

Calipari was laying the foundation for a winning program. As luck would have it, the 1997 NBA Draft had three future legendary players: Chauncey Billups, Tim Duncan and Tracy McGrady. The Nets held the no. 7 overall draft position and acquired no. 21 via the trade made with the Lakers earlier that year. Duncan and Billups were off the board when New Jersey was on the clock. Calipari opted for yet another Villanova product, the Paterson, New Jersey native Tim Thomas, over the high school sensation McGrady. Fourteen picks later, the Nets selected Anthony Parker out of Bradley. Neither player appeared in a Nets uniform, as Calipari sent both rookies to Philadelphia, along with Eric Montross and Jim Jackson for Keith Van Horn, Lucious Harris, Michael Cage and Don MacLean. Van Horn, a six-foot, ten-inch sharpshooter out of Utah, was the no. 2 pick in the draft, wedged between Duncan and Billups. He provided a shot in the arm for the Nets, who rushed to a 4-0 start to the season. The rookie started in all 62 games he played after missing the first 17 due to a preseason ankle injury and led the team in scoring (19.7 points per contest). For his outstanding efforts, Van Horn was named to the NBA All-Rookie First Team and played in the Rookies Game All-Star Weekend. Jayson Williams was selected to the 1998 NBA All-Star Game for grabbing a league-high 6.8 offensive rebounds per game.

The Nets reached a 31-21 record, marking the first time they had reached 10 games over .500 since the second half of the 1992–93 campaign. Cassell's leadership at point guard can't be overstated, as he averaged 19.6 points and 8 assists, facilitating the offense with poise and precision. On February 19, Calipari orchestrated yet another trade, sending Dare, Edwards, David Benoit and a 1998 first-round draft choice to Orlando for Rony Seikaly and Brian Evans. Seikaly played in just nine regular-season games before a foot injury sidelined him for the remainder of the regular season. The veteran returned for the playoffs, but his minutes and impact were limited due to ongoing recovery from his injury.

Keith Van Horn was a driving force in the Nets' run to the 1998 playoffs. *Steven Lipofsky/ LipofskyPhoto.com.*

As the calendar turned to March, the Nets dropped 7 straight games to come crashing near the .500 mark and in jeopardy of missing playoffs. The Knicks, Nets and Wizards were clustered at the bottom of the Eastern Conference playoff picture, and New Jersey needed a win on the final day of the season to secure its first playoff berth since the 1993–94 season. Grant Hill, Jerry Stackhouse and Joe Dumars headlined a gritty Detroit team that arrived at the Meadowlands looking to play the role of spoiler, but the Nets were up to the task. Gill poured in 27, Van Horn 25 and Kittles 22 to help the team secure the final spot in the Eastern Conference playoff picture. Gill looks back fondly on that do-or-die scenario. "The one is when we beat the Detroit Pistons on the last day of the season to go to the playoffs to play the Bulls. That was the one highlight that I'll always remember. We needed that game and I had given up a lot of offense throughout the season to fit these other guys in, but that game I was just like, 'F--- it, I'm going back to the old Kendall.' I had like 27 and outdueled Grant Hill to get us into the playoffs."

Remarkably, the Nets stayed above the .500 mark throughout all 82 regular-season games for the first time since joining the NBA. Van Horn was a rookie sensation, Jayson Williams terrorized the glass and the backcourt duo of Cassell and Kittles were the team's second and third leading scorers, respectively. Gill could go off for 20-plus points on any given night. New Jersey ranked as the top-scoring offense in the Eastern Conference at 99.6

points per game but had its hands full facing the East's crown jewel in a Bulls dynasty looking to capture its second three-peat of the decade. In the teams' four regular-season meetings, the Bulls won three by way of double-digit blowouts. Much like the rest of the NBA, the Nets had no answers for the scoring prowess of Jordan and Pippen.

Gill and New Jersey embraced the role as underdogs in the series, as they put a scare into Chicago in Game 1, staging a furious fourth-quarter comeback to force the game into overtime. With just under fifty seconds left in overtime and the game tied at 91, Kittles had the ball at the top of the key with a chance to give the Nets the lead, but Jordan swooped in and stripped the ball from the second-year guard and converted a fast-break dunk plus the foul on his way to a game-high 39 points. The Bulls closed out the Nets, 96–93, in the extra session, but Calipari's crew got Jordan and company's attention. In Game 2, Chicago jumped out to another double-digit lead in the first half, but the Nets kept scratching and clawing their way back into it midway through the fourth quarter. But Chicago's defense persisted, with key stops and forced turnovers each time the Nets pulled to within a two-possession game to hold on for a 96–91 victory. New Jersey returned to the Meadowlands for Game 3, a place where they went 26-15 during the regular season, but the Bulls smelled blood in the water and won the game going away, 116–101, in front of a packed house of more than twenty thousand Nets loyalists mixed with Bulls fanatics. Cassell's strained groin limited him to just 27 minutes in the entire series, yet surprisingly, super-sub Sherman Douglas emerged as the team's leading scorer in the playoff round (18.3 points per contest), followed by Kittles (16.3). Van Horn was questionable entering Game 1 with a stomach virus and appeared to feel the ill-effects of that and a tenacious Bulls' defense, posting 13.3 points per game in just 77 minutes played for the series. While the poor health of the Nets' two leading scorers from the regular season is an often-overlooked factor contributing to the 1998 playoff sweep at the hands of the Bulls, Gill contends that the officiating in favor of Chicago had as much to do with the series' outcome as anything.

They see the New Jersey Nets and they don't take you seriously and that's why we became serious. I can tell you that in that game, the calls were distinctly in favor of the Bulls. I got fouled, six or seven times, and I should have gone to the line. Most of the time in Games 1, 2 and 3 I was in foul trouble most of the time because you can't even sneeze around Michael in the playoffs or else it's a foul. Not only were we playing against the greatest team possibly ever, and the greatest NBA player ever, but they went in with a distinct advantage as far as the foul calls. I always felt that way in that series.

ALL TOLD, THE 1997–98 campaign put the franchise back on the map, but that off-season would usher in changes regarding the team's ownership group and previously imposed restrictions on relocating the team. While Calipari and his staff were preparing for free agency and the draft, several notable developments unfolded beyond basketball operations that would shift the course of the organization forever.

Ironically, it was a pending sale in 1997 involving the New York Knicks that opened the door for the Nets' ownership group—which at that time expressed interest in selling the team—to field offers from multiple parties. The Knicks were a constant roadblock to the Nets, whether it was imposing territorial rights issues dating back to Arthur Brown's founding of the franchise or forcing them to trade Erving by imposing additional financial fees on joining the NBA. As part of the merger agreement, the Knicks restricted the Nets' ability to relocate anywhere outside the state of New Jersey, but a series of business dealings by the Knicks needed the approval of all NBA teams, including the Nets. So, the tables had finally turned in New Jersey's favor. Back in 1994, Gulf and Western, the owner of Madison Square Garden, was acquired by Viacom. As part of that transaction, Viacom ended up selling MSG's properties to Cablevision and International Telephone and Telegraph (ITT), with both companies holding a 50 percent ownership interest. Three years later, ITT sold its stake to Cablevision, founded by Charles Dolan and eventually run by his son James, as Executive Chairman of the Madison Garden Sports Company. The Knicks had a track record of playing hardball with the Nets and stymieing them at every turn in their mission to establish roots in the New York metropolitan area beyond New Jersey state lines. So, before Cablevision could take control of the Knicks and MSG properties, the Nets needed to approve the sale. As Rowe recounts, an enlightening phone call from NBA Commissioner Stern opened his eyes to the vast opportunity his team had to pressure the Knicks to make a monumental concession regarding territorial rights restrictions that they had so staunchly defended in the past.

One of my basketball mentors was Willis Reed, my other basketball mentor was David Stern. The Knicks needed the Nets' approval, and when I got a phone call from the commissioner, he said, "David Checketts wants to talk to you and needs your approval." David made it sound like we needed to get it done in the next week or two before the board meeting. He said, "What are you going to ask him for?" I've only known about this question for ten seconds, and I haven't really thought about it. What are you talking about? "They need your approval. What are you going to ask them for?" This is big. What do you want? After five minutes of David Stern knowing the answer to the question and him working me through until I actually voiced it, he said, "That's correct, Michael, you want permission to move anywhere you want in the Metropolitan area." Because they had restricted our ability to move anywhere. Once that happened and we got it approved, we then met with the Garden executive, Mark Lustgarten, who since passed away, and he actually convened a meeting with David Checketts and I and we were actually trying to figure out how to get together. Months earlier, they had held control over us that we couldn't move anywhere outside of New Jersey, and now here we are sitting table to table talking about if we could fit inside of the Garden. Technically, the answer was yes, but eating up 40–50 dates that are prime booking dates for concerts and stuff just didn't make sense for the Garden. The extra locker rooms, the extra practice times, and stuff that everybody seemed to work out by having practice facilities in the building and two courts in the building didn't exist at the time. During the time I was there, there were a couple highlights of things that our team had done, one of them that was largely unknown was getting approval from the Knicks to relocate, which allowed us to begin to field offers from the Islanders, and [Bruce] Ratner and [Ray] Chambers and anybody else that wanted to move the team out of New Jersey.

That phone call from the late NBA Commissioner to the Nets' Team President in 1997 had a lasting impact on the course of the franchise, in that it paved the way for the team's eventual move to its current home in Brooklyn. In the immediate aftermath of the territorial restriction being lifted, it was open season for bidders to purchase the franchise from the Secaucus Eight. What transpired during the bidding process can only be characterized as chaotic and frenzied, with ownership entertaining offers that included a bevy of potential scenarios: a return to Long Island to share a new venue with the Islanders; a move to MSG to share a building with the archrival Knicks; a co-venture with the Devils at a future arena in Hoboken; and a move to Newark at an arena to be built as part of a community redevelopment project. Essentially, all options were on the table. After a prolonged period of ownership and venue stability, the Nets were once again putting the wheels in motion to abandon Werblin's romantic vision for the Meadowlands Sports Complex and search for a host city in a populous area with better infrastructure and more convenient access to public transportation to recruit more fans to the games. The Nets finished eighteenth in the league in attendance in 1997–98, drawing barely over 718,000 fans in the country's top market.

The winning bid to buy the Nets saw a new ownership group led by Ray Chambers, a noted philanthropist and co-founder of Wesray Capital Corporation, a private equity holding company, along with Lewis Katz, an attorney and businessman who owned Kinney Parking Company and served as chairman of Interstate Outdoor Advertising. Both businessmen had altruistic sides. Katz had established the Katz Foundation to support charitable, educational and medical causes by donating to several youth programs dedicated to Jewish entrepreneurs in his hometown of Camden. Chambers' efforts focused on revitalizing his hometown of Newark by supporting the Boys and Girls Club among other youth initiatives while serving as chairman of the New Jersey Performing Arts Center. Chambers aimed to create a cultural and entertainment beacon for the poverty-stricken and crime-laden city of Newark. Rowe outlines the hectic but exciting time in the franchise's history and indicates that while the offer presented by Chambers and Katz was not as lucrative as other offers made at the time, it was the consensus pick among the Secaucus Eight. After some creative political and financial maneuvering, Chambers and Katz set a new course for the franchise to follow.

In 1998, a group led by Ray Chambers, who was a philanthropist and smart businessman, was a visionary for the redevelopment of Newark, New Jersey. He had envisioned this world-class arena, maybe even a soccer stadium in Newark, as an entertainment capital to revitalize housing and to get the businesses to come back into Newark and maybe put it near the train station. A group led by Ray Chambers purchased 80 percent of the Nets in 1998. The Secaucus Eight came along and were part of that group, in May or June of '98, he received approval to purchase the Nets to bring them to Newark. He then met with Governor Christie Whitman at the time and talked to her about his plans. She indicated to Ray that it was difficult for her as the head of the state to try and come up with two arenas, because the Devils were looking to build an arena, as they wanted out of the Meadowlands also and they wanted to go to Hoboken. She explained to him that it wouldn't work for her to build two arenas. She encouraged Ray to come back to her with a one-arena solution for both teams. Ray spoke to then-owner of the Devils, John McMullen. John did not want to go to Newark. Ray did not want to go to Hoboken, because he purchased the team to move it to Newark. Faced with needing to go back to the governor with a one-arena solution, he made an offer and bought the Devils. That created the one-arena solution. Ray couldn't get his partners, which now included at this time the Yankees, together to the point where everybody wanted to move to Newark, so he ultimately sold the team to Bruce Ratner, who had a vision for what you now see as Barclays Center.

So, the Nets, at that particular point, had notified the Meadowlands that they were leaving and wound up playing their interim years in Newark. It was a short-term situation. You were not going to sell season tickets. There was no reason to invest in 41 games because you were only going to be a season-ticket holder for two years. Ticketing services were now allowing you to buy the best games and the best seats by buying single tickets, whether it was StubHub or any other reseller, so the value of being a season-ticket holder, which is a real estate play, was gone. The Nets had two very, very rough years in Newark. I don't think they could have made them any better. What Ray Chambers ultimately envisioned for Newark has come into play. There is housing and restaurants, and a lot of good things are happening in Newark. It's just his team isn't playing there. The Nets aren't there. He ultimately sold his share of the Devils and so did Jeff Vanderbeek to Harrison Blitzer, who owns it now. Before Ray Chambers bought the Nets, there was a meeting in New York, I was at the meeting and we were meeting with the owner of the Islanders, Charles Wong. It was the same month as we met with Ray Chambers, I want to say it was April of 1998. We met with Charles Wong in New York, and Charles made an offer to buy the team. Wong made a substantially higher offer than the Nets ultimately sold to Ray Chambers' group for and wanted to move the Nets to Long Island and use the Nets and the Islanders as leverage to have a brand-new arena out in Long Island. We shook hands in the conference room, at a hotel in Midtown Manhattan. We agreed to sell him the team. We went downstairs and there were three of us in the room from the Nets, two owners and myself, and we went down and we called the other majority owner, one of the eight owners, and we said, "Great news, we got more than we wanted."

We're ready to have a board meeting. The owner said, "I'm sorry, I'm not voting with you. I'm not moving the team out of New Jersey." So, we ultimately sold to Ray Chambers, who couldn't get the team to stay in New

Jersey, through no fault of his own, and sold it to Ratner, who moved it out of New Jersey. Very weird little piece of the nomadic Nets; we were almost the Long Island Nets all over again. We were literally days away from closing that deal. There are more details that will take forever to explain to you, but we actually began the due diligence on selling the team, and I was out at Computer Associate's offices while my Nets owners were negotiating with Ray Chambers to sell them the team to move it to Newark. It was another piece of the Nets move that just didn't happen.

Building consensus among the Secaucus Eight was a nearly impossible feat, even though the team was on the doorstep of a move back to Long Island or entertaining serious thoughts of playing its home games at MSG. Lengthy discussions and handshake agreements were made, but without the blessing of all eight owners, particularly the two majority owners, Cohen and Taub, to move outside New Jersey, the unofficial deals were dead on arrival. The convoluted ownership structure created a power struggle within the organization. As Nets franchise history tells us, the path to reach the final destination in Brooklyn was not a direct flight, but more like a connecting flight with three layovers, including being rerouted unexpectedly to Newark. The new ownership group brought about a welcomed change, in that there seemed to finally be a unified vision for the team. But staying in the Garden State and building a state-of-the-art arena in the state's largest city, Newark, to become the team's new home didn't pan out as Chambers and Katz anticipated, according to Rowe.

Before we sold the team to Ray, we almost moved to Madison Square Garden. We had begun discussions with the Garden ownership about whether a second team could play in the building. We had very serious discussions about whether the Knicks and Nets could play in the same building as the Rangers. I remember at least a half a dozen meetings where we were trying to work it out. So, the Nets' owners were trying to sell the team. We had a couple offers to sell it, but we got most serious with Charles Wong, shook hands on a deal, and then at least one of the majority owners said, "Look, I'm not moving the team out of New Jersey. We bought this team to move it to New Jersey, we're not going back to Long Island." So, Ray Chambers' group moved front and center, Ray got half of what he wanted done. He wanted to have an arena in Newark as part of the renaissance, and he did. He's a smart guy, he just didn't have his basketball team with him.

9

NBA LOCKOUT DISCORD, MORE COLLATERAL DAMAGE

1998–99 through 1999–2000

With an imminent move to yet another host city—and with that a new home arena hovering over the Nets, the NBA had its own issues to sort through that off-season. In March of 1998, NBA owners were dissatisfied with the league's salary-cap system, thereby reopening the collective bargaining agreement (CBA). The National Basketball Players Association made raising the league's minimum salary a top priority. The two sides hit a stalemate about how the league's basketball-related income should be split.

Despite a lockout looming, free agency and the NBA Draft went on as scheduled, but for the first time in franchise history, the Nets did not have a first or second-round pick, as they had sent both via trade, including their first-rounder, to Orlando earlier that year. The Magic selected Matt Harpring with the pick acquired from New Jersey. Following June's draft, the labor dispute officially started on July 1, with Stern imposing a January 6 deadline for a potential cancellation of the season.

That off-season was out of the ordinary for all NBA franchises. On January 6, 1999, the two sides finally came to an agreement on a 50-game season to commence on February 5. As part of the new six-year CBA, both sides made concessions, with owners getting the majority of what they wanted. Player salaries were reduced from a maximum of 57 percent of the league's income to a maximum of 55 percent. On the players' side, they were able to negotiate a rookie pay scale that coincided with the position selected in the draft class.

Jayson Williams (*far right*) celebrating with teammates during the 1998–99 campaign. *Steven Lipofsky/LipofskyPhoto.com.*

As part of the new CBA, teams were permitted to spend above the maximum limit allowed by the salary cap but were required to pay a luxury tax for doing so. The NBA instituted an all-encompassing drug-testing policy that provided yearly testing for performance-enhancing drugs and marijuana.

With hardball negotiations over, the NBA's shortened off-season saw the Nets make few roster changes. Douglas left in free agency to join the Clippers. The team signed undrafted rookie Earl Boykins, Eric Murdock and Scott Burrell, in addition to re-signing Jayson Williams to a monster seven-year, $100 million contract.

New Jersey traded Michael Cage and Don MacLean to Seattle for Jim McIlvaine. The Nets were an offensive force in the East the season before, but during the first 20 games of the lockout-shortened season, they were among the worst scoring offenses in the league. Calipari's bunch scored 99 or more points twice over that 20-game span. Following a stunning 3-17 start to the season, the team's third-year head coach was fired. Assistant Don Casey stepped in. Just when it looked like Calipari was putting his fingerprints on the Nets' roster and developing a winning culture, the bottom fell out. With a new ownership group led by Chambers and Katz, Calipari was not able to foster the same relationship he had with Taub, Cohen and the rest of the Secaucus Eight.

Stephon Marbury evolved into an All-Star with the Nets. *Steven Lipofsky/LipofskyPhoto.com.*

Just three days before Calipari was fired, on March 11, the lame-duck coach signed off on a mega three-team trade between the Nets, Bucks and Timberwolves. The Nets acquired Stephon Marbury, Chris Carr, Bill Curley and Elliot Perry. The Bucks received Cassell, Gatling and Paul Grant and the Timberwolves received Brian Evans, a 1999 first-round draft pick from New Jersey, and Terrell Brandon from Milwaukee. The centerpiece of that trade, at least from the Nets' perspective, was Marbury. A Brooklyn native, Marbury was named Mr. New York Basketball as a senior at Abraham Lincoln High School. The Georgia Tech product was the no. 4 overall pick in the 1996 NBA Draft and instantly became the Nets' leading scorer at 23.4 points per contest while dishing out 8.7 assists and starred alongside Van Horn, who produced stellar averages of 21.8 points and 8.5 rebounds during that campaign.

In fact, Van Horn was featured on the cover of the NBA Jam 99 video game that debuted in the fall of 1998 for N64 and Game Boy Color. In addition, Van Horn was the first white athlete to appear on the cover of *SLAM* magazine, in the April 1998 issue, alongside teammates Cassell, Gill, Kittles and Williams. The Nets were acquiring and drafting players with untapped All-Star potential, and that tack—directed by ownership and executed by the front office—paid major dividends in the seasons to follow. As Rowe notes, the impact of Marbury's acquisition goes well beyond the numbers he produced throughout the 172 games in which he donned a Nets uniform.

According to Rowe, the three-team trade for the electrifying point guard enabled New Jersey to develp a budding star and positioned the team to eventually trade for a generational player who instantly carved out his place in the Mount Rushmore of Nets legends.

> *Kerry Kittles was our first draft pick, Keith was our second one and we had, at that particular point, got Stephon Marbury on the team, which to me was probably one of the most pivotal acquisitions that we had. Keith Van Horn is sitting next to Stephon at the end of one game, and he says, "Hey Steph, how's your arm?" Steph says, "My arm's fine." "No, really, how's your arm?" Steph says, "It's fine. Why?" "Well, you took so many f--- shots, I have no idea why your arm just hasn't fallen off." We were developing that kind of fun enjoyable kind of thing, which didn't exist in the prior structure we had. Everyone was on pins and needles. Some of the All-Stars didn't have that warm and fuzzy relationship with the other players, and the team started to develop a little bit of chemistry, which was aggravated by us making a lot of changes, unfortunately. We were starting to get better than good people who were good players. We didn't have any great players, but we were getting players that other teams would want, and they became puzzle pieces for other teams.*

After the disastrous 3-17 start under Calipari, the Nets play improved significantly under Casey, and with Marbury in the fold, they finished the remainder of the strike-shortened season 13-17. Casey's eighteen years of NBA coaching experience, including two as head coach of the rebuilding Clippers, had a stabilizing effect on the team.

Unfortunately, on April 1, Williams suffered a gruesome right leg injury in a game against Atlanta and underwent career-ending surgery in which five screws and a plate were inserted to stabilize his leg. The once-promising

Left: Stephon Marbury was the centerpiece of the trade that brought Jason Kidd to New Jersey. *Steven Lipofsky/LipofskyPhoto.com.*

Right: Keith Van Horn was traded right after starring in the Nets' miraculous run to the 2002 NBA Finals. *Steven Lipofsky/LipofskyPhoto.com.*

Nets big man was forced into early retirement, which he announced in June 2000 at just thirty-two years of age. The highlight of the year came on April 3 in a game against Miami, with Gill securing a triple-double with 15 points, 10 rebounds and 11 steals (tying an NBA record). He was named the NBA's season leader in steals at 2.68 per contest.

1999–2000

After Calipari's departure, John Nash assumed the acting General Manager position and prepared for the 1999 NBA Draft without the first-round pick shipped out in the Marbury trade. The Timberwolves selected Wally Szczerbiak, while the Nets took Northwestern product Evan Eschmeyer early in the second round at no. 34 overall.

The off-season was eerily quiet for the Nets, aside from signing one ex-Net and trading for another in Sherman Douglas and Johnny Newman. Casey finished the 1998–99 campaign on somewhat of a high note, and there was optimism that the team could get back into the playoff conversation heading into the upcoming season. Instead, New Jersey started with a miserable 2-15 record, suffering 8 double-digit losses during that early rough patch. Casey and company rebounded to pull to within 5 games of the .500 mark after a win over the Clippers on January 13. Despite dropping to 9 games under .500 on March 30, the team was still within range of the final playoff spot. From there, the team went into a tailspin, losing 11 straight games to end the year. Casey was fired at the conclusion of the season, and the team sought out top General Manager candidates.

On the ownership side, in October of 1999, Chambers and Katz forged a merger between the Nets and Yankees, known as YankeeNets LLC. The merger came about following the Yankees' failed acquisition by Cablevision in 1998, with the Nets' owners proposing and successfully forming a joint holding company. The merger was bumpy from its inception, with both ownership groups failing to seeing eye to eye on team management strategy and philosophy regarding player contracts, among other issues. The merger ultimately dissolved in 2003. Shortly thereafter, the Nets were sold to Brooklyn Basketball LLC, owned and operated by Bruce Ratner. As part of the agreement, the Nets retained stake in the YES Network, as the main aim of the original arrangement had been to bolster both franchises' bargaining powers when it came to new stadium deals and television rights contracts. The Nets never fully realized the true synergistic benefits of the merger. However, New Jersey's pre-merger local television broadcast partner, FOX Sports Net New York, transferred to the newly formed YES Network in 2003, and as part of the sale to Ratner, the team signed a long-term deal for the network to broadcast the team's games. This outcome translated to a tangible, longstanding impact in the broadcasting realm for the Nets. The short-lived YankeeNets partnership never fulfilled the vast power of influence it held to negotiate a favorable new arena deal for the Nets, which eventually fell into Ratner's purview as he developed a vision to station the team in Brooklyn.

10

NBA CHAMPIONSHIP PURSUIT

2000–01 through 2003–04

The long-term host city for the franchise was unpredictable, and things were even more indefinite on the basketball operations side of the equation. New Jersey was in dire need of a seasoned executive to direct the upcoming free-agency and draft period.

To that end, on June 2, 2000, the Nets hired Rod Thorn to be the team's next General Manager. Thorn had been an assistant coach under Loughery for four seasons, including the Nets' second ABA championship team in 1975–76 and the Nets' first season in the NBA in 1976–77. Loughery and Thorn were teammates in 1963–64 on the Baltimore Bullets of the ABA, and the two saw their paths cross again in the NBA. When Thorn was General Manager of the Bulls, he hired Loughery to be the team's head coach for two seasons beginning in 1983–84. Thorn spent seven seasons in Chicago's front office and was part of the brain trust that selected Jordan with the no. 3 overall pick in the 1984 NBA Draft.

As luck would have it, the Nets secured the top overall pick in the 2000 NBA Draft, and just one day before the rookie class was selected, they finalized the hiring of their next coach, Byron Scott. A three-time NBA champion with the Lakers, Scott had just two years of coaching experience, having served as an assistant to Rick Adelman in Sacramento. Scott was a neophyte head coach, and while the Nets were showing flashes of a talented roster with two All-Star-caliber players, New Jersey was not considered a coveted destination for free-agent players or coaches. The Nets added Lawrence Frank alongside holdovers Eddie Jordan and Mike O'Koren on Scott's staff.

Byron Scott was a three-time champion with the Lakers during his playing career. *Steven Lipofsky/ LipofskyPhoto.com.*

For the first time since 1990, when they selected Coleman, the Nets held the no. 1 pick, taking Kenyon Martin out of Cincinnati. Under the tutelage of Bearcats coach Bob Huggins, Martin blossomed as a senior to lead the team to the nation's no. 1 overall ranking at the end of the regular season. Things took a devastating turn for the promising senior when he suffered a fractured right fibula and ligament damage in his right knee in the opening round of the Conference USA Tournament. The injury put an end to Cincinnati's NCAA Tournament title hopes, and for Martin, he faced a long recovery with an unknown impact on his upcoming NBA Draft stock. Thorn and New Jersey felt comfortable enough in Martin's recovery and refused to pass up on his undeniable talent. The Nets made Martin the top overall selection of the 2000 NBA Draft and used their second-round pick on seven-footer Soumaila Samake of Mali.

A new regime in New Jersey should have ushered in a renewed sense of hope, but attendance figures hit an all-time low. Continental Airlines Arena posted the NBA's second-fewest number of fans that season at 556,573. Infrastructure problems, the lack of a megastar main attraction, as well as a tenuous future at the venue, were all mitigating factors relating to fan engagement. During free agency, center Aaron Williams signed a six-year contract with the team, and Stephen Jackson signed a one-year deal with the Nets. Under Scott's leadership, the Nets jumped out to a 6-4 start, led by a starting five of Marbury, Gill, Jackson, Martin and Eschmeyer. Kittles missed the entire campaign following reconstructive right knee surgery—his fourth procedure on that knee in his young career. Injuries sidelined many key contributors,

Rookie Kenyon Martin (*left*) alongside veteran Kendall Gill (*right*) during the 2000–01 campaign. *Steven Lipofsky/ LipofskyPhoto.com.*

including Gill, who missed a total of 51 games, and Van Horn (33 games). New Jersey lost 9 consecutive games and 17 of 20 overall after the 6-4 start. Unsurprisingly, the Nets endured several prolonged losing skids after the All-Star break. Marbury enjoyed the best all-around season of his NBA career, including a career-high 50 points against the Lakers on February 13. He earned a nod for the 2001 NBA All-Star Game by producing averages of 23.9 points, 7.6 assists and 3.1 rebounds at the age of twenty-three. Another youngster, Martin, produced 12 points, 7.4 rebounds and 1.9 assists per contest and played in the Rookie Challenge at NBA All-Star Weekend while being named to the NBA's All-Rookie First Team. New Jersey finished at 26-56 and drew the no. 7 slot on the 2001 NBA Draft board.

2001–02

The summer of 2001 can only be characterized as the most consequential period of any the franchise experienced since joining the NBA. Of the Nets opening-night starting five from the 2000–01 season, only Martin remained in his role, as creative free-agency maneuvering, complex but effective draft-day trades and injury recoveries for Van Horn and Kittles seemingly transformed the Nets overnight from a lottery team into one of the league's most improbable Cinderella stories.

As for the longest-tenured Net at that time, Gill's six-year run with New Jersey came to an end. The free-agent guard inked a deal with Miami. Kittles was right on track to return to the lineup, so Gill knew the writing was on the wall for him to leave in free agency. Gill looked back fondly on his time with the Nets and playing at Continental Airlines Arena.

> *One of my favorite things to do as a New Jersey Net was to look over at New Jersey from my apartment in Manhattan and say, "I'm probably the only professional basketball player that lives in the city right now and I don't play for this team, the Knicks, I play for that team over there across the river." I loved every day getting up, driving through the Lincoln Tunnel, getting over to East Rutherford, New Jersey, going to practice and coming back through the Lincoln Tunnel to Manhattan. I loved it. I loved being in the traffic jam. I loved going through the tunnel paying four dollars back then each way. I absolutely loved the New York metropolitan lifestyle, and I didn't have to be a Knick to enjoy it.*

Historically speaking, New York had the upper hand in the area rivalry. Even during the Nets' championship runs in the ABA, the Knicks won two NBA titles (1970 and 1973) with considerably more fanfare and excitement surrounding it. In the ten years predating the 2001–02 NBA season, the Knicks strung together ten consecutive seasons with a winning record, each campaign accompanied by a playoff berth, including six 50-plus win seasons. The Knicks ousted the Nets in the first round of the 1994 playoffs and finished as the runner-up in the 1994 NBA Finals to Houston and the 1999 finals to San Antonio. That span in the 1990s was a microcosm of the largely one-sided battle between the two adversaries on each side of the Hudson River. The Nets would flip the script on the Knicks in the next two seasons and the better part of the following twenty years.

Kendall Gill relished all six seasons he played for the New Jersey Nets. *Steven Lipofsky/LipofskyPhoto.com.*

The 2001 NBA Draft saw the Nets select Seton Hall guard Eddie Griffin with the no. 7 overall pick. The former Pirate was barely a Net long enough to put his draft night hat on before he was sent to Houston for Richard Jefferson and Jason Collins—both four-year college players at Arizona and Stanford, respectively—with Brandon Armstrong as the final piece coming to the Nets. New Jersey also used its second-round pick, no. 35 overall, to select eventual fan favorite Brian Scalabrine out of USC. Jefferson and Collins were immediate impact players for the team in the upcoming regular season and eventual mainstays in the starting lineup for the next seven years.

With a monumental draft night in the books, Thorn's first major trade became the single most transformative move since Dr. J's acquisition during the team's ABA days.

Michael Rowe's five-year tenure as president of the team came to an end in 2000, yet the Nets' executive indicated that the organization's core philosophy regarding team-friendly, high-character signings and the strategic building of draft capital helped facilitate Thorn's ability to execute the momentous trade.

So, Jason Kidd had a problem in Phoenix, and Jerry Colangelo had to move Jason Kidd. As you know in the basketball divisions, the West teams and the East teams only play each other twice, once at home and once away. You try not to trade within your division, because you don't want to see that player come back four or five times and be good and have four and five reasons to try and kill you. If he's going to turn out to be a better player, you want him to go away where you'll only see him twice, so Jerry Colangelo had to call an Eastern Conference team and he had to find a serviceable, immediate star point guard, and we had one, Stephon Marbury. I don't think we could have gotten Jason Kidd without Stephon, I don't think Sam Cassell or Chris Childs or even Kenny Anderson, who would have been four years older at the time, would have been something Jerry wanted. When he called our then–General Manager Rod Thorn at the time, I could imagine Rod's enthusiasm and how hard it would have been for him to just not say, "We'll pick him up in two minutes, yes." What we were doing over the years, they call it affectionately rebuilding, but we were trying to get better not by breaking the team down, but by moving parts in and out while keeping the train running. Some teams crash the train down, bring it to a halt, a few other teams like the 76ers have done that successfully, but our owners didn't want to do that, so we made subtle changes, all with the criteria of getting good players who were good people, who didn't mind playing 48 minutes of basketball a night. We didn't have any prima donnas, we tried to get rid of players who were writing on their sneakers, who were getting into trouble in town with various social things that are around a team that plays in a New York market. We largely did that and became a team right after I left, but I think the reputation was developed by our ownership and our staff. We became a team people wanted to be on, like Kendall Gill, who had good thoughts about the team. We were looking for those kinds of players.

New Jersey netted an embattled superstar whose team-first attitude permeated the locker room, while his endearing charisma with the fans and media instantly transformed him into a franchise icon. Professional athletes are often lionized and held to unreasonably high standards, and Jason Kidd was no different. But the 1994–95 Co–Rookie of the Year battled his own demons that prompted his abrupt exit from Phoenix. Kidd was drafted no. 2 overall in 1994 and spent parts of three seasons in Dallas before being traded to the Suns following a purported rift with Mavericks teammate Jim Jackson. In Kidd's five seasons in the Valley of the Sun, the team failed to advance past the first round of the playoffs on four occasions and clinched one semifinal berth during the 2000 playoffs before bowing out in 5 games to the Lakers. The California native's numbers were gaudy, but it remained to be seen whether the multifaceted point guard could lead a team into championship contention. Before he had a chance to answer those questions with Phoenix, in January 2001, Kidd was arrested and pled guilty to spousal abuse of his wife at the time, Joumana. The twenty-seven-year-old was fined and ordered to undergo anger-management classes.

Lawrence Frank, who served as Scott's lead assistant, recalled the summer that the Marbury-Kidd trade transpired, as the stars aligned for an agreement to take place.

Even during the Chicago pre-draft, where we were with Rod [Thorn], John Nash was still with the team, Ed Stefanski and the coaching staff, and I remember having dinner and Rod saying, "I don't know if we're going to be able to make many changes." It wasn't a real uplifting dinner, you know, but as good fortune would have it in our way, Jason became available. Unfortunately, I think Phoenix felt pressure to move him because of the domestic situation with his wife at the time, and they had interest in Marbury, and that move obviously changed the entire trajectory of the franchise.

This development prompted Suns General Manager Jerry Colangelo to seek out trade partners for the talented but troubled floor general. As Rowe outlined, New Jersey's breadth of young standout performers was vast, and Thorn was able to acquire the four-time All-Star, eventually a ten-time All-Star, for a relatively modest asking price. On July 18, 2001, Marbury, Newman and Samake were dealt to Phoenix, with Kidd and Chris Dudley coming to the Meadowlands. Lawrence Frank depicts Kidd's leadership as nothing short of extraordinary.

> *The first day that Newark Airport opened back up* [after September 11], *I was on a plane flying to see Jason and spent around five days with him. They had just had their twin girls, so that's why he was in Phoenix the entire time and didn't come to Jersey. So, I spent around five days working out with him. We did three-a-days, we did basketball workouts, Pilates, and then we'd do something at night, whether it was playing tennis or whatever, just working on conditioning. The first time anyone else saw Jason was the night before our first practice. He showed up and we had a team dinner before training camp started. Byron spoke, Rod spoke and Jason, who wasn't a person of many words, and no one really knew him, but he said something to the effect of: "We're not the same old Nets, we're making the playoffs." Then his first practice, it was obvious this dude was on a whole different level. Diving for loose balls, he played it like it was a playoff game that first practice and set an unbelievable tone for everyone to follow. That group was a really, really special group, but he just changed the whole tenor of the franchise. When people talk about culture, your culture is always based on who your best players are. Your coach can contribute to it, but if his best players aren't modeling the right player and they're not uniting the team with their play, then it puts a limit to where you're at.*

New Jersey represented a second chance for Kidd, and right from the get-go he set the tone in training camp with an up-tempo style that rewarded his running mates with alley-oops and other aerial attacks on the fast break. New Jersey was not an offensive juggernaut by any stretch, finishing thirteenth in the league at 96.2 points per contest, but its opportunistic defense forced opponents into turnovers that led to run-outs and easy baskets at the other end. The Nets were accustomed to slow starts, even during playoff seasons under Larry Brown, Albeck, Fitch, Daly and Calipari, and so the 7-1 start to the year represented the franchise's best eight-game start to a season since joining the NBA. All of Kidd's teammates were reaping the benefits of his selfless play, but Martin flourished the most in the open court with jaw-dropping finishes to the tune of 14.9 points and 5.3 rebounds per game.

The preseason odds for the Nets to win the NBA title sat at +6,000, meaning a $100 bet on New Jersey to take home the Larry O'Brien Trophy would net a bettor $6,000!

To say the Vegas sportsbooks were not bullish on the Nets to make a championship push would be the understatement of the century. So, when the Nets finished the pre–All Star break portion of the schedule at a scintillating pace of 32-15, it was the first time the team was at least 15 games over .500 heading into the break since the 1982–83 season, when they were 33-18.

Jason Kidd showing the poise of a true leader. *Photo by Andrew Bernstein.*

During All-Star weekend, Martin participated in the Rookie Challenge for the sophomore squad, while Kidd played in the All-Star Game.

The pixy dust wore off in the second half under Larry Brown's watch back in 1982–83, but Kidd's first season at the helm was fairytale-esque. Despite wavering levels of fan support at home games, the Nets finished with the East's best home mark at 33-8 and ran roughshod over the East at 35-16 to finish as the conference's top seed at 52-30. New Jersey won its first ever Atlantic Division crown, besting Boston by 3 games, and set the new NBA franchise record for regular season wins.

According to Frank, Kidd's intangibles truly made the Nets' point guard special. "That was Kidd's greatest skill, it was that uncommon will. Even though over the course of time his shot improved, he wasn't a great shooter. The advantage we had with Kidd is that first year he played the game with this inner rage about him that was basically, "How was I ever traded from Phoenix?" Because guys like him don't get traded very often. We got the ultimate-best version of him during that year."

The 2002 playoffs saw New Jersey up against Larry Brown's Indiana Pacers, who were just two years removed from an NBA Finals appearance. An aging yet effective Reggie Miller starred alongside Brad Miller and Jermaine O'Neal, rounding out a not-so-typical eighth-seeded foe. Brown admitted that there was added motivation facing his former club, given the circumstances surrounding his exit from New Jersey as well as Calipari's firing. "The Nets were getting better and better and better. I had a real close connection with Calipari since he worked for me. When he got fired by the

Nets, I hired him. There was a little bitterness from me for them getting rid of John. I always looked at New Jersey, Indiana, San Antonio and Denver as a league of their own. It was always unbelievable pride for me, and I think you could ask any of those other guys and they'd feel the same way I did. The Nets got better and better."

Indiana stunned the Nets in Game 1 behind 30 points from Jermaine O'Neal to hand New Jersey just its ninth home loss of the year. Kidd and company regained their footing to win Game 2 handily, and by virtue of a Kittles clutch 3-pointer with 22.5 seconds left in Game 3 captured a 2–1 series lead with an 85–84 victory. The Pacers held serve at home in Game 4 to force an epic Game 5 that took two overtimes to settle the score. The game looked to be in the Nets' grasp as Jefferson stepped to the charity stripe for two with his team leading, 96–93, and 5.1 seconds remaining. One make would all but close the book on Indiana, but the rookie missed both attempts, and the ball found the hands of the man nicknamed "Miller Time," who swished through a remarkable thirty-nine-footer to tie the game and send it to overtime.

Lawrence Frank recounted the elimination game against Indiana and its significance to the history of the franchise.

> Now it's a Game 5 and literally this could determine our whole entire path. If you go back and remember that game, that's the game where Reggie Miller shoots the half-court shot after the buzzer went off, but it was before instant replay, so the shot never should have counted, and it put the game into overtime and that game wound up going to the second overtime.
>
> That game changed the whole historical path of that team, if we lose that game [f---] there was always a negative sentiment or thought with the Nets.

Miller prolonged the game yet again in overtime, converting a dunk with 3.1 seconds remaining to tie it. Kidd shot a midrange jumper as time expired that clanked off the rim to send the game to a second overtime. This time, the young legs of the Nets outlasted the gritty Pacers, as New Jersey outscored Indiana, 13–2, to win 120–109 in double overtime and advance to the semifinal round.

Awaiting the Nets in the second round was a Hornets team coached by the legendary ex-Net assistant Paul Silas and directed by point guard Baron Davis. Kidd's mastery of the court was on full display, as he outdueled the fellow California native and carried New Jersey to a 4–1 series win and the franchise's first-ever trip to the NBA Conference Finals.

In Game 3 of the series, Kidd's face was bruised and bloody after he collided with ex-Net David Wesley, but remarkably he returned to finish and played the next two games of the series, including closing out Charlotte in Game 5. The powerful message of resiliency that the charismatic point guard delivered to the Nets' locker room is not something that Lawrence Frank will soon forget.

> *Then we go to Charlotte, I think everyone will always remember the collision between David Wesley and Kidd. At that time, Charlotte's visitors' locker room was one of the worst in the league. They gave you this one room, so literally the training table is in the middle of the locker room. The training table is always in another room adjoining the locker room, but this one was right in the middle, so there's blood all over the floor, and they're literally stitching him up at halftime, while Byron and the rest of the coaching staff is talking to the team. And he comes back, and he plays, now we lose that game, Game 3. But, in terms of toughness and courage, that was an indelible mark for the best player and leader of the team to take that sort of blow and come back.*

The stage was set for the cream of the crop in the Atlantic Division to face off, as a Celtics team that featured Paul Pierce, Antoine Walker and former Net great Kenny Anderson looked to play spoiler. The Nets split the first two games at Continental Airlines Arena, and Game 3 in Boston would go down as a catastrophic loss for New Jersey. Leading 74–49 with fifty-four seconds remaining in the third quarter, it seemed almost unfathomable for the Nets to be on the wrong end of the worst collapse in playoff history up to that time. Unfortunately, that nightmarish scenario is exactly what transpired, to the horror of the Nets and their fans. Boston erupted for 41 points to New Jersey's 16 in the final stanza, with 18 of the Celtics' points coming at the free-throw line. On the verge of regaining home court with a 2–1 series lead, New Jersey faltered mightily for the first time under Kidd's leadership. The Boston faithful were especially brutal to Nets players in the aftermath of the shocking breakdown, and Kidd became the recipient of vitriol from the opposing fans, who referenced his domestic-violence episodes via vulgar chants and handwritten signs in a not-so-subtle reminder of his missteps in his personal life.

According to Frank, New Jersey turned the page quickly from the painful comeback loss. "I remember in the ballroom when we got the guys together the next day, Byron did not really say much about the game. I think what happened after that game, I like to say a couple of our players went to the hotel restaurant just sat together and had some food and some drinks, but kind of got the loss out of their system."

Kidd found a way to pick his team up off the mat, and the Nets jumped out to an early 13-point first-quarter lead in Game 4. By halftime, that lead had shrunk to 6 points, and New Jersey found itself in a fourth-quarter dogfight on the precipice of facing a daunting 3–1 series deficit. The free-throw line was particularly advantageous for the Celtics, who went 33 of 39 from the charity stripe in Game 3. But Game 4 saw a cruel twist of fate for Pierce. After a pair of Lucious Harris free throws gave the Nets a 94-92 edge with just 6.6 seconds remaining, Pierce drew a shooting foul on Van Horn with just 1.1 seconds left. Just 16.0 seconds earlier, Pierce had knocked down two free throws to tie the game, and the capacity crowd at Fleet Center fully expected the clutch captain to send the game to overtime. Instead, Pierce missed both free throws, and Tony Battie's offensive rebound and put-back rolled off the rim to send the boisterous home crowd into stunned silence. The Nets survived in monumental fashion by salvaging the road game in Beantown and headed back to the Meadowlands with a chance to recapture the series lead.

In Game 5, the Nets jumped out to another double-digit first-quarter lead when their advantage swelled to 15 points. As was the case throughout the series, it came down to the fourth quarter, with 3 points separating the teams. New Jersey opened the final frame on a 22–5 spurt and did not look back on the way to a 103–92 victory.

It was unimaginable that the Nets would have a chance to punch their

Jason Kidd knocks down an open 3-pointer. *Photo by Andrew Bernstein.*

first-ever ticket to the NBA Finals on the same court where they had blown a 21-point fourth-quarter lead just two games earlier, but the resilient squad behind Kidd's steadfast leadership was primed for a championship berth. Things did not look promising early on for New Jersey, as the Celtics raced to a 14–3 advantage and built a 10-point halftime cushion. The Nets battled back, and a pair of Martin free throws gave them their first lead of the second half, 70–69, by the end of the third quarter. After a Pierce 3-pointer knotted the contest at 72 early in the fourth quarter, Jefferson splashed through two free throws to give New Jersey a lead it would not relinquish.

Keith Van Horn had ice water in his veins in Game 6 of the 2002 Eastern Conference Finals against Boston. *Steven Lipofsky/LipofskyPhoto.com.*

Van Horn hit a clutch long-range jumper to push the Nets lead to 6 with fifty seconds left, and the final seconds ticked off the clock with Kidd being swarmed by teammates to the tune of a 96–88 triumph and a 4–2 series win. The nomadic Nets were the NBA's Cinderella story, and the franchise's improbable conquest of the Eastern Conference was complete in dramatic fashion.

Thorn, alongside Kidd, Martin, Kittles, Van Horn, Jefferson and the rest of the bunch were the embodiment of the team's newly formed winning culture. Scott, Frank and the entire coaching staff celebrated a remarkable postseason run to the championship round. Awaiting David in the 2002 NBA Finals was the league's Goliath. Shaquille O'Neal, Kobe Bryant and Phil Jackson aimed to crystallize a Lakers dynasty and complete a three-peat title run.

In Game 1, Los Angeles raced out to a 15-point first-quarter lead as O'Neal wreaked havoc on the Nets in the paint. Collins and Todd MacCulloch put up little defensive resistance in the interior. New Jersey was the Little Engine that Could, but Shaq was the diesel-powered locomotive shredding and pulverizing anything in his way.

Despite the dominance of the Lakers' seven-foot, 320-pound center, Kidd's triple-double of 23 points, 10 rebounds and 10 assists kept the Nets within striking distance. Martin added 21 points, including two free throws with 4:47 left in the game to close the gap to 84–81. O'Neal singlehandedly refused to let New Jersey get any closer, as his 14 fourth-quarter points and 36 points overall along with 16 rebounds proved to be too much in the end.

In Game 2, Shaq went for 40, and the Lakers cruised to a 106–83 victory. The Nets were hopeful that a return home to the Meadowlands would signal a change in fortune. Despite Los Angeles leading 2–0 in the series, Bryant was kept largely in check by producing 22 and 24 points in those games, but a change of scenery unleashed his full scoring potential, and he poured in 36 and O'Neal continued with his rampage, dumping in 35. Once again, Kidd led the Nets with 30, and Martin's 26 saw New Jersey grab an 80–78 edge in the early moments of the fourth quarter. The Nets maintained a narrow advantage over Los Angeles until a Robert Horry 3-pointer with 3:04 remaining swung the momentum back in favor of the two-time defending champs, 98–96. Kidd drained a 3-pointer to close a 4-point hole to just 1 with 5.2 seconds left. Rick Fox sank two free throws to extend the lead to 3 points with only 3.5 seconds on the clock. With no timeouts, Kidd was forced into a desperation heave from twenty-nine feet to try to send the game to overtime, but it ricocheted wide left off the backboard. Suddenly, his squad was on the verge of elimination.

Lawrence Frank tipped his cap to one of the NBA's most imposing centers of all-time, who wreaked havoc on New Jersey.

> *Everything was game planned around Shaq. Shaq was just so incredibly dominant, and we had no answers for him. Just between MacCulloch and Collins, he was just too massive.*
>
> *The Lakers were just dominant, they were just much better than us. You need to have unwavering belief all the way up to the point, and once we lost Game 3, that was the first time it was really shaken, but the Lakers were just the better team.*

New Jersey's championship pipe dream had all but faded to black, and the Lakers smelled blood in the water in Game 4. As Kidd's crew had shown all season, they brought tremendous fight and refused to go quietly. The championship pedigree and experience of Bryant and O'Neal (series MVP), and Phil Jackson's coaching, proved too much for New Jersey to overcome. Martin's 35 points and Kidd's 13 points and 12 assists were not enough to avoid a finals sweep. Bryant celebrated emphatically on the same court he almost called home when Calipari had him teed up as the team's potential first-round selection less than six years earlier. Not a single prognosticator predicted the Nets would be standing between the Lakers and a three-peat. New Jersey's storybook season failed to culminate in a title, and the empty feeling following its playoff elimination served as the impetus for the franchise's continued pursuit of its first NBA championship.

Thorn was named the NBA's Executive of the Year, as the team doubled its regular-season win total from 26 to 52 and advanced to its first NBA Finals. Kidd was named to All-NBA First Team and All-Defensive First Team. The Nets captured the hearts and imaginations of casual and hardcore basketball fans alike while generating disdain and jealousy from the Atlantic Division rival Knicks and Celtics in the process.

2002–03

In the 2002 NBA Draft, Thorn selected Serbian seven-footer Nenad Krstić, who stayed overseas with Partizan Belgrade to hone his skills. At no. 54 overall, the Nets took Marshall product Tamar Slay as a potential swingman scoring option off the bench. It's not often that an executive will trade two of his starting five players on a title-contending team, but Thorn was hell-bent on finding a defensive stopper capable of contending with the dominant big men in the Western Conference, namely Shaq and Duncan. Thorn sent MacCulloch and Van Horn to Philadelphia for thirty-six-year-old future Hall of Fame shot blocker Dikembe Mutombo. The Nets started the season 10-6, with Mutombo averaging then-career lows of 5.8 points, 1.5 blocks and 6.4 rebounds with his minutes restricted to stay fresh for the playoffs. After 16 games, Mutombo underwent surgery to repair a torn ligament in his right wrist, and his potential availability for the playoffs was in serious jeopardy. He eventually returned to the team in late March and played sparingly in eight games as a tune-up to for the playoffs. After it was announced that Mutombo would undergo surgery on December 3, the Nets went 15-2, including 10 wins in a row, to climb to an NBA-best 26-9 with Jefferson and Collins starting. At the All-Star break, New Jersey sat at 34-15 but finished the season a disappointing 15-18 for a 49-33 regular-season mark and the no. 2 seed in the East. Kidd led the NBA in assists with 8.9 per contest to earn NBA All-Star honors, an All-NBA Defensive Second Team selection and All-NBA Second Team recognition.

The 2003 playoffs were largely a cakewalk through the Eastern Conference, but to the surprise of many, Milwaukee put a scare into the Nets in the first round. Led by future Hall of Famers Gary Payton and Ray Allen, ex-Net Cassell and coached by George Karl, the Bucks poured in over 100 points three times during the series on the league's best defense that season. In Game 3 of the first round, Rodney Rogers hit a game-winning shot from inside the arc in the final seconds to break a 1–1 series tie. Starting in the 2003 playoffs, the NBA expanded the first round from best of five to best of seven. New Jersey led, 3 games to 2, entering Game 6 at Bradley Center. Martin, who averaged 22.3 points and 10 rebounds for the series, dumped in 29 points and 9 rebounds, while Kidd's triple-double (22 points, 11 rebounds and 11 assists) lifted the Nets to a hard-fought first-round conquest. New Jersey would not lose another game in the next two series against reigning Eastern Conference runner-up Boston and the top-seeded Detroit Pistons.

The Nets won a tightly contested Game 1 against the Celtics, 97–93, and proceeded to win Game 2 by 9 and Game 3 in an 18-point blowout. Game 4, the clincher, went into double overtime before the Nets prevailed by 9 to sweep through to the conference finals.

Facing a stingy Pistons' defense that held home-court advantage, the Nets refused to even blink, as Kidd hit a heroic fadeaway jumper from the right baseline to break a tie late in Game 1 to propel New Jersey to a 76–74

Kenyon Martin elevated his play in three playoff runs with New Jersey. *Steven Lipofsky/ LipofskyPhoto.com.*

road win. The Nets held Detroit to just 11 points in the fourth quarter of the opener, and while they faced a 9-point fourth-quarter deficit in Game 2, Kidd and company locked down defensively again and outscored the Pistons, 30–19, including holding them to just 5 points in the final 5:45 of the contest. Chauncey Billups missed a potential game-winning 3-pointer, and the Nets escaped with 2 road wins against ex-Net player and assistant coach and now Pistons head man Rick Carlisle.

New Jersey cruised to a pair of double-digit wins in Games 3 and Game 4 and, for the second straight year—this time in the friendly confines of the Meadowlands—celebrated an Eastern Conference title with Kidd, Martin and Jefferson leading the charge. New Jersey was riding a 10-game winning streak into an NBA Finals matchup with the Spurs, who were just four years removed from hoisting the Larry O'Brien Trophy in the lockout-shortened 1998–1999 season. San Antonio fashioned a powerhouse roster with the twin towers of Duncan and David Robinson, the latter in his NBA farewell tour, as well as young international phenoms in French-born point guard Tony Parker and Argentinian super-sub Manu Ginóbili. Duncan won the MVP race over Kidd in the 2001–02 season and once again following the 2002–03 season. The point guard's best case for earning the honor came on the heels of his superb 2001–02 campaign. Duncan received 57 percent of the first-place votes to Kidd's 45 that year, and the Spurs' big man amassed 954 voting points to the Nets' floor general's 897 out of a possible 1,260 points.

The championship clash between the Nets and Spurs held historical significance, as it marked the first time in NBA history that two former ABA teams met in the NBA Finals. In Game 1, Kidd had the worst shooting performance of the 2003 playoffs, going 4 for 17 from the field. Thorn acquired Mutombo to neutralize the NBA's dominant big men, specifically Duncan and O'Neal, but the Nets' center played less than six minutes, and Duncan dazzled with 32 points, 20 rebounds, 7 blocks and 6 assists. San Antonio steamrolled New Jersey behind a 32–17 third-quarter barrage for a 101–89 win. The narrative had quickly changed, from a Nets team enjoying a double-digit win streak entering the series to a desperate bunch hoping for the franchise's first NBA Finals game win. Kidd got back on the horse and carried the scoring load in Game 2 by dropping 30, while Mutombo played nearly 20 minutes and made his presence felt on the defensive end by limiting Duncan to 19 points on 8 of 19 shooting.

Ex-Net Stephen Jackson drilled a 3-pointer with just under ten seconds left to pull the Spurs to within 1 point, 86–85. Kidd stepped to the charity stripe and missed the front end and sank the second attempt. San Antonio raced up the court with no timeouts remaining. The ball found Jackson for an open left-wing 3-pointer, but this time the basketball gods were on the Nets' side, and the ball fell off the iron. For the first time since their Game 6 win over Denver in the 1976 ABA Finals, the Nets had a taste of a championship-round win, albeit it was just one game. Following a twenty-six-year drought without so much as sniffing a finals berth, Kidd accomplished two franchise milestones in his first two seasons with the team. The series would shift back to the Meadowlands for 3 straight games, as the NBA Finals followed the

2-3-2 format adopted in 1985 that would last until 2014 before moving to the 2-2-1-1-1 format. Celtics legendary coach Red Auerbach was a driving force in adopting the 2-3-2 format, with Boston and Los Angeles traveling coast to coast throughout the 1980s.

New Jersey tied San Antonio's 2003 regular-season home record at 33-8 but winning 3 consecutive games against a Spurs team with an uncanny championship pedigree proved to be a daunting task. Despite an announced crowd of 19,280, Continental Airlines Arena failed to sell out for the potential series-shifting game. Suffice it to say, the lack of fan support for the franchise's biggest game since joining the NBA was disappointing. In reality, it wasn't all that unexpected for a venue that drew the seventh-fewest fans fresh off a magical run to the 2002 NBA Finals. The Nets jumped out to a 6-point first-quarter lead in Game 3, but things came to a grinding halt in the second quarter, as they scored just 9 points on 4 of 14 from the field while committing 6 costly turnovers. Scott's team had a penchant for strong third quarters, and Game 3 of the NBA Finals was no different. Kidd and company splashed in 27 points and committed just 1 turnover to regain a 3 point lead heading into the fourth. Parker's blazing speed had given Kidd fits on the defensive end, and the Spurs' point man erupted for 11 points in the fourth and outscored New Jersey's captain by 9 singlehandedly to spur his team to a road victory. Lawrence Frank recalls the gut punch that Game 3 was for his team. "Really the swing game for us was that Game 3. Kenyon had a real tough night, Duncan was really, really good defensively. Kidd had a real tough night shooting the ball. That was the game, we played harder than heck. After Game 1, we put Kittles on Tony Parker."

Much like Game 2 in San Antonio, Game 4 was an instant classic that featured another nail-biting finish. The Nets' defense was in especially rare form, limiting the Spurs to a 28.9 field-goal shooting percentage with Parker going 1 for 12 for just 3 points. Parker, Ginobili, Bruce Bowen and Jackson combined to go 7 of 40 from the field for an unheard-of 17.5 shooting percentage. Even with San Antonio's futile shooting performance in concert with the Nets' swarming defense, New Jersey held just a 73–72 advantage with 54.1 seconds left. On their ensuing offensive possession, the Nets failed to score but grabbed two critical offensive rebounds and forced the Spurs to send Kidd to the line with 9.1 seconds remaining. Kidd was true on both attempts, and after Duncan dropped in a layup, the Nets' point guard sank another two free throws with 4.8 remaining to reestablish a 3-point lead. Gregg Popovich drew up a play that set Ginobili up for a game-tying 3-pointer, but after pump-faking to get Kidd out of his face, the Argentinian

Jason Kidd willed the Nets to a Game 4 victory over the Spurs in the 2003 NBA Finals. *Steven Lipofsky/ LipofskyPhoto.com.*

missed the open shot. Duncan converted a 2-pointer as time expired for a window-dressing effect in New Jersey's 77–76 win.

Just like that, the 2003 NBA Finals was gridlocked at 2–2, and the Nets had an opportunity to pull to within 1 win of capturing the franchise's first NBA championship. In an overt attempt to rekindle the magic and mystique of the Nets' ABA glory days, New Jersey showcased its ABA "stars and stripes" home uniforms to conjure up the good karma it needed to hand San Antonio a second straight loss. Kidd played all forty-eight minutes of Game 5, scoring 29 points and dishing out 7 assists to go along with 7 rebounds; Jefferson added 19 points, while Martin added merely 4 points. In the end, the Nets ended up with more turnovers (16) than assists (15). The Nets briefly grabbed a 54–53 lead with 3:47 remaining in the third quarter, but 37 seconds later, the Spurs recaptured the advantage and never relinquished it. The Nets pulled to within a two-possession game at

87–81 with 45 seconds left, but Parker, Kerr and Ginobili combined to go 6 of 8 from the line down the stretch to put the game out of reach and held on to prevail, 93–83. An immense opportunity to gain control of the series went by the wayside. The Nets then faced an uphill climb to win two road games against a budding Spurs dynasty.

Kidd's squad had defied the odds the previous two seasons, and backed into a corner, they came out punching to the tune of a 25–17 first-quarter lead. The stellar play of San Antonio's bench was a prevalent theme in the series and a major factor in the outcome of Game 6. New Jersey maintained the upper hand throughout the first three quarters, building 12 points of separation that shrank to 6 entering the fourth. Martin was in foul trouble throughout the series, and even with him on the bench to start the fourth, New Jersey led, 72–63, following a Rogers 3-pointer with 8:55 left. From that point on, a Spurs barrage slammed the door on the Nets' title dreams.

Behind a monstrous effort that included 17 bench points in the frame, the Spurs went on a 25–5 run to end the game and put a shocking and abrupt end to New Jersey's championship run. Kidd went for 21 points, 7 assists and 4 rebounds; Kittles dropped 16; and Jefferson scored 13. Martin struggled mightily from the field on a brutal 3-of-23 performance for just 6 points and 10 rebounds. The power forward on the winning side, Duncan, almost notched a rare quadruple-double (21 points, 20 rebounds, 10 assists and 8 blocks).

Tim Capstraw, former head coach at Wagner and 1993 Northeast Conference Coach of the Year, joined the Nets' radio broadcast booth alongside longtime play-by-play man Chris Carrino at the start of the 2002–03 season. Capstraw also filled in as a color analyst for YES television broadcasts with partner Ian Eagle and had a front-row seat throughout that magical run that ended in bitter defeat.

First of all, that was my first year and I was just all ears. I would listen to Chris Carrino, Ian Eagle or whoever was with us and had experience going with us the previous year going to the finals. What happened in the first year and this happens to teams quite a bit, you can be overwhelmed by the details of what goes into playing in the finals, whether it be extra family members coming to games, extra planes going out to the West Coast, and everybody said the second year the Nets were much more prepared for all the outside distractions that occur during the finals. They seemed much more prepared for it. Getting there the year before against the Lakers and getting swept was a very good lesson in how to be a little bit more prepared. I think if you review the games, it was a 4–2 series, and the Nets were getting ready to make it a Game 7. In Game 6 they were up double digits in the second half. Speedy Claxton just jumps out to me because I was familiar with him in high school, but he was ridiculous during that time. It was just unfortunate.

The Nets really had a shot. It's Game 6, you're up in San Antonio double digits in the third quarter. Yes, there was a time when you thought you could get this to a Game 7, and anything can happen in a Game 7.

2003–04

Just like his MVP races with Duncan the previous two years, Kidd fought valiantly but ultimately failed to walk away with the requisite hardware to validate his remarkable season. Duncan was named the NBA Finals MVP, and with Kidd's contract expiring, the 2003 off-season was dominated by speculation that the Nets' captain would ultimately join forces with Duncan and replace Parker as the Spurs' starting point guard. There were many versions of this rumored deal, including a sign-and-trade scenario in which New Jersey would ship Kidd to San Antonio in exchange for Parker and draft assets. During that summer, the Nets' leader visited with San Antonio and was all but ready to join the burgeoning Western Conference juggernaut, but Thorn showed a willingness to make roster maneuvers and opened the organization's checkbook to convince Kidd to return to the Nets. On July 16, 2003, Thorn announced that the team had signed free-agent center Alonzo Mourning to a four-year, $22.6 million deal. The acquisition of the aging Mutombo in 2002 did not pan out the way Thorn anticipated, and Kidd's decision to return to the Nets was made easier by the fact that the franchise finally signed a center still in the prime of his career. On July 24, 2003, the Nets and Kidd agreed to a six-year, $103 million deal as they embarked on a third straight quest for the NBA Finals.

Prior to finalizing Mourning's and Kidd's contract agreements, New Jersey selected Croatian guard Zoran Planinić at no. 22 overall and future All-Star sharpshooter Kyle Korver at no. 51 overall in the 2003 NBA Draft. Korver was immediately dealt to Philadelphia for cash considerations. On-court success was aplenty the previous two years, and the Nets were a likeable underdog nationally but still played second fiddle to the Knicks locally and remained an afterthought in the vast New York sports landscape. Hampered by an arena lacking accessibility to mass transit and stationed in a fragmented hometown of East Rutherford, New Jersey, it made generating an expansive, loyal base of season-ticket holders a nearly impossible task. The upcoming season rumors circulated about the pending sale of the team to yet another ownership group, as Continental Airlines Arena drew the fourth-fewest fans among all NBA venues, even with the franchise pursuing a third straight trip to the NBA Finals. In October 2004, the New Jersey Devils' pending move to Newark and planned construction of a new arena in Brick City was approved by the city's council, and they broke ground on the project nearly one year later. Chambers' vision of a renaissance in his birthplace of Newark with an arena shared between the Nets and Devils at the city's epicenter nearly came to fruition. Instead, Jeffrey Vanderbeek, former executive vice-president at Lehman Brothers, who had owned a minority stake in the Devils since 2000, officially bought the team outright in 2004. Vanderbeek expediently orchestrated the hockey club's move to Newark, the construction of a new arena and the eventual pseudo-revitalization of the City of Newark, sans Chambers, Katz and the Nets. The cloud of uncertainty surrounding the Nets' future at the Meadowlands evolved from a scenario of "if" they would move to a "when" scenario. Before Chambers and Katz sold their ownership stakes in the team in January 2004, Kidd's Nets were consumed with unfinished business on the court and attempting to three-peat as Eastern Conference champs.

New Jersey appeased Kidd by signing Mourning to fortify its interior presence, but just 12 games into his Net career, the center was diagnosed with kidney disease. Complications forced him to undergo a transplant, effectively ending his season and jeopardizing his NBA career. Even with Mourning in the fold, New Jersey went 5-7, with the seven-footer tallying then-career lows in points, rebounds, assists, blocks, minutes and field-goal percentage while coming off the bench. Clearly impacted by his gloomy diagnosis, the integral role that Thorn and Kidd envisioned for Mourning took a devastating turn, as the Nets dipped to under the .500 mark for the first time since the point guard joined the team. Reports began to surface regarding philosophical differences between Kidd and Scott, while Thorn had been contemplating making a coaching change after the team's loss in the 2003 NBA Finals. With the 2004 All-Star break fast approaching, the Nets suffered a lopsided 85–64 defeat in Miami on January 23. Thorn informed Scott that he was being relieved of his coaching duties after a win over Boston on January 25. During his tenure, Scott compiled a 149-139 (.591) regular-season record with a 25-15 (.625) playoff mark. Scott left as the winningest coach in the team's NBA history after three and a half seasons. Prior to Scott's arrival, the Nets had compiled a pitiful regular-season record of 776-1,160 (.401) and a 9-30 playoff mark (.231) without a single Eastern Conference championship appearance, NBA Finals appearance or Atlantic Division title in twenty-four seasons since joining the NBA.

As is often the case when a coaching change is made, a new voice in the locker room provided a jolt in morale and had a rallying effect on the players and staff. The man hired to replace Scott, Lawrence Frank, had served as Scott's lead assistant all four seasons he coached, and he developed a reputation for being extremely detail-oriented in his preparation for opponents and was a hands-on coach during practices and film sessions.

The Nets enjoyed their longest winning streak in their NBA history, stringing together 13 straight wins, which stood as a North American pro sports record for a rookie head coach. New Jersey's total win steak spanned 14 games with a win over Boston just prior to Frank's appointment as interim head coach. The Nets were riding high off a spectacular pre– and post–All-Star Game stretch that boosted their record to 35-20, near the top of the Eastern Conference.

Just days before Scott's firing, the Nets' ownership group, led by Chambers and Katz, reached a tentative agreement to sell the team for $300 million to New York real estate mogul Bruce Ratner, who publicly expressed interest in relocating the franchise to the borough of Brooklyn. Ratner's bid bested that by an ownership group comprising Charles Kushner and former New Jersey governor Jon Corzine, which aimed to keep the team in East Rutherford.

As part of the transaction, Ratner recruited rapper, philanthropist and Brooklynite Jay-Z as part owner of the team for a reported price tag of $1 million. For the first time since 1977, the notion of the franchise returning to New York became a distinct reality. Ratner's real-estate career, born out of his family's construction materials business, started in the 1920s, eventually evolving into Forest City Ratner. This venture became the driving force for the MetroTech business epicenter, later known as Brooklyn Commons, that currently stands in Brooklyn's downtown, which was sold to Brookfield Asset Management for $6.8 billion in 2018. Prior to his real-estate career flourishing, Ratner worked for the New York City Mayor's Office (1974–82) within the Consumer Protection Division under John Lindsay and then as consumer affairs commissioner under Ed Koch. While there, Ratner cultivated deep political connections throughout New York City and its five boroughs, utilizing this networking along with his experience protecting the public from corrupt businesses to build a real-estate empire. He needed every ounce of business acumen and every political connection to pave the way for the Nets' eventual move to Brooklyn in 2012. Issues regarding eminent domain, funding concerns and an economic recession, among other obstacles, impeded Ratner's progress, as the Nets did not break ground at Barclays Center until March 11, 2010, over six years from when Ratner tentatively reached an agreement to buy the team. The painfully elongated period of transition left a team that was already struggling to build a fan base in New Jersey in limbo and without a clear path to a permanent home. Remarkably, to that point, the Nets had called the Meadowlands home for over twenty-two years, and that prolonged stay extended far beyond the franchise's six-year run (1971–72 through 1976–77) at Nassau Coliseum in Long Island. New Jersey's basketball product finally had a sense of stability, but its long-term prospect of playing at the Meadowlands was bleak at best. So, while it appeared that yet another move for the franchise was imminent, those who followed the team's wanderings over the decades understood that there would likely be a series of twists and turns that could set the franchise off its intended course.

The impending move and ownership transition served as the backdrop to New Jersey's championship pursuit as it entered the post–All-Star break portion of the 2003–04 schedule as the hottest team in the NBA. For the first time in his career, Martin was named an All-Star, playing alongside Kidd as a reserve for the East. The team finished an underwhelming 12-15 over the final 27 games, and the late-season swoon dropped them to the third spot in the Eastern Conference, still enough to repeat as Atlantic Division champs and set up a compelling matchup with a Knicks team that had shuffled through three coaches that season (Don Chaney, Herb Williams and Lenny Wilkens). The Nets, meanwhile, still carried the redheaded stepchild label in the metropolitan area by playing in an arena dropped into the middle of New Jersey's swamplands. The Nets had a small, loyal fan base compared to that of the Knicks, whose brand gained national and international appeal. None of that mattered when the two teams met in the 2004 playoffs, as the Nets dominated the series with an average margin of victory of 12.8 points. Martin shined, averaging 23.3 points and ripping down 14 rebounds in the series. A backcourt of ex-Net Marbury and ex-Magic star Anfernee Hardaway put up little resistance, with New Jersey finally besting New York in the playoffs. The first round sweep of the Knicks amounted to a mere tune-up for the Nets, as one of the East's heavyweights, the Detroit Pistons, awaited Lawrence Frank and company in the semifinal round.

Coaching along the Pistons sidelines was Larry Brown, who had replaced Rick Carlisle, despite Carlisle leading Detroit to a 50-win season and a no. 1 overall seed in the East in 2002–03 before getting swept out of the conference finals at the hands of the Nets. From the opening tip of the 2004 Eastern Conference Semifinals, it was clear that Detroit had grown by leaps and bounds, as the franchise netted star big man Rasheed Wallace in a four-team mega-trade with Atlanta, Boston and Portland following the 2004 All-Star break to shift the balance of power in the conference. Detroit finished with the no. 2 overall defense during the regular season, allowing only 84.3 points per contest.

In Game 1, New Jersey shot an abominable 27.1 percent from the field, with Kittles and Martin the only players on the team to reach double figures in scoring. The Nets fell, 78–56. The Palace of Auburn Hills drew the most fans in the NBA that season (872,902), and Game 2 was more of the same for New Jersey, as Rasheed Wallace and frontcourt-mate Ben Wallace stymied the Nets' offense to the tune of a 95–80 win. The Nets held serve at home, winning the next two games, but Kidd's shooting woes continued. In Game 4, he cracked double digits in scoring for the first time in the series. Game 5 was the outlier of the series, as the Nets scored 127 points compared to a 136-point running total they had produced in the first two games in the Motor City. The colossal game featured 24 lead changes, 21 ties and 3 grueling overtime periods. With 3.9 seconds left in the fourth and the Nets leading, 87–85, Jefferson blocked Billups at the rim. The ball found Kittles, who was immediately fouled and sent to the line. New Jersey's shooting guard split a pair to put his team up, 88–85, with 2.9 seconds remaining.

With no timeouts left, Tayshaun Prince inbounded from under his own basket to Billups, who pushed up the court and launched a miraculous shot from just inside the halfcourt line that banked off the glass and fell through the nylon to send the game into overtime.

After picking their jaws up off the floor and preparing for the extra session, the Nets needed to manage a frontline that was decimated by foul trouble. Martin, Collins, Aaron Williams and Rogers all eventually fouled out, resulting in the most unlikely of all playoff heroes to emerge off the team's bench. Scalabrine became a fan favorite with the Nets' faithful despite playing roughly twenty-four minutes combined in the first 4 games of the series and totaling a mere 6 points. The third-year

Kerry Kittles averaged 14.4 points for the Nets during 2004 NBA Playoffs. *Steven Lipofsky/ LipofskyPhoto.com.*

forward broke out for 17 points, including 9 in the three overtime periods in just under twenty-four minutes to give New Jersey the energy boost it sorely needed. Scalabrine went 4 for 4 from 3-point range and 6 of 7 from the field overall as the Nets outlasted Detroit, 127–120, in a three-overtime marathon. Frank detailed his humorous exchange with the improbable star of the game.

We were always a team that fouled when up three, always. I think we were a little shellshocked that we missed the free throw, and we didn't have the pickup point with Chauncey high enough, and in that situation we would always foul, but we didn't. He gets it off, makes the epic shot right past half court. That could have been it and yet that game we went small, since you had a number of people foul out of that game: Rodney Rogers fouled out, Kenyon fouled out, Jason Collins fouled out. Scalabrine tells an unbelievable story, it is his version, which is really funny. Rodney fouls out, I'm looking down the bench basically saying, "Who the f---, can I put in the game?" I see Scalabrine. Now Scalabrine's version is, he sees me turn to him and mouth the words, "Oh f---." You know, like, "Oh f---, I have to put him in the game?" I put him in, and he's pissed off at me that this dude goes on an epic, epic run, he scored 17.

With a chance to close out the series in the Meadowlands, the Nets entered another defensive slugfest and faced a 3-point deficit at the start of the fourth quarter. New Jersey absorbed Detroit's rush, with the lead ballooning to 9 halfway through. New Jersey pulled to within 2 points on four separate occasions over the final five minutes, but every Nets run was answered with a Detroit counterpunch, as a masked Richard Hamilton hit a clutch jumper with 15.5 seconds left and Billups and Lindsey Hunter combined to make four free throws down the stretch to solidify an 81–75 Pistons win. Prior to Game 6, Rasheed Wallace guaranteed a Detroit victory, and with that promise fulfilled, the Nets faced the prospect of a playoff elimination by an Eastern Conference opponent for the first time since Game 5 of the 2002

Jason Kidd races up the floor, with Richard Jefferson trailing the fast break. *Photo by Andrew Bernstein.*

playoffs against Larry Brown's Pacers. Game 7 was virtually over before it started, with the Pistons romping New Jersey, 90–69, in an embarrassing season-ending loss. For the first time in his career, Kidd scored 0 points, shooting a then–NBA record-low 14.7 percent from 3-point range for the series. New Jersey's point guard missed 15 games with nagging knee injuries during the regular season, and it was determined that he needed to undergo microfracture surgery on his left knee in the off-season. Clearly hampered by injury, Kidd still led the NBA in assists at 9.2 and earned All-NBA First Team and All-Defensive Second Team honors. The Pistons, meanwhile, knocked off Carlisle's top-seeded Pacers in the conference finals and stunned the star-studded Lakers in the NBA Finals, as Brown captured his first NBA title as head coach.

Kidd's microfracture surgery dominated the off-season chatter. The track record of athletes returning to peak form following surgery was not all that encouraging. The Nets' floor general needed extended time for recovery and rehabilitation, and he missed the first 16 games of the 2004–05 season.

Lawrence Frank recalls the courage Kidd showed to play through the pain and delay knee surgery until after the 2004 playoff run. "He needed microfracture during the year, and he wanted to play through it. He went to go see different people, he got different therapy, therapy now that is in vogue, that back then wasn't. He was going to do everything because he thought we had an opportunity to win a championship. He actually hurt his knee during the year and was playing with a knee that required microfracture for a while."

11

BIG THREE ERA IN NEW JERSEY

2004–05 through 2006–07

I n the 2004 NBA Draft, the Nets selected Russian prospect Viktor Khryapa in the first round and immediately traded his draft rights to Portland for Eddie Gill. Aside from Kidd's injury recovery, the most notable development of that off-season was the free-agent status of Martin, who was seeking a max contract to remain with the franchise. Given the money New Jersey committed to Kidd and Mourning in the previous off-season, coupled with the attendance woes and pending move to Brooklyn, the likelihood of bringing back the starting power forward was slim. Thorn was in a predicament and made the best of an untenable situation by completing a sign-and-trade agreement with Denver. As part of that deal, Martin signed a seven-year, $95 million maximum contract to join the Nuggets, and the Nets received a 2005 first-round pick and a pair of 2006 first-round picks in return. New Jersey lost a major centerpiece of its championship-contending teams. Martin contends that the decision not to tender him a contract offer came from over Thorn's head and was initiated by ownership. The former Nets power forward reflected on the circumstances surrounding the trade in an April 2011 interview with Randy Zellea of Back Sports Page.

That's their decision. It was the same decision they made when they let me go. New Jersey didn't want to keep this thing going. They didn't want to keep winning. I think that's the choice that was made when they opted not to re-sign me. It just went downhill from there. Have they been to the playoffs since I left? They've been to the playoffs only a couple times since I left if I'm not mistaken. It wasn't the people who are making the decisions now; it was other people who had no basketball knowledge whatsoever. Do I feel sorry for them? No. I feel sorry for Rod [Thorn], I feel sorry for the coaches, my former teammates, and I felt sorry for Kiki [VanDeWeghe]. But as far as everybody else, it was their decision, and I don't feel sorry for them at all.

Martin was the heart and soul of the early 2000s Nets teams, bringing an unparalleled defensive intensity and an uncanny ability to burst out on the fast break with Kidd and finish at the rim with authority. The Nets' defensive-minded leader created turnovers that led to easy points on the other end. With Martin gone, the DNA of New Jersey changed forever, according to Capstraw.

I thought he was a huge piece of the identity of the Nets. I don't know if they ever really recovered from that part of it that well. You wanted the big body to throw down to at the power forward position. The Nets were a modern team. They were up-tempo. Jason Kidd was going to be great if they were in the open floor. The games would be even and then there would be a few steals, a few long rebounds and the Nets would break the game open by making people pay with turnovers and finishing on the other end. I thought a big part of the identity changed when Kenyon wasn't there. I thought those players might have helped, but I don't think their greatness was going to be there, because they weren't going to be able to fly up and down the floor like they did previously.

Martin spent the remainder of his prime years in Denver, but his offensive production never reached the heights it did when Kidd was distributing him the ball in masterful fashion. The Kidd-Martin duo would go down as arguably the franchise's most potent combination, and while Thorn eventually acquired another perennial All-Star that upcoming season, the void Martin left behind was never truly filled. The front office made another somewhat surprising move by sending Kittles to the Clippers for a 2005 second-round pick as the thirty-year-old's knee problems forced him into retirement at the end of the 2004–05 campaign. Rodney Buford and Jacque Vaughn signed contracts with the team that off-season to build guard depth behind Kidd and to resupply the roster without Kittles. Lucious Harris was waived prior to the start of the season, and like Kittles, he would play one more season in the NBA before calling it a career. Suddenly, Kidd, Jefferson and Collins were the only cogs remaining from New Jersey's NBA finals

Left: Kenyon Martin's departure left a major void in the Nets' frontcourt. *Steven Lipofsky/ LipofskyPhoto.com.*

Right: Kenyon Martin playing for the Denver Nuggets during the 2004–05 season. *Courtesy of Wikimedia Commons.*

runs, signaling a new era for the team. On August 13, Jefferson signed a six-year, $78 million contract extension with the Nets. On January 17, 2005, Brett Yormark was hired as CEO of the Nets, having previously served as NASCAR's Vice-President of Corporate Marketing for eight years. Yormark, under Ratner's direction, became a major driving force in pushing along the agonizingly slow move to Brooklyn.

Meanwhile, still in New Jersey, the Nets floundered with Martin gone and Kidd missing the start of the season, tumbling to a 2-11 start. Jefferson, fresh off a summer playing for Team USA, flourished as the team's leading scorer for the first half of the season. Kidd's return to the court gave the Nets an instant boost, but it took until his seventeenth game on January 7 against Golden State for him to register his first double-double. In the following game, against Orlando, he registered his first triple-double with 22 points, 11 rebounds and 11 assists. Kidd gradually regained his form, but with a diminished supporting cast, the early season hole saw the team remain under .500 most of the year. Mourning returned to the court to start the year after

Vince Carter slams it on his former club, Toronto. *Photo by Andrew Bernstein.*

a kidney transplant and registered twelve double-digit scoring performances, including four double-doubles in 18 games played, but he grew disgruntled with the overall direction of the organization. Thorn used this development as an opportunity to net a perennial All-Star who had fallen out of favor with his organization in Canada. Just prior to an 89–84 loss to Memphis to drop the team to 7-15, Thorn orchestrated a trade to send Mourning, Aaron Williams, Eric Williams and first-round draft selections in 2005 and 2006 to Toronto for superstar Vince Carter. Much like Mourning, Carter became disenchanted with the direction of his club, the Raptors, who were coming off a playoff-less season. Toronto's ownership made many unfulfilled promises to him. Carter joined a Nets club with a nucleus of Kidd and Jefferson to form a big three in New Jersey. The former UNC standout was an electrifying high-wire act, winning the 2000 Slam Dunk Competition with the true flair and dramatics of a world-class entertainer. In the soon-to-be twenty-eight-year-old, New Jersey was landing one of the league's premier players still in the prime of his career.

Carter's Nets' debut came on December 27. He scored 23 points and dished out 5 assists, but New Jersey fell in an overtime bout to the reigning champion Pistons. Ironically, the Nets' big three played only eight regular season contests together that year, as Jefferson suffered a torn ligament in his left wrist when he was undercut by Billups on a layup attempt in that game. The injury sidelined Jefferson for the team's remaining 49 games as he underwent wrist surgery, but he returned in time for the 2005 playoffs. In 33 games, Jefferson averaged 22.2 points, 7.3 rebounds and 4.0 assists for his best all-around NBA season, albeit in a small sample size. On February 14, Thorn swung a trade with Golden State to acquire Clifford Robinson for a 2005 second-rounder.

Even without Jefferson in the lineup, the Nets' backcourt duo of Kidd and Carter was arguably the league's best, but with less than a week until the playoffs started, the team was still under .500 and not guaranteed a playoff spot. As fate would have it, Carter made his long-anticipated return to the Air Canada Centre on April 15 and was greeted by an unruly crowd with signs and props vilifying him and antagonizing the ex-Raptor star. The man nicknamed "Vinsanity" went off for 39 points, 9 rebounds and 4 assists and was booed vociferously every time he touched the basketball. Capstraw recounted the rowdy scene surrounding Carter's hostile reception at the arena he once called home. "It was unbelievable. It was wild. I had never been to pro wrestling when the villain comes out. When the bus pulls in, they didn't have Jurassic Park back then, they just had a lot of people, and a lot of yelling. This idea of Canadians being nice people, forget about that. They were going off. There were tons of signs, and it was unbelievable with the signage and baby bibs and all these other things people had. It was wild, man."

The 101–90 win over the Raptors pulled the Nets to within 1 game of the .500 mark and it was the start of New Jersey's 4-game winning streak. New Jersey needed a win on the final night of the regular season to clinch the playoff berth, and Carter led the way with 37 to fend off the Celtics, 102-93. The Nets (42-40) narrowly edged out LeBron James' Cavaliers (42-40) by virtue of the head-to-head season tiebreaker for the final playoff spot in the East.

The Nets did not reach above the .500 mark until the second-to-last game of the season and were slated for a first-round matchup with a familiar foe in Shaquille O'Neal and rising superstar Dwyane Wade with the Heat. Jefferson returned to action, but with barely a few practices to develop chemistry with Carter and no regular-season games to help serve

Vince Carter was vilified by the Raptors' faithful for jumping ship from Toronto to an Atlantic Division rival. *Steven Lipofsky/LipofskyPhoto.com.*

as a tune-up. Miami lived up to its billing as the best team in the East that year and defeated the Nets handily in Games 1 and 2 at American Airlines Arena with Jefferson contributing off the bench. New Jersey put up a huge fight in Game 3 back at the Meadowlands, with Kidd, Carter and Jefferson combining for 75 of the team's 105 points. Tied at 90 with 2.2 seconds remaining in the game, Kidd missed a potential game-winning 3-pointer, and the game went to overtime. It looked as though New Jersey was on the verge of its third straight playoff loss, with Carter clanging a 3-pointer off the rim and the Nets trailing, 99–97, as Eddie Jones secured the rebound with 11.9 seconds left. Jones, an 80.6 percent free-throw shooter, took a trip to the foul line with a chance to ice the game, but he missed both attempts, and the Nets had second life. The ball would be in Carter's hands with a chance to win the game, and for the second time in two possessions, he

Richard Jefferson returned for the 2005 NBA playoffs just three months after wrist surgery. *Photo by Andrew Bernstein.*

misfired on a 3-pointer, then Krstić missed a tip attempt, but the Nets secured the rebound and took another timeout with 2.3 seconds remaining. On the ensuing offensive possession, Kidd inbounded the ball from the baseline to Carter, who launched a deep 2-pointer from the right corner that swirled around the rim before falling through to send the game to a second overtime. Miami outlasted New Jersey in the second extra session, 108–105, to take a commanding 3–0 series lead. Jefferson returned to the starting lineup hoping to get New Jersey to salvage a game in its own building in Game 4, but Wade scored 34 to lead the Heat to a 110–97 rout and a series sweep.

The newly formed Nets trio played in just eight regular-season games together and four playoff games, producing a 3-5 regular season record and 0-4 playoff record. Jefferson's wrist injury and Kidd's prolonged recovery from knee surgery hindered the team's chances of a deep playoff run, but the evolution of Krstić became an encouraging trend. Krstić rounded out his first season in the NBA averaging 10 points and 5.3 rebounds in 75 games, and he started in 57 contests.

2005–06

With New Jersey's big three returning healthy, Thorn looked to uncover quality depth in the 2005 NBA Draft and free agency and used the no. 15 overall selection to pick six-foot, seven-inch swingman Antoine Wright out of Texas A&M and took a flyer on another Serbian big man in Mile Ilić in the second round. With Kidd in his ear, Thorn engaged Portland in a sign-and-trade scenario for power forward Shareef Abdur-Rahim. The twenty-eight-year-old was offered a six-year, $38 million deal, but he failed his team physical. Several doctors expressed concerns over his arthritic knees. New Jersey backed out of the deal with its $4.9 million trade exception expiring, much to Kidd's chagrin.

Thorn tried to pick up the pieces and sent a 2006 conditional second-rounder to the 76ers for center Marc Jackson, while adding free-agent small forward Lamond Murray, power forward Scott Padgett and point guard Jeff McInnis as free agents.

The Nets avoided a repeat of the disastrous start of the season prior but sat at a subpar 9-12 following a disconcerting defeat to the lowly Charlotte Bobcats on December 14.

Frank stuck to his guns and rode out the starting five of Kidd, Carter, Jefferson, Krstić and Collins. The Nets won their 10th game of the season on December 16 against ex-Net Martin's Nuggets and 9 more thereafter to build an impressive 10-game win streak. On December 23, Vinsanity tied a career high with 51 in a 95–88 win in Miami. New Jersey's tenth consecutive win came on January 8, with Carter hitting a buzzer-beating 3-pointer to cap a 42-point eruption for a rousing 105–104 over his ex-club, Toronto. Kidd leapt into his arms for one of the duo's signature moments.

AMAZINGLY, IT WAS NOT the hottest stretch of that season, as Lawrence Frank and company compiled 14 straight victories spanning March 12 through April 6. Just prior to the trade deadline, the Nets dealt Marc Jackson, Linton Johnson and cash to the New Orleans Hornets for Slovenian-born small forward Boštjan Nachbar. Carter represented the Nets in the 2006 All-Star Game, and for the fourth time in five seasons, the franchise won the Atlantic Division title. Kidd was named to the NBA's All-Defensive First Team.

New Jersey clinched the third seed in the East and was pitted against a Pacers club led by Jermaine O'Neal and ex-Nets Stephen Jackson and Anthony Johnson. Indiana stole Game 1, 90–88, as Jefferson missed a potential game-tying jumper as time expired. Kidd scored just 5 points on 2-of-11 shooting in the series opener, and his scoring woes carried into Game 2 with just 6 points on a 3-for-10 clip from the field to go along with 13 assists and 11 rebounds. Carter's 33, Jefferson's 21 and Krstić's 20 were enough to power the Nets to a 90–75 Game 2 win. The Nets split Games 3 and 4 in Indiana. Back home in New Jersey for Game 5, Carter delivered a virtuoso performance (34 points, 15 rebounds and 7 assists). New Jersey closed out Indiana on the road in Game 6 by hitting clutch free throws up by only two points with 56.6 seconds left. Carter averaged a scintillating 29.2 points and Jefferson 23.5. Kidd averaged a pedestrian 8 points in the series but contributed in other ways, with 10.2 assists and 7.5 rebounds. New Jersey slipped past a gritty Pacers squad.

Nenad Krstić rocks the rim. *Photo by Andrew Bernstein.*

A rematch with Shaquille O'Neal, Wade and the Heat awaited the team in the second round.

In the 2005 playoffs, the Heat demolished the Nets by 18 points and 17 points in Games 1 and 2, respectively, at American Airlines Arena. This time around, the Nets' big three put together their best playoff performance to that point, as Kidd emerged out of his shooting slump for 22 points. Jefferson dumped in 20, and Carter led all scorers with 27 in the series opener. New Jersey jumped out to an impressive 38–21 lead at the end of the first quarter and maintained a double-digit advantage on its way to a 100–88 upset win. The tenor of the series looked to be vastly different from the teams' last playoff matchup, but Wade and O'Neal kicked things into high gear, blasting New Jersey by 22 points in Game 2. Miami won Games 3 and 4 by 11 and 10, respectively. Miami bludgeoned New Jersey in the fourth quarter of games and feasted at the free-throw line. The Nets' season ended in Game 5, as Kidd threw an errant pass that was stolen by Wade in the final seconds. The Heat advanced by virtue of a narrow 106–105 triumph. The 2005–06 campaign saw the Nets' powerful trio of stars finally stay healthy. Despite a division title and a playoff-round win, the season ended in eerily similar fashion to the one preceding it: a lopsided series loss to the Heat. Miami won the 2006 NBA Finals over Dallas for the franchise's first championship. Meanwhile, Kidd and the Nets were still chasing that elusive first NBA title for the player and the franchise, and with the legendary point guard at the end of his prime and set to turn thirty-three at the end of the year, New Jersey's championship window was closing fast.

2006–07

The Nets held two first-round selections in the 2006 NBA Draft, no. 22 via the Clippers in the Kittles trade and their own at no. 23. Thorn and Stefanski elected to take college teammates at UConn in point guard Marcus Williams and power forward Josh Boone.

Future All-Star point guards Rajon Rondo and Kyle Lowry bookended the Nets' picks, and future four-time All-Star power forward Paul Millsap was taken no. 47 overall by Utah. The Nets took Hassan Adams out of Arizona in the second round. As for the franchise's top pick, Marcus Williams had a litany of off-the-court issues while at UConn, including being placed on academic probation during his freshman season and being booted from the program for several months in his junior year for stealing laptops on campus.

Thorn and Stefanski signed sharpshooter Eddie House and sent a 2009 second-rounder to Seattle for Mikki Moore, who had previously played four games with the Nets in 2003–04. Frank's crew got off to an inauspicious 5-9 start, suffering a six-game slump against Western Conference opponents to wrap up November. Just when the team was making strides, with Moore replacing Collins as a starter and Krstić posting a career-high 16.4 points and 6.8 rebounds per contest, injuries started to inflict the

Josh Boone skying for the throwdown against Seattle. *Photo by Andrew Bernstein.*

team. On December 7, two future Nets coaches clashed, as Kidd's 38 points, 14 rebounds and 14 assists came in a double-overtime classic opposing Steve Nash and his 42 points and 13 assists. Nash carried the Suns to a 161–157 marathon triumph.

On December 22, during a 99–95 defeat to the Lakers, Krstić suffered a torn ACL in his left knee and missed the remainder of the season. Fourteen games later, Jefferson underwent ankle surgery and was sidelined for 21 games. Just before Jefferson went down, the Nets finally pulled to the .500 mark at 20-20 and went 8-13 in his absence to sink further in the standings. Carter hit a Herculean buzzer-beater on January 29 in Utah, sinking a 3-pointer just inside half-court for a stunning 116–115 result.

Kidd and Carter once again represented the Nets in the All-Star Game, while Williams played for the All-Star Rookie Team. But without the offensive dynamism of the team's second-leading scorer (Jefferson) and the soft touch of their third-leading scorer (Krstić), the Nets were buried in the Eastern Conference rankings. Carter carried the scoring load in Jefferson's absence, tallying at least 30 points twenty-five times to set a new franchise mark.

On April 7, in an overtime win over Washington, Carter and Kidd became the first players in franchise history to each record a triple-double in the same game. Upon his return to the lineup, Jefferson provided an instant jolt, as New Jersey went 13-8 down the stretch, including 8-2 over the final 10 games of the season to secure the no. 6 seed in the East at 41-41.

As fate would have it, Carter faced his old squad, Toronto. While Carter had a penchant for punishing the Raptors, the sharpshooter was unable to find the bottom of the net in Game 1, converting just 5 of 19 field-goal attempts for 16 points as the sellout crowd at Air Canada Centre savored his struggles. Jefferson picked up the scoring load with 28 points, and Nachbar added 16. Kidd's 8 points, 15 assists and 10 rebounds paced New Jersey to a 96–91 road upset. Chris Bosh, Anthony Parker and Morris Peterson bounced back in Game 2 to outscore the Nets, 31–20, in the fourth to even

Above: Marcus Williams appeared in 79 games during his 2006–07 rookie campaign. *Photo by Andrew Bernstein.*

Left: Vince Carter's pregame ritual of kissing the rim. *Photo by Andrew Bernstein.*

Boštjan Nachbar was an X factor for the Nets in the 2007 NBA Playoffs. *Photo by Andrew Bernstein.*

the series with an 89–83 win. New Jersey held serve in the next two home games with a pair of double-digit wins to take a 3–1 series advantage heading back to Toronto.

Carter shined in Games 3 and 4 at the Meadowlands, dropping 37 and 27, respectively, while shooting a blistering 24 of 38 in that span. The former Raptor savior needed to show he could take his show on the road in a hostile environment, and he did not disappoint, scoring 30 points on 10-of-22 shooting, but New Jersey still trailed 95–94 after Carter smoothly sank a 3-pointer with 27.6 seconds left. From there, the Nets played the foul game and trailed by 2 with 14.9 seconds left to potentially eliminate Toronto with a 3-pointer. The ensuing position was disjointed, as Kidd found Nachbar for a 3-pointer who misfired at the buzzer. In Game 6, Carter's shooting woes crept up again; he went just 6 for 19 from the field for 21 points, but the Nets were sitting pretty after three quarters with a 75–68 advantage. Bosh and company refused to go quietly, as the former Georgia Tech star hit a clutch midrange jumper with 47.9 seconds remaining. The Raptors jumped ahead, 97–96.

Carter missed a contested jumper on the ensuing possession. After New Jersey staged a defensive stop, the Nets had 15.5 seconds left with Carter expected to play the role of hero. Instead, Nachbar inbounded to Kidd, who fed Jefferson on the wing. He converted a spinning layup for a 98–97 edge with 8.3 seconds left. Jefferson was once again the man of the hour on Toronto's ensuing offensive possession, deflecting a pass from José Calderón intended for Bosh into Kidd's hands. Kidd dribbled out the final seconds. The series victory was extra meaningful for Carter, and dethroning the Atlantic Division champions was just another superior feat accomplished by New Jersey's big three. The Nets advanced to the semifinals against LeBron James and the Cleveland Cavaliers. Much like the first-round series with Toronto, the Nets were on the verge of stealing the opening game. They trailed, 79–77, after Carter sank a pair of free throws with 32.3 seconds left. Kidd and company needed to stop James, but the Akron native forced his way inside the paint and hit a short-range shot to extend the lead to 4 points, where it remained for an 81–77 final.

In Game 2, Carter's 26, Jefferson's 22 and Kidd's 17 were not enough to dethrone "King James" in his building. He went for 36, including 12 in the fourth quarter to spur the Cavs to a 102–92 victory. New Jersey won Game 3 at Continental Airlines Arena, with Kidd, Carter and Jefferson all going for 23 and the defense holding James to 18 in the 96–85 final.

In Game 4, Kidd, Carter and Jefferson combined to shoot 11 of 48 from the field and scored 5, 25 and 15, respectively. Moore dropped a playoff-

Jason Kidd surging ahead of LeBron James for a layup. *Photo by Andrew Bernstein.*

175

Richard Jefferson's clutch basket and steal sealed the Game 6 win over Toronto. *Photo by Andrew Bernstein.*

high 25 on 11-of-14 shooting to keep the Nets in it. Down 86–83 with 11.4 seconds left, Carter drew a foul on Eric Snow and drained both free throws to narrow the margin to 1. After James split a pair, Carter had the game in his hands once again, but he committed an untimely turnover in the final seconds to hand Cleveland a 3–1 series advantage. New Jersey had posted a subpar 17-24 road record during the regular season. Facing elimination in Cleveland did not bode well for Lawrence Frank's crew. Despite New Jersey scoring just 6 points in the fourth quarter, the Nets put on their most brilliant defensive performance of the playoffs, holding Cleveland to just 72 points. Kidd's 20 points led the Nets to an 11-point Game 5 victory. Still backed into a corner, the Nets were steamrolled in the first quarter of Game 6, 32–15. Even with the disastrous start, they outscored Cleveland, 45–29, over the next two quarters to find themselves down just 61–60 entering the fourth.

As was the case throughout the series, when the Cavaliers needed to shut the door defensively, they locked in. Cleveland outpaced the Nets, 27–12, in the fourth quarter to clinch the series. At that point, Kidd became the only player in NBA history to average a triple-double for a playoff stretch of 10 games or more, posting averages of 14.6 points, 10.9 rebounds and 10.9 assists in the 12-game run.

After four straight seasons of Kidd and his team failing to get back to the conference finals or the NBA Finals, Game 6 of the 2007 playoffs marked the last playoff game for Kidd in a Nets uniform and the final time the team made the playoffs in New Jersey.

12

PLAYING OUT THE STRING IN THE GARDEN STATE

2007–08 through 2011–12

New Jersey's captain, Jason Kidd, entered the fifth year of the six-year contract extension he had signed following the run to the 2003 NBA Finals, and even with shrewd maneuvering on the part of Thorn and Stefanski, the franchise was sliding further down the Eastern Conference pecking order. At that point, New Jersey had secured six straight playoff seasons for their best run in the team's NBA history. Aside from Kidd's seemingly imminent departure from the team, 2006–07 also marked the final season that the Nets and Devils shared an arena in the Meadowlands. The hockey club christened its new digs, the Prudential Center in Newark, in October 2007. With the Devils leaving, the Nets' future at the Meadowlands was murky at best. Bruce Ratner had every inclination of moving the team to Brooklyn. Continental Airlines Arena opted out of its naming-rights agreement at the conclusion of the 2006–07 season. Ahead of the Nets opener on October 31, 2007, the arena was renamed Izod Center, with the clothing brand signing a five-year naming-rights deal and paying $1.4 million for the first two years of the agreement and $750,000 for the remaining three.

Just prior to the start of the 2006–07 NBA season, the Nets, and the governing body of the Meadowlands Sports Complex, NJSEA, agreed to a lease extension to run until 2013, but it included an out clause for the Nets to leave as soon as 2009 if the intended move to Brooklyn and potential arena project were completed. Chambers' dreams of moving the Nets to Newark went by the wayside due to political and financial

Sean Williams rocks the rim versus the Cavs. *Photo by Andrew Bernstein.*

forces beyond his control, and Ratner needed to persevere through a host of similar issues in his quest to get the team to Brooklyn. The Nets' proposed move back to New York was only a part of Ratner's overall plan to bolster his real-estate empire in the borough, with an arena and basketball team as the focal point of the redevelopment project. So, while substantial barriers to the team's potential move existed, several media reports suggested that Ratner was fielding offers for the team, and ownership's intended move became a true spectacle.

With all the dizzying developments, Thorn, Stefanski and the rest of the Nets' basketball operations group had their work cut out for them to appease an aging cornerstone piece in Kidd. With the no. 17 pick in the 2007 NBA Draft, New Jersey selected center Sean Williams out of Boston College. The former Golden Eagle developed a reputation as an elite shot-blocker but had a multitude of issues, including a suspension from the team during his sophomore year and eventual dismissal from the club his junior year for drug violations. Thorn added center Jamaal Magloire, guard Darrell Armstrong and forward Malik Allen. Krstić's recovery from knee surgery went better than expected, and he was ready to return to the team's starting lineup for the season opener against Chicago. New Jersey won the opener in a thrilling 112–103 overtime contest and raced out to a 4-1 record with rookie Sean Williams becoming part of Lawrence Frank's rotation.

After a 99–88 win over Seattle on January 9, the Nets maintained a winning record at 18-17 but went into a freefall from that point on, losing 9 straight from January 11 to 27. Jefferson finished as the team's leading scorer at 22.6 points per game, followed by Carter's 21.3, but Krstić's scoring output was down nearly 10 points from the year before. Kidd's 11.3 points per game was third on the team. The rest of the supporting cast did not carry its weight. On February 4, Collins was sent to Memphis in exchange for Stromile Swift in a harbinger of sweeping moves to come.

Lawrence Frank coaching the final season with Jason Kidd, Richard Jefferson and Vince Carter together. *Photo by Andrew Bernstein.*

In the 2008 NBA All-Star Game, Kidd represented the Nets for the fifth and final time. The East toppled the West, 134–128, in New Orleans. Kidd was inactive for the final two games leading up to the break, fueling speculation that his days in New Jersey were numbered. Several reports linked Kidd to the Lakers, with the Nets receiving Andrew Bynum in return. On February 19, New Jersey officially dealt Kidd back to the team that drafted him, the Dallas Mavericks. The Nets' captain, along with Antoine Wright and Malik Allen, were sent in exchange for Devin Harris, Trenton Hassell, Keith Van Horn, a 2008 first-round draft pick and a 2010 first-round draft pick, along with Maurice Ager and DeSagana Diop. Van Horn never suited up for the Nets and was waived following the season. As for Kidd, he singlehandedly changed the culture and perception of a franchise that had endured countless losing seasons sprinkled with fleeting success. New Jersey reached back-to-back NBA Finals, won four division titles and earned six straight playoff berths under his leadership, all unprecedented feats for the team. Kidd was a triple-double machine in an era dominated

Jason Kidd willed the Nets to unprecedented heights. *Photo by Andrew Bernstein.*

by big men and defensive-centric play. Unlike Erving before him, Kidd's impact on the team could not be strictly quantified in the box score, and he was not capable of acrobatic dunks that would demoralize opponents. Instead, the Nets' floor general had an innate basketball sense on both sides of the floor. No. 5's cerebral approach and pass-first nature empowered his teammates to go the extra mile on and off the court, as they knew he would create unique scoring opportunities. The captain held intangible qualities and a knack for raising the level of play of his teammates. While his championship aspirations were foiled in New Jersey by the Lakers and Spurs dynasties, Kidd's prodigious transformation of a franchise that had been an afterthought in its own market into the talk of the basketball world was simply remarkable. The book was closed on Kidd's playing career with the Nets, but it was left slightly ajar for his eventual return in a prominent role with the organization in the not-so-distant future.

Kidd reflected on his Cinderella NBA Finals runs in the Garden State with Randy Zellea in a 2011 exclusive interview for BackSportsPage.com.

Devin Harris slashing to the rim against the Bucks. *Photo by Andrew Bernstein.*

My time in Jersey, I have no complaints. We were a talented team, and we had a great group of guys on and off the court. We were young and we sprinkled in a couple veterans, including Lucious Harris and myself, and then you sprinkle in a couple young guys, RJ, K-Mart, Jason Collins. So, from that point it was a fun team. We played defense, we got out and ran, some nights we didn't score a lot of points, but we weren't going to give up a lot of points either. So, we had some success and some of those playoffs I can remember, if I recall correctly, we lost I think the second game against Milwaukee, and then after that series we swept everybody back to the Finals. But that was a good group of guys. You rarely have that type of team where everybody gets along on and off the court.

In the immediate aftermath of the trade, the Nets gained the services of a twenty-four-year-old point guard with All-Star potential, as well as valuable draft assets. For fans, saying farewell to a Nets legend was not easy, but Thorn once again made the most of a delicate situation. New Jersey's point guard of the future, Devin Harris, was two years removed from an NBA Finals appearance with Dallas as a key reserve and was clearly on the upswing of his career. After drafting Harris at no. 5 overall in 2004, Washington immediately traded him along with Jerry Stackhouse and Christian Laettner to the Mavericks for Antawn Jamison. Harris made his Nets debut in a 120–106 win over Milwaukee on February 28, scoring 21 points in just under twenty-one minutes off the bench. Marcus Williams served as the starter in seven games that year before Harris entered the starting five. Boone started in 53 games at center, averaging 8.2 points and 7.3 rebounds with the Nets' youth movement in full force. Harris achieved then-career highs in points per game (15.4) and assists (6.5) in 25 games with New Jersey. The Nets' young stud was just scratching the surface. The next season brought with it more achievements and personal accolades. Capstraw acknowledged how Harris exceeded expectations but was in an unenviable position, trying to live up to the standards set before him by a franchise legend.

> *There were some amazing moments with him, and he had some pretty big games, but to compare anybody to Jason Kidd wasn't fair. It was not going to be the same. Although, I remember on night number one we might have been playing the Bucks, he scored in the [20s]. You thought it was going to be another great move and a great situation that might work out. Over time you realized how great Jason Kidd was. A special, special guy. Although Devin Harris was a fine player at the time, it was going to be tough to recover from that.*

The retooling Nets finished 34-48 for the 2007–08 regular season, 3 games behind the eighth-seeded Hawks.

2008–09

On May 8, the Nets officially hired Kiki VanDeWeghe as special assistant to Thorn in the front office. A former two-time NBA All-Star, VanDeWeghe enjoyed a standout fourteen-year playing career with stops in Denver, Portland, New York and with the Clippers. Prior to joining the Nets in the role of special assistant to Thorn, VanDeWeghe served as the Nuggets'

Yi Jianlian sharpening his shooting skills during the Nets pregame warmups. *Rick Laughland/ NetsInsider.com.*

General Manager (2001–06) and was one of the driving forces in the sign-and-trade between Denver and New Jersey centered on Martin.

Even with a front-office shakeup, it was clear that the Nets' path to success was via the draft. And with two All-Stars—Carter, thirty-one, and Jefferson, twenty-eight— part of the rebuilding club, two-thirds of the Nets' once-vaunted big three were gone by draft day. The Nets held the no. 10 pick in the 2008 NBA Draft. Calipari's prized player at Memphis, Derrick Rose, went first to Chicago.

Intuitively, Carter appeared to be the player with the highest trade value and the most sought-after contributor for a contending team. But the piece that ultimately moved was Jefferson, who was coming off a career year and had more prime years ahead of him. The Nets could broaden their horizons and potentially acquire building blocks for the future. Additionally, and perhaps most importantly, Jefferson was entering the fourth year of his six-year, $78 million contract. These factors resulted in the Nets shipping out the talented forward to Milwaukee for center Yi Jianlian and Bobby Simmons.

With that, the last remaining star of New Jersey's championship finals teams played the remainder of his NBA career elsewhere. Curiously, Thorn was unable to finagle any draft picks out of a Milwaukee club that became NBA Draft Lottery eligible three of the next four seasons. Unfortunately for Jefferson, despite averaging over 22 points per game in two different campaigns over his seven seasons with the Nets, the small forward never got an All-Star nod or the opportunity for the organization to build around him the way they did with Kidd at a similar age.

Often overshadowed by Kidd's all-around mastery and Carter's flair for the dramatic, Jefferson quietly built an All-Star-caliber career in New Jersey, even if he did not have the recognition to show for it. At twenty-one, Jefferson played a key role off the bench in the Nets' first NBA Finals appearance and was an integral part of the starting lineup on the second leg of the championship run that fell two games shy of glory. His departure

Brook Lopez calling for the ball from Chris Douglas-Roberts. *Photo by Andrew Bernstein.*

signaled a changing of the guard, with Carter the only remaining veteran with significant playoff experience.

On draft day, the Nets selected Stanford standout center Brook Lopez at no. 10 and stretch-four Ryan Anderson out of Cal at no. 21, the latter pick acquired in the trade that sent Kidd to Dallas. Under Thorn, the Nets drafts largely failed to produce starting-caliber talent, but Lopez and Anderson quickly bucked that trend with breakout rookie seasons. The former evolved into a franchise center for the better part of the next decade. In the second round, Thorn and VanDeWeghe targeted another one of Calipari's finds in Memphis standout Chris Douglas-Roberts. New Jersey signed a pair of veterans in Eduardo Nájera and Jarvis Hayes and acquired the rights to Keyon Dooling from Orlando. Two years after drafting him, the Nets sent Marcus Williams to Golden State for a 2011 second-rounder and a 2013 first-rounder. Remarkably, Carter, Sean Williams and Ager were the only players who remained on the roster from opening night of the 2007–08 season. New Jersey was not retooling its roster; it was overhauling it with wholesale changes and a fresh new voice and perspective alongside Thorn to influence trades, signings and draft selections in VanDeWeghe. The Nets were coming off their first playoff-less season since the 2000–01 campaign, and the team's final four seasons in New Jersey saw them devolve into a perennial lottery team. New Jersey ushered in a youth movement, with rookies Lopez and Anderson starting 75 games and 30 games, respectively, alongside Harris, Carter and newcomer Jianlian. Lopez was an instant difference-maker, producing 13 points, 8.1 rebounds and 1.8 blocks per game to finally give the Nets the well-rounded inside presence they had long desired. Carter's scoring output dropped to the second-lowest since his rookie season. It would be the last time in Carter's storied career that he reached the 20-point-per-game plateau. To the delight of the Nets, Harris thrived in his new role as franchise point guard, to the tune of a team-high 21.3 points, 6.9 assists and 1.7 steals per game, including a sizzling 47-point, 8 assist, 7 rebound outburst in a 117–109 win over Phoenix on November 30. Just nine days before the superb outing from Harris, Carter haunted his former team once again, hitting a game-tying 3-pointer in regulation and game-winning dunk in overtime on his way to a 39-point night as the Nets overcame an 18-point deficit to stun Toronto, 129–127.

With Devin Harris' meteoric rise and Vince Carter's production dipping, New Jersey's point guard was named to the 2009 NBA All-Star Game for the first time in his career. Lopez played for the All-Star Rookie Team and was named to the NBA All-Rookie First Team by season's end. After the All-Star break, the Nets posted a 10-19 record. Highlights were few and far between during that stretch. Harris etched his place in Nets' history when he splashed through a miraculous half-court shot at the buzzer at Izod Center on February 23 to shock Philadelphia, 98–96. New Jersey drew the sixth-fewest fans that season, but an announced crowd of 13,236 went bonkers as Harris' heroics capped his 39-point onslaught. New Jersey finished at the identical mark as the year before, 34-48. The Nets were out of playoff contention, and the state of the franchise slipped deeper into an abyss of historic proportions in the upcoming campaign.

2009–10

The Nets held the no. 11 pick in the 2009 NBA Draft, and Rick Pitino's most highly touted draft-eligible player, Terrence Williams, was selected by Thorn and VanDeWeghe. That was not the most significant move,

Vince Carter dribbles across the Nets half-court logo at the Izod Center. *Photo by Andrew Bernstein.*

however, as the Nets sent Carter and Anderson to Orlando for Rafer Alston, Tony Battie and Courtney Lee. In a nearly identical fashion to when the team shipped out Jefferson on draft day in 2008, Carter was this year's roster casualty as the team cleared out its high-priced, aging players. "Vinsanity" had spent five seasons in New Jersey, amassing averages of 23.6 points, 5.8 rebounds and 4.7 assists, and the team compiled an 11-16 playoff record and earned two playoff series wins. But Carter was unable to topple the giants in the East in Miami and Cleveland. His prime years in the Garden State were showstopping entertainment as his high-wire act defied gravity and harkened back to Dr. J's ABA heyday with the Nets. Carter, who idolized Erving and modeled his game after the legend, was spectacular in every facet, but for many reasons, the Nets were unable to achieve the playoff success they enjoyed prior to his arrival. Carter left the franchise second all-time in scoring with 8,834 points, trailing only Buck Williams. (Lopez eventually notched 10,444 points in the years ahead.) The man nicknamed "Half-Man/Half-Amazing" was a superhuman scorer and rightfully cemented his place in the Mount Rushmore of Nets legends.

Prior to the beginning of the new season, it was announced that Bruce Ratner had reached a tentative agreement to sell 80 percent controlling interest in the team and a 45 percent stake in the yet-to-be-constructed arena to Russian oligarch Mikhail Prokhorov for $223 million, who assumed $160 million in team debt . Under the newly formed partnership agreement, Forest City Ratner, Nets Sports and Entertainment and Prokhorov's Onexim

Group served as the impetus for pushing through the Atlantic Yards Project and arena construction in Brooklyn. Obstacles and hurdles still created a bumpy pathway to the borough, but with the deep pockets of a Russian billionaire as his safety net, Ratner assembled an ownership power play to push the project full steam ahead. By December 16, Ratner cleared a major hurdle by selling more than $500 million in tax-exempt bonds to help finance the new arena As for Prokhorov's questionable business practices, he amassed his fortune in the precious-metals sector as many previously highly regulated industries became privatized after the collapse of the USSR. The Russian oligarch, along with business partner Vladimir Potanin, capitalized on this macroeconomic development by acquiring shares of Norilsk Nickel at well-below market value from employees. Prokhorov then became chairman of the board at Potanin's Onexim Bank, which served as a depository by holding government bonds and auctions that were, in fact, illegitimate and resulted in many titans of Russia's industries being acquired by small banks at a fraction of their market value. This disreputable route to fortune saw Prokhorov's shares in Norilsk Nickel and other previously state-controlled industries proliferate into the billions of dollars.

The sale of the Nets required league-wide approval, and the Nets' regular season commenced with another pending ownership change and transport to another arena in the offing.

New Jersey had endured its share of disastrous starts over the years, most notably its second year in the NBA, when it posted a 3-22 record in 1977–78 campaign, as well as a 3-18 start in 1987–88 and a 3-18 mark in 1998–99. But none of those catastrophic starts compared to the futility of 2009–10 squad. Even the most pessimistic prognosticators pegged the Nets at 17 wins heading into the season, putting them with the highest odds for the NBA Draft Lottery's top pick. What transpired that regular season rewrote the NBA record books for all the wrong reasons and provided the clearest indication to that point that, from ownership on down, winning was far down the list of the organization's priorities. The Nets opened their season on the road in Minnesota on October 28, with Lopez scoring 27 points, ripping down 15 rebounds and blocking 5 shots, powering New Jersey to a 14-point advantage heading into the fourth quarter. Minnesota stormed back behind an 18–6 run over the final 5:33, with Damien Wilkins hitting a game-winner with 0.2 seconds left to hand the Nets a season-opening loss, 95–93. New Jersey would drop its next 15 contests in lopsided fashion and parted ways with its seventh-year head coach, Lawrence Frank, who had been with the organization as an assistant since the 2000–01

Left: Terrence Williams dishes to an open Trenton Hassell during the 2009–10 campaign. *Photo by Andrew Bernstein.*

Below: View from the stands at Izod Center prior to tipoff between the Nets and Clippers. *Rick Laughland/ NetsInsider.com.*

season. The 0-16 start under Frank's watch pushed his overall regular-season record with the team to sub .500 at 225-241. Assistant coach Tom Barrise, a Paterson, New Jersey native and Fairleigh Dickinson University alum, had been with the Nets organization since 1996. He took over as the interim head coach for the next two games. The Nets dropped both contests and clinched the unpleasant distinction as achieving the worst start in NBA history at 0-18. VanDeWeghe had seen enough and rose out of his executive chair and onto the team's bench to coach the remainder of the year. Initially, the Nets responded well, beating Charlotte in his debut as coach on December 4 to snap the dry spell. They won against Chicago on December 8 to post a 2-1 mark after a monumental losing streak. Things turned downright ugly from there, as the team went 2-29 leading up to the All-Star break with separate skids of 10, 11 and 8 games for an unfathomable record of 4-48.

Bobby Marks recalls the team going to bizarre and unusual lengths to help players stay mentally strong throughout a brutal campaign.

> *It was a crazy year. We wound up bringing Del Harris on as an assistant coach, and I think there were mixed signals that Del was eventually going to get the job and Kiki was going to go back to the front office, but that never happened. We had a voodoo expert come in when we were really playing poorly to do like a spiritual exercise with our players to the point where he wound up sticking a needle into the side of his jaw just to show that there is no pain as far as what these guys were going through.*

In the final 30 games of the season, the Nets desperately wanted to avoid being on the wrong side of NBA history, yet again. They were on pace to break the league's mark for futility set by the 1972–73 76ers (9-73). New Jersey's win percentage to that point was an unheard-of .077, and the team needed to finish at least 5-25 to simply tie the pitiful benchmark set by Philadelphia. Immediately after the 2010 All-Star break, the Nets reached an agreement with NJSEA to opt out of their lease at the Izod Center early and, in so doing, paid a penalty of $4 million over two years to move out of the arena they had called home since 1981. The Nets planned an interim move to Newark at the Prudential Center, to share it with the Devils for only the 2010–11 and 2011–12 seasons while the arena in Brooklyn was being constructed.

New Jersey went 8-22 over the final 30 contests to clinch the worst regular-season record in franchise history (12-70) but avoided tying or breaking

Philadelphia's miserable record. Lopez started all 82 games and led the Nets in scoring (18.8), but the rest of the roster vastly underachieved and underwhelmed, contributing to the team's downfall. The Nets played their final game at the Meadowlands on April 12 against the Bobcats and, in fitting fashion, dropped that contest, 105–95, to leave the building they had called home for twenty-nine seasons on an ultimate low.

2010–11

Lopez and Humphries were the only two players from the 2009–10 campaign who remained on the team for the entirety of the 2010–11 season. The franchise cleaned house in preparation for an interim move to Newark and geared up for its best chance yet at the no. 1 overall pick via the 2011 NBA Draft Lottery. New Jersey held a bevy of cap space to sign free agents in a class led by All-Stars LeBron James, Dwyane Wade, Chris Bosh, Amar'e Stoudemire, Joe Johnson, Rudy Gay and Carlos Boozer.

On July 14, Thorn announced that he would step down from the organization and accept an offer with the 76ers to become their Team President and reunite with Stefanski. With new majority ownership, Mikhail Prokhorov proclaimed that VanDeWeghe would not return. The team was setting its sights on a new head coach and General Manager to carry it through the stopover in Newark. Thorn remained with the organization to manage the hiring process and handle the upcoming draft before the next General Manager was in place. Prokhorov's right-hand man, Dmitry Razumov, became a key figure in basketball operations throughout the draft process and in pitches to marquee free agents that off-season.

On June 10, New Jersey formally hired Avery Johnson to the head-coaching position. Johnson had led the Mavericks' coaching efforts from 2004–05 through 2007–08, including the franchise's first NBA Finals appearance in 2006. Nicknamed the "Little General" for his demonstrative disposition but small stature by NBA standards, Johnson was an integral part of the Spurs' 1999 championship as a player and compiled nineteen seasons in the NBA. After a brief stint as a television analyst with ESPN, he was snatched up by the Nets to develop a winning attitude and culture for a franchise that had gone belly up.

In fact, in a culture-changing marketing campaign, Prokhorov appeared alongside Jay-Z on a huge wallscape across from Madison Square Garden with the tagline "Blueprint for Greatness." While the mural had the city buzzing and stoked the fire between the two fan bases, Irina Pavlova, president of Onexim Sports and Entertainment, indicates that Prokhorov and Jay-Z were not part of the originally planned ad. "The billboard was meant to have John Wall on it. It was going to be a big wall for John Wall. We were expecting to get him in the draft, and we did not get him. I'm not sure whose genius idea it was to put Mikhail and Jay-Z on the wall, but it was basically, we have this gigantic wall, so what do we do with it? So, we did that."

In the 2010 NBA Draft, New Jersey drew the no. 3 lottery pick, two spots shy of Wall, and had its sights set on Georgia Tech forward Derrick Favors. The Nets took Jordan Crawford later in the first round and Tibor Pleiß in the second round, only to immediately send both players to Atlanta for Damion James. With the draft in the books, Thorn and Prokhorov narrowed down the General Manager search to two finalists, coincidentally former Duke teammates, Billy King and Danny Ferry. King was awarded the GM vacancy with a clear-cut advantage in the experience department, having served in that same role with Philadelphia (1998–2007). King's legacy as an executive was mixed in the City of Brotherly Love. He was the architect of the 2000–01 Eastern Conference champion team with Allen Iverson as the franchise cornerstone piece, but the 76ers failed to win a single playoff round in six of the next seven seasons. King was a standout player in college at Duke. He was a leader of the 1988 Blue Devils team that cinched an NCAA Final Four berth. But that sterling reputation as a player contrasted with the harsh criticism directed at him for orchestrating several head-scratching moves during his tenure in Philadelphia and, more glaringly, in his years ahead with the Nets. Prior to King's arrival, the Nets front office went on a free-agent spending spree under the direction of Razumov, with Prokhorov's approval, despite all the top-tier talent signing elsewhere. The Nets made a series of cap-clearing moves in the weeks leading up to the July 1 free-agency period, sending Jianlian to the Wizards for Quinton Ross after just two seasons with the team.

The Nets had nearly $30 million in cap space available, and with some additional roster maneuvering, the possibility existed for them to sign two max-salary players. The former swamp-dwellers—and soon to be Newark tenants and eventual Brooklyn residents—were unable to lure prized free agents, despite using Prokhorov's wealth and Jay-Z's celebrity as recruiting tools. Even with a billionaire owner, money alone was unable to sway any of the league's premier players to roll the dice on the nomadic Nets. With all the shiny free-agent pieces off the table, New Jersey resorted to the bargain bin in the first two weeks of July, signing Travis Outlaw to a five-year, $35 million deal; Johan Petro to a three-year, $10 million deal; and Jordan Farmar to a three-year, $12 million agreement.

Pavlova was front and center during the team's ownership transition—the final year at the Meadowlands, the interim move to Newark and at the final stop in Brooklyn.

> *First of all, when we came in, that being Mikhail's team, the team was contingent on eminent domain going through and the arena actually being built. If there was not going to be a new arena, there was not going to be a new deal. I caught the tail end of it, but I was not really affected by it. I knew that from the time that I started to interview for the job, which was late November 2009, I knew that there was a high probability that the deal might not happen because they needed to raise pilot bonds and get approvals and eminent domain. So, once it went through, I really wasn't worried about it. Also from Mikhail's perspective, the beauty of having Bruce as a partner was Forest City was taking care of all the permits, government relations and all that stuff that none of us knew how to handle. I don't think we were affected by any of that.*

The first stepping-stone to the relocation in Brooklyn was the Nets opting out of the lease agreement at the Meadowlands early and joining the Devils in Newark. While it was understood from the get-go that Newark was not in the organization's long-term plans, there were serious challenges trying to appeal to a fan base that would ultimately be left behind for the bright lights of New York City. Without a long-term commitment to New Jersey, the organization was in a bind from a marketing, sales and sponsorship standpoint. Cultivating and retaining a loyal customer base with so many rapid changes in the works was far from easy, according to Pavlova.

> *Moving to Newark had some personal history, since I worked in Newark from 1992 to 1994. When I left in 1994, I told myself, I'm never setting foot in that city again. Lo and behold, I get this job twenty years later and I'm back there and the arena is literally two blocks from my former office. I was at the last game in the Meadowlands, and this is before the deal was officially consummated. Seeing Prudential Center, I could see it was a step up from the Meadowlands. I thought we would be ok. Then the whole experience of just going there, I would take the PATH most of the time and*

especially coming back, it wasn't a nice environment. We were definitely very enthusiastic about moving to Barclays once it was completed.

From the marketing perspective, we were kind of all in flux. We knew that we were moving to Brooklyn, so the construction was going on at the same time, and that's a huge project as you can imagine. At the same time, thinking about the transition, the rebranding, the name of the team, the colors, and Brett [Yormark] was great at figuring out how to sell tickets at the time.

We basically guaranteed seat selection to the people that bought tickets in Newark, and they were cheap then, where we guaranteed their seat selection when Barclays Center opened.

The Nets enjoyed a few fleeting moments of excitement during their final two years in the Garden State, but philosophically, the organization shifted all of its fan-engagement practices and marketing muscle away from its base in New Jersey and aimed to establish a Brooklyn-centric brand. Yormark, hired back in 2005 as CEO, was most overtly the catalyst for the marketing department's concerted efforts to whitewash the team's thirty-six seasons of history in New Jersey (one season in the ABA, thirty-five in the NBA) from any branding, uniforms, merchandise and promotional materials. The franchise had finally started to break ground on the new arena on March 11, 2010, but Yormark's directives centered on looking ahead to the team's next step instead of honoring—or at least acknowledging—its lengthy history in the Garden State. The Jets and Giants currently practice and played in New Jersey, yet they are branded as New York teams. A sizeable opportunity was missed for the Nets to build a brand in the greater metropolitan area. Instead, the Nets' CEO unleashed a hyperfocused campaign aimed at the borough of Brooklyn and parts of Manhattan that shunned fans from New Jersey and Long Island, where the team had established its roots. The Nets launched the "Jersey Strong, Brooklyn Ready" campaign—one of the rare examples of the club referencing New Jersey, but only as an afterthought.

The Nets' distancing themselves from the state they had called home for thirty-six total seasons only intensified after their arrival in Brooklyn—a move that hit multiple snags due to eminent-domain cases and financial difficulties following an economic recession.

As the team geared up for its second-to-last season in New Jersey, it executed a pair of trades, acquiring dead-eye shooting guard Anthony Morrow from Golden State for a protected 2011 second-round pick and a four-team trade involving Houston, New Orleans and Indiana in which New Jersey unloaded Lee and received smooth-shooting seven-footer Troy

Murphy. A star from Sparta, New Jersey, Murphy showcased his talents at Delbarton High School in Morristown before a decorated collegiate career at Notre Dame. An off-season filled with the potential of the draft's top pick and top-flight free-agent talent joining the team amounted to serviceable NBA players coming into the fold instead. The Nets opened their first—and, coincidentally, second-to-last—season at the Prudential Center with wins over the rebuilding Pistons and Kings to find themselves one-sixth of the way to their win total from the 2009–10 season. Things regressed from there. The team dropped 25 of the next 32 contests. Lopez took a major step forward in his burgeoning NBA career by topping the 20-points-per-game average plateau. Harris produced at a superb level, but his scoring was down almost 6 points per contest from his All-Star campaign in 2008–09. The Nets flirted with the idea of acquiring Dwight Howard. Several iterations of a deal were on the table, centering on Lopez, expiring contracts and picks. The Magic star opted in to his deal and ended the Nets' pursuit of him. That would not be the last of trade talks between the Nets and Magic centered on Howard. The never-ending saga was dubbed "Dwightmare."

When the Nets slipped to 7-19, Billy King engaged in a three-team deal sending Joe Smith, 2011 and 2012 second-rounders to the Lakers for Sasha Vujačić and a 2011 first-rounder. As part of the deal, the Nets also traded Terrence Williams to Houston and received a 2013 first-rounder in exchange. All-Star weekend came and went without a single Net representing the organization in Los Angeles. The team was marginally improved but far from must-see basketball. After the All-Star break, New Jersey sat at 17-40, and King set his sights on a floor general who clashed with legendary coach Jerry Sloan in Utah. That player, Deron Williams, became the centerpiece of a trade that brought him to New Jersey and sent Harris, Favors, 2011 and 2013 first-round picks and cash to the Jazz. Deron Williams was in the second year of a four-year, $70 million contract extension signed with Utah back in 2008. The no. 3 selection in the 2005 NBA Draft out of Illinois, as a junior, Williams powered the Fighting Illini to a 37-1 record heading into the NCAA championship game before falling to UNC. The Nets were taking a gamble with a franchise-caliber point guard who would become a free agent the summer before the team's anticipated move to Brooklyn.

With no assurance that Williams would be part of the team's eventual relocation, it made marketing the star doubly difficult. To make matters even more complicated, while still with the Jazz Williams injured his wrist during a January 26 loss to San Antonio and missed 4 games before returning to action with his former club, Utah. The injury lingered throughout the season, and Williams filled a distributor role upon his trade to New Jersey with his shooting hand ailing. On March 14, Williams hit a clutch 3-pointer in the final minute to knock off the powerhouse Celtics and propel the Nets to a 5-game winning streak. The moment went viral when a gleeful young Nets fan was caught on camera rejoicing to the heavens. Nets broadcaster Ian Eagle dubbed the moment, "Jubilation in Newark."

For the 2010–11 campaign, Williams had 35 double-digit assists games (27 in 53 games with Utah and 8 in 12 games with New Jersey), including a whopping 21 dimes and 18 points in the Nets' 107–105 victory over Minnesota on April 5. Coincidentally, that performance was Williams' final action of the season. He opted for season-ending surgery to clean out loose bodies in his wrist. In just 12 regular-season games, he averaged 15 points and a career-high 12.8 assists as a Net.

The Nets finished tied for the NBA's fifth-worst record (24-48) but doubled their win total from the nightmarish final season at the Meadowlands. The Nets drew the third-fewest NBA fans in a Devils-centric venue filled with Seton Hall branding and only sprinkled with Nets banners.

2011–12

For the second consecutive year, the Nets earned the third spot in the NBA Draft Lottery, but the pick was already sent to Utah as part of the Deron Williams acquisition. New Jersey selected Purdue product JaJuan Johnson at no. 27, then immediately sent him and a 2014 second-rounder to Boston for Providence guard MarShon Brooks. Billy King then sent a 2013 second-round pick and cash to Minnesota for Bojan Bogdanović, who remained overseas. The off-season had all the makings of a team that was simply playing out the string in New Jersey and looking ahead to a new era of basketball in Brooklyn. In near-perfect symmetry to the Nets' first season in the NBA, the team's final season in New Jersey was met with virtually no fanfare, hoopla or anticipation. Many Garden State residents felt betrayed by the team's deliberate efforts to phase out the team's thirty-six-season run in the state, while the Nets' brass grew increasingly frustrated with the political, economic and social pushback that temporarily sidetracked the move to Brooklyn—a move that was more than seven years in the making.

The NBA's 2011–12 campaign was a lockout-shortened year, with teams playing a 66-game regular-season schedule. On February 24, Morrow participated in the 3-point contest wearing a throwback Dražen Petrović jersey but was eliminated with a score of 14 points in the first round. Lopez was emerging as a potential All-Star talent, but he suffered a broken foot in the preseason against the Knicks, forcing him to miss the first 32 games.

The Nets' big man played well in his return, but after just 5 games, he injured his ankle. The team decided to shut him down with the Nets completely out of playoff contention at 12-26 following a March 4 victory over the lowly Bobcats. In that very same contest, Williams' signature moment in a Nets uniform came when he dazzled to the tune of 57 points on 16 of 29 shooting, including an astonishing 21 of 21 from the free-throw line. The point guard set a single-game franchise scoring mark (57 points), breaking the previous record (52, set by Mike Newlin and Ray Williams). Deron Williams was the Nets' lone All-Star that season, posting 21 points and 8.7 assists per game. On March 15, the Nets acquired Gerald Wallace from Portland for Mehmet Okur, Shawne Williams and a 2012 first-rounder. The Trailblazers would select Damian Lillard sixth overall with that pick. He developed into one of the NBA's premier players and clutch shooters.

Lopez being sidelined opened the door for Humphries to dominate inside, with 13.8 points and 11 rebounds per contest, while Brooks, Morrow and Gerald Green all averaged over 12 points. The Nets played their last game in New Jersey on April 23 against the Philadelphia 76ers at the Prudential Center, with 18,711 fans saluting the end of an era.

Several former Nets legends were in attendance for the Jersey swan song during a halftime ceremony that paid homage to the pinnacle moments and integral players during the franchise's thirty-five seasons as the New Jersey Nets. As for the contest, New Jersey led, 5–2, with 9:39 left in the first quarter, but they never led again, suffering a lopsided 105–87 loss to Philadelphia. Perhaps fittingly, the team scored just 2 points over the final three minutes of the game. When the final buzzer sounded, the Nets' staff collected all the team banners hanging from the rafters, and any Nets-centric branding was removed from the building in preparation for the move to Brooklyn. In the final game of the regular season, the Nets played a forgettable road contest in Toronto, a 98–67 thrashing to drop the Nets' record to 22-44. Petro scored the final basket of the New Jersey Nets era. For the fifth consecutive season, the Nets were lottery-bound. That off-season saw a flurry of changes for a franchise aiming to form a new identity and unleash a new branding campaign in one of New York's most storied boroughs.

13

HELLO BROOKLYN!

2012–13

C hief among the organization's objectives was finalizing the nickname of the newly relocated franchise. Just one week after playing the final home game in New Jersey, new branding was unveiled at an official press conference on April 30. Plenty of dialogue between Nets ownership, the marketing department and the NBA league offices contributed to the final product showcased at the event. With "Hello, Brooklyn" plastered all over team promotions, the franchise was putting the borough front and center and attempting to create a lifestyle brand to turn Brooklynites, who were largely well-established Knicks fans, into Nets fans. To its credit, the franchise's brain trust did not attempt to reinvent the wheel in terms of gimmicky nicknames to replace "Nets," but it added new-age flair to the moniker it had adopted prior to the 1968–69 season, its second year of existence.

"I can't say exactly why it was the shield," noted Pavlova.

> Like I said, it was a lot of iterations, there were a lot of options we were looking at. I like this font, but not that font. I like "Brooklyn" written out this way, but not that way. It wasn't like it has to be a shield because of a, b and c, it was just that it looked good. Definitely every team name was being discussed. I think Brooklyn Knights was probably a top contender, well, I can't even say a top contender because from what I remember it wasn't really a long discussion on a name. It was more like, we're going to have a new city name with Brooklyn versus New Jersey or [New York] State, but this team has a lot of history. We should probably keep "Nets" for continuity since they go back to the ABA with Dr. J, and you don't want it to be completely new. So, keeping the Nets in the name was the way of providing that continuity and connection to history.

The Nets were far from a franchise steeped in history and adept at promoting its legendary players throughout the years. With a new chapter of Nets basketball set to get underway in Brooklyn, the relocation and rebranding was essentially being hyped as the start of an entirely new franchise. Merchandise marked with "Brooklyn Nets est. 2012" turned its back on the journey the team took to get back to its roots in New York. In fact, while in New Jersey, the Nets hardly ever harkened back to their days in Long Island, aside from the red, white and blue stars-and-stripes jerseys they showcased during the Kidd, Martin and Jefferson years to mark the twenty-five-plus seasons since the ABA glory days.

While the Nets brand was trying to expand its horizons and create new inroads in one of New York's largest boroughs, Billy King and Razumov on the basketball operations side were positioning the product on the court to get the team back in the playoff conversation. During the 2011–12 campaign, King made a series of transactions that reshaped the identity of the roster, including waiving a high-priced free-agent signing from the summer of 2010, Outlaw. Without their first-round selection from the Gerald Wallace

The Brooklyn Bridge from the Manhattan side of the East River. *Kristen Laughland/NetsInsider.com.*

trade, the now–Brooklyn Nets took Turkish big man İlkan Karaman in the second round as a project player in the 2012 NBA Draft. King then traded cash to Portland for Tyshawn Taylor. The Nets' "Dwightmare" saga entered another chapter, with rekindled talks taking place that summer, but the Magic ultimately spurned King's offer centering on Lopez and multiple unprotected first-round picks in favor of a four-team deal between the Magic, Nuggets, Sixers and Lakers that, among many moving parts, saw Howard dealt to Los Angeles and Andrew Bynum to Philadelphia. The biggest cliffhanger for the organization was the free-agent status of Deron Williams, for whom King gave up a haul to anoint as the rebranded Nets' franchise player.

On July 3, Williams agreed to a five-year, $99 million contract to remain with the team, even though he was hotly pursued by Dallas during that summer. Lopez re-signed with the club on a four-year, $61 million deal to put an end to the Dwightmare drama that had hovered over the team the previous two seasons.

Brooklyn cut bait with several key pieces of the summer of 2010 free-agent spending spree, shipping Farmar, Morrow, Petro, DeShawn Stevenson, Jordan Williams, a 2013 first-rounder and a 2017 second-rounder to the Atlanta Hawks for Joe Johnson. The smooth-shooting guard was entering the third year of a six-year, $124 million deal he had signed in the summer of 2010 with Atlanta. With Johnson as the Hawks' max player costarring alongside Josh Smith, Al Horford and Jeff Teague, Atlanta failed to get out of the second round of the playoffs, despite holding the distinction as a perennial playoff team in Johnson's final five seasons with them. The former Razorback standout was selected tenth overall by the Celtics in the 2001 NBA Draft. He played just 48 games with the Celtics before being traded to Phoenix in February 2002. Even with Johnson as the third scoring option in the Valley of the Sun behind Shawn Marion and Stephon Marbury upon his arrival and eventually behind Steve Nash and Amar'e Stoudemire, Phoenix failed to conquer the Western Conference giants in the playoffs during his three and a half seasons there. The Nets committed nearly $223 million to a backcourt of Johnson and Williams, who were key contributors on playoff teams, but neither player advanced to a single NBA Finals nor was in a serious hunt for a league MVP award. The moves had the league buzzing, but many felt that neither Johnson's nor Williams' bodies of work warranted the near-max deals they netted. Nonetheless, the backcourt on paper looked to be among the most dynamic in the game. And with an inside presence like Lopez, the Nets became an intriguing team to keep an eye on in the upcoming season.

To fortify the bench, King signed a quartet of proven veterans: Andray Blatche, Jerry Stackhouse, Keith Bogans and C.J. Watson, while trading for rebounder extraordinaire, Reggie Evans. The Nets also signed Bosnian sensation Mirza Teletović, who had spent over eight years with professional stints in Bosnia and Herzegovina, Belgium and in the EuroLeague. Williams, Lopez, Humphries and Brooks were the only roster holdovers from opening night of the 2011–12 campaign, and the rebuilt and rebranded Nets were set to open their newly constructed venue at the crossroads of Brooklyn, Flatbush and Atlantic Avenues. The last professional franchise to call Brooklyn home, the Dodgers, had several alternate nicknames over the years and played at two stadiums both named Washington Park in South Brooklyn before moving to the neighborhood of Brownsville at Eastern Park. By 1913, the team had settled into the Flatbush neighborhood at the famed Ebbets Field, which they called home until the franchise's departure for Los Angeles in 1957. The Dodgers were woven into fabric of the Brooklyn community, and their heated rivalry with the New York Giants and New York Yankees culminated in twelve National League pennants and a World Series title in 1955 over the Pinstripes while still residing in the borough. The owner of the Brooklyn Dodgers, Walter O'Malley, was pushing for the team to build a new stadium in the early 1950s within the immediate vicinity of where Barclays Center currently stands, but he was rebuffed by the city and thus shifted his sights to Los Angeles.

Brooklyn Nets franchise point guard Deron Williams. *Photo by Dexter Henry.*

So, while the fourteen-mile move from the New Jersey Meadowlands to Downtown Brooklyn was a hard pill to swallow for many Garden State basketball diehards, the 2,800-mile trek from the East Coast to the West Coast was nothing short of gut-wrenching for fans of a baseball team that had been founded in Brooklyn way back in 1883.

The former Hudson River rivalry between the Nets and Knicks was now billed as the "Battle of the Boroughs." There was curiosity as to how the Nets planned to convert a borough programmed to follow and root for the Knicks since their inception in 1946 into Brooklyn Nets loyalists. By promoting and elevating the borough in all of its marketing and public-relations efforts, the Nets' brass emphasized the pride that over 2.5 million

Brooklynites intrinsically held for the borough. Pavlova illuminated the flaws in the Nets' initial marketing plans after the move to Brooklyn that many fans in New Jersey and Long Island objected to then and continue to criticize to the present day.

> *I think a lot of it was common sense. Just looking at it from the distance from New Jersey to Brooklyn and the fact you have to take a bridge or a tunnel, we realized that not a lot of New Jersey fans were going to make it over there. Also, there also were not enough New Jersey fans to begin with to sustain the team, so that's why it had to move. So, the main push was to establish the Brooklyn brand, and it was all Brooklyn all the way. Black and White from day one. Hello Brooklyn Campaign. Jay-Z being instrumental at that point and the King of Brooklyn. So, at that point, New Jersey kind of got left behind for obvious reasons. You have to allocate your budget and you're not going to market to New Jersey that you just left because New Jersey couldn't sustain it. So, we started marketing to Brooklyn.*
>
> *I don't know if Mikhail meant this when he said we're going to make Knicks fans into Nets fans. My personal feeling based on my personal experience is, it's much easier to groom new fans from scratch than to convert fans from your competitors. I personally didn't have very high hopes for converting Knicks fans. That's not what fandom is about. If you're a real fan, you should not be easily converted. The Knicks are lucky to have those*

The Manhattan Bridge connecting Lower Manhattan to Brooklyn.
Kristen Laughland/NetsInsider.com,

fans. Rain or shine, no matter how bad they are, MSG always sells out and they're passionate. That's the way fans should be. It takes a while. I don't think Brooklyn is there yet. It's growing slowly. To be honest, I think at this point, it's a mistake to just keep pushing Brooklyn. That should have been done the first two or three years max, and after that you have to go to the Nets brand. That's where you have your old fans from New Jersey, and also I've met a lot of people that say, "I'm from the Bronx and I don't care about Brooklyn. I'm from Queens, I'm not going to wear Brooklyn on my jersey." I think at this point it makes sense to be more inclusive and promote the Nets brand more than Brooklyn. I don't think they're there yet.

When Ratner made public his intentions to move the franchise to Brooklyn, he shared illustrations of the planned arena, set to be designed by renowned architect Frank Gehry. The proposed $3.5 billion, twenty-two-acre sports, entertainment and residential development project was delayed more than three years from its initially targeted start date, while the arena alone was originally planned to open in 2006. The proposed timeline for the project shifted, and Barclays Center was then set to be built in time for the start of the 2009–10 NBA season. The economic recession in 2008 created financial difficulties for Ratner, but bringing Prokhorov into the fold as majority owner provided the requisite capital to infuse into the project during the downturn. However, Ratner was forced to abandon the extravagant designs devised by Gehry and pivoted to another architecture firm to plan the world-class arena, SHoP Architects along with AECOM. The venue was completed in September 2012 at a cost of $1 billion for the eighteen-thousand-seat, 675,000-square-foot arena. Gehry's initial design, while ostentatious and eye-popping, also featured a cavernous layout with wasted space at an exorbitant cost. Gehry's futuristic and galactic elements were replaced with a more industrial yet sleek look to reflect the grit and heritage of the borough. Above the main plaza entrance, a signature, gargantuan oculus brims with digital signage for team promotions and sponsorship branding.

The façade features twelve thousand panels of A588 alloy steel that underwent a specialized coating process to create a weathered, rusty effect, giving the impression that the structure had been part of the community for many decades. Within the arena, the team's black-and-white color scheme is pervasive, with dimly lit concourses illuminated by a crystal-white glow. The main lobby of the arena showcases direct sightlines to the hallmarked herringbone patterned court situated below the street level.

Barclays Center's signature oculus. *Rick Laughland/NetsInsider.com.*

Ratner reportedly wanted the arena to be modeled—at least in part—after Conseco Fieldhouse (later renamed Gainbridge Fieldhouse), built as home to the Indiana Pacers in 1999. To that end, the lower bowl seating is situated so that even fans in the last row have unobstructed and clear views of the court, while the steep, thirty-six-degree slope of the upper bowl is intended to give fans in the upper rung the feeling that they are on top of the action. The bars, clubs and concourses are characterized by distinct urban elements indicative of Brooklyn's history and culture, while Jay-Z's Suite Level 40/40 club was unveiled on September 28, 2012, with the rap star kicking off the arena's opening-night ceremonies with an epic concert. The world-class arena shouts "Brooklyn" and gives off big-city vibes throughout. Nearly $150 million in improvements were made to the Atlantic Yards Transit Center that comprises both subway and rail service through the MTA and LIRR, bringing fans to the doorstep of the main entrance. The arena is in no way conducive to fans attending via car, as street parking is hard to come by. No team-owned or -operated parking decks translate to higher fees even for season-ticket holders. Those factors, along with the concerted marketing efforts to shift away from the New Jersey fan base, discouraged longtime followers of the franchise from outside New York City from attending games. Back in 2007, Ratner's Nets created a bidding war for the naming rights to the proposed arena. Universal bank Barclays, based in London, placed the winning bid, over $400 million for a twenty-year term.

"Dr. J" signing a jersey for Nets super fans "Mr. and Mrs. Whammy." *Photo by Doug Bearak.*

The Brooklyn Nets played their first regular-season home game of a new era on November 3, 2012, in a spirited 107–100 opening-night triumph over the Toronto Raptors. Brooklyn lost its next 2 games but rebounded in 10 of the next 12 contests to jump out to a superb 11-4 start. Just when it appeared the team was turning the corner and ready to make noise in the Eastern Conference, Avery Johnson's crew lost 10 of the next 13 games to slide back to .500. Following a 108–93 defeat at the hands of Milwaukee on December 26, the Nets parted ways with their coach after just 28 games and in the middle of his third season with the team. While the decision was curious to many, Brooklyn was sending a clear message to its fans and the rest of the NBA that new standards were being set.

The Nets filled the vacancy from within, slapping the interim head-coaching tag on Johnson's lead assistant, P.J. Carlesimo. The well-respected coach spent three seasons apiece as head coach in Portland and Golden State at the start of his NBA coaching career beginning in the 1994–95 season.

During the 1997–98 campaign with the Warriors, star forward Latrell Sprewell infamously choked Carlesimo during practice. Teammates and coaches were forced to pull Sprewell off his coach. After his challenging stint in Golden State, Carlesimo spent the next five seasons as Gregg Popovich's assistant in San Antonio before his third head-coaching opportunity came in the Supersonics' final year in Seattle and carried into the first 13 games in Oklahoma City the following season, when he was fired after a 1-12 start. Carlesimo's NBA résumé was a mixed bag, but his success as a collegiate coach at Seton Hall in a run that spanned twelve seasons was astounding. With the Pirates, Carlesimo clinched six NCAA Tournament berths. His most successful campaign came in 1988–89, when he lost in the National Championship Game, 80–79, in overtime to powerhouse Michigan.

Much like the jolt in player morale that the coaching change from Byron Scott to Lawrence Frank delivered during the 2003–04 campaign,

The Main Plaza Entrance at Barclays Center in Brooklyn. *Photo by Doug Bearak.*

early returns were promising for Brooklyn. In Carlesimo's first 14 games, the Nets posted a 12-2 record, and the offense played through Lopez, with the backcourt duo of Joe Johnson and Deron Williams dazzling. The Nets were in the driver's seat for a top-five spot in the East as the All-Star break approached, with Lopez being named a first-time All-Star. Blatche was a sparkplug off the bench to help the team finish with a top-ten offensive rating in the league. The Nets continued stacking wins after the All-Star break and rounded out the campaign winners of 6 of their last 7 games to tie the franchise's second-best NBA regular season record at the time (49-33), good enough for the fourth seed in the East. The Nets made a remarkable one-year transformation, from 22 games under the .500 mark in 2011–12, and it became abundantly clear that the modus operandi in Brooklyn contrasted with that of the last few seasons in the Garden State. Brooklyn was a divisional runner-up to the 54-win Knicks led by Carmelo Anthony, Stoudemire and ex-Nets Kidd and Martin.

The Nets drew an unfavorable matchup against a Bulls squad that was decimated by injuries but led by a hard-nosed, defensive-minded coach, Tom Thibodeau. Derrick Rose missed the entire campaign due to a torn ACL, Luol Deng missed 2 games in the series due to an undisclosed illness and Kirk Hinrich was sidelined 3 games with a calf injury. Joakim Noah battled through flu-like symptoms and plantar fasciitis, which slowed down his activity level considerably. Brooklyn cruised to a 106–89 Game 1 win as Barclays Center hosted in first playoff game, but the wire-to-wire Nets' win was not predictive of the rest of the series. Thibodeau's crew bounced back for a 90–82 road win by holding the Nets to just 11 third-quarter points in Game 2. Chicago protected its home court in Game 3 by staving off a late comeback attempt by Brooklyn. For the first time in their NBA history, the

Brook Lopez meets the media during the Nets' first season in Brooklyn. *Photo by Dexter Henry.*

Nets had finished with an above .500 mark on the road (23-18) in the regular season, but playoff basketball at the United Center was a whole new ball of wax for Carlesimo and crew. Game 4 wound up as one of the wildest and most crushing losses in the Nets' playoff history. The three-overtime marathon was a scoring parade for Chicago's sixth-man extraordinaire Nate Robinson as well as Brooklyn's shooting guard Joe Johnson, who aptly carried the moniker "Iso-Joe" for being unstoppable in one-on-one situations. With 2:59 left in Game 4, the Nets held a commanding 109–95 lead and looked well on their way to tying up the series heading back to Barclays Center. The Bulls outscored the Nets 16–2 in the final few minutes, with Robinson exploding for 12 points. Despite the late-game collapse, Brooklyn had two chances to win the game in regulation, but Williams missed a contested midrange jumper, and Wallace's put-back attempt was blocked by Jimmy Butler. Robinson and Johnson traded clutch shots as the Nets' shooting guard tickled the twine with a midrange jumper to tie the game at the end of the first overtime. With fatigue playing a factor, each team scored just 6 points in the second overtime, and the contest was deadlocked at 127, now entering a third overtime. Robinson fouled out, but the rest of Chicago's lineup outlasted the Nets, 142–134. Back in Brooklyn for Game 5, the Nets were able to wash away the bitter taste of brutal defeat by powering their way to a 110–91 victory, outscoring the Bulls 33–18 in the final quarter. Williams and Lopez each posted a double-double.

The Nets carried the momentum they had built in Game 5, trading blows with Chicago. After three quarters, they held the upper hand at 75–71 in

Game 6. The gritty Chicago squad pulled to within 93–92 at the 25.2-second mark, with Nazr Mohammed punishing the Nets inside the paint. On the Nets' ensuing offensive possession, Blatche drew a foul and calmly drained both attempts despite fashioning a measly 68.5 percentage during the regular season. Brooklyn finally got the stop they needed after forcing a miss on a Marco Belinelli potential game-tying 3-pointer. The series evolved into a 7-game classic. The Bulls took on the personality of their resilient coach by jumping out to a 17-point halftime advantage in the series finale.

To its credit, Brooklyn refused to go quietly. A Lopez bucket shrank the deficit to 95–90 with 1:17 left, but the Nets failed to pull closer than 4 points in the final few possessions of the game.

In their first playoff season since the 2006–07 campaign, the Nets showed progress but needed to vastly improve if they aimed to ascend into the upper echelon of the East. Immediately following the Nets' playoff ousting, Billy King announced that Carlesimo would not be retained as head coach. The ensuing off-season can only be characterized as the hastiest in team history, as the shortsighted thinking of the front office, ushered along by an impatient owner, had reverberating long-term effects on the team.

14

BIG THREE ERA NO. 2 GONE AWRY

2013–14

When Mikhail Prokhorov took over as majority governor of the team in May 2010, he issued a public pledge to Nets fans that the team would return to the playoffs that upcoming season and deliver a championship parade within a five-year window. Prokhorov indicated that if his team failed to fulfill his promise of a title, the lifetime bachelor would vow to get married. This self-imposed "penalty" drew a few laughs, but it mostly elicited incredulous reactions from fans.

Prokhorov's playoff decree went unfulfilled, and the Nets were entering year four of the five-year championship blueprint outlined by the team's misguided owner. While Brooklyn was fresh off a playoff berth, it was far from the title favorite. Brooklyn already boasted the league's most expensive backcourt, and Prokhorov pushed all his chips to the middle of the table by paying hefty luxury-tax fees and parting ways with valuable draft capital to orchestrate a mega-deal with the Boston Celtics during free agency.

Prior to the draft and free agency, the Nets had a coaching hire to make, and while Billy King compiled a wish list of candidates to interview, it was Razumov's preferred hire who would ultimately gain approval of ownership. After the move to Brooklyn left some Nets fans in Jersey feeling like they were left in the dust, the former all-time legendary point guard who had electrified the Meadowlands, Jason Kidd, joined as the team's head coach just months removed from his retirement from the Knicks. Kidd's success with the Nets was well chronicled, but the cerebral, team-oriented leader endured a steep learning curve transitioning to the coaching profession.

Jason Kidd taking on Atlantic Division foe Kevin Garnett in 2007–08. *Photo by Andrew Bernstein.*

Kidd hired his former coach in New Jersey, Lawrence Frank, as his lead assistant and sounding board in his first season at the helm. For the first time in eons, the Nets were not a lottery team and instead held the no. 22 overall selection. King picked center Mason Plumlee from his alma mater, Duke. The Nets turned the page to free agency and, on July 11, signed backup point guard Shaun Livingston and re-signed Blatche. The next day, Brooklyn signed veteran forward Andrei Kirilenko, whom Prokhorov was familiar with. More importantly, Kirilenko had played brilliantly with Deron Williams in Utah. But that was hardly the most notable transaction of the day. Billy King announced a blockbuster deal with Boston that saw the Nets ship out Bogans, Brooks, Humphries, Kris Joseph, Gerald Wallace and first-round picks in 2014, 2016, 2017 and 2018 for aging superstars Kevin Garnett, Paul Pierce, sixth-man extraordinaire Jason Terry, D.J. White, a 2017 first-round pick and a 2017 second-round pick.

On the surface, the Nets were acquiring two future Hall of Famers, but Pierce (thirty-six), Garnett (thirty-seven) and Terry (thirty-six) were all well past the prime years of their careers. King did not trade a single All-Star from his team, but the Nets' General Manager failed to safeguard his future draft picks by not designating them as top-five or top-ten protected selections. The nine-player trade, which included the exchange of six draft picks, became the talking point of NBA pundits and fans in the immediate aftermath and for many seasons to follow. Another factor to consider surrounding the transaction was the exorbitant luxury-tax bill that the Nets' billionaire owner absorbed. As part of the acquisition, Prokhorov forked over nearly $70 million in taxes by virtue of the league-approved changes to the salary- and luxury-cap rules collectively bargained back in 2011 that went into effect ahead of the 2013–14 season. Prokhorov had nearly $170 million tied up in the team's payroll, and it's not hyperbolic to think that the Nets had genuine championship-or-bust expectations. Money and draft picks were no object to Prokhorov, as the Nets' trio of former All-Stars made waves at that off-season's media day, hosted at the Barclays Center. The 2013–14 training camp was truly a three-ring media circus, with the Nets garnering national attention for the splashy off-season trade with Boston.

Upon Kidd reuniting with the organization, now as a coach, the Nets planned to honor his playing career with the team by retiring his no. 5 jersey in the building's rafters. Since the former team captain wanted little fanfare and hoopla that would create more of a distraction for the Nets, Kidd opted to hold his retirement ceremony during the preseason, prior to Brooklyn's October 17 contest against Miami. Kidd would later buy a small stake in the franchise from minority owner Jay-Z to further illustrate his recommitment to the organization.

Joe Johnson, Kevin Garnett, Deron Williams and Brook Lopez (*left to right*) at 2013 Nets' Media Day. *Photo by Dexter Henry.*

Prior to his hiring by the team, the Nets' head coach pled guilty to driving while impaired stemming from an incident on July 15, 2012, when the Cadillac Escalade he was driving crashed into a telephone pole in the Hamptons at approximately 2:00 a.m. The NBA announced on October 4, 2013, that Kidd would be suspended the first 2 games of the season following the misdemeanor.

Brooklyn opened on the road against Cleveland, with the Nets suffering a narrow 4-point defeat. They regrouped and returned

Jason Kidd enjoyed his fair share of playoff battles against LeBron James. *Photo by Andrew Bernstein.*

home for a highly anticipated matchup with the Heat's big three of Dwyane Wade, Chris Bosh and LeBron James. There was no love lost between the two clubs, as the former Celtics and current Nets trio had endured epic playoff battles against James' Cavaliers teams and the super teams he spearheaded in Miami. To stoke the fire, former Celtics sharpshooter Ray Allen joined the crew from South Beach prior to the 2012–13 campaign, drawing the ire of Garnett and Pierce.

Miami was coming off back-to-back NBA championships and stood head and shoulders above the rest of the competition in the East. The first regular-season matchup between the newly formed Brooklyn Nets and Heat featured a playoff-like atmosphere. The Nets escaped with a 101–100 triumph. After the home opener and until the end of the calendar year, Kidd's crew floundered mightily. Brooklyn's offense was stagnated by a collection of aging talent devoid of athleticism. The team's former and current All-Stars were not dynamic acrobats or speedsters on either side of the floor. The result of this roster composition was a team that scored 100 or more points just twelve times over its first 31 games and looked two steps slow on the defensive side of the ball. Things got even worse for Kidd. He garnered attention for all the wrong reasons in the closing seconds of a 99–94 loss to the Lakers on November 27. Brooklyn's coach instructed second-year guard Tyshawn Taylor to bump into him and spill his drink to create a stoppage in play when the team had no timeouts left. Kidd used the delay in action to huddle up his team and draw a potential game-tying 3-point play. On the Nets' ensuing possession, Pierce misfired on a quality look from deep as Brooklyn lost the contest and Kidd walked away a bit lighter in the wallet after being fined $50,000 by the league.

Barely over a week later, Kidd grabbed back-page headlines again. He reportedly kicked assistant coach Frank out of a December practice when philosophical differences came to a head in a heated moment with his former mentor. The team announced that Frank would be reassigned from his assistant coaching role to avoid further conflict.

Brooklyn fell to 9-17 after a lackluster 121–120 overtime loss to Brent Brown's rebuilding Sixers on December 20. During the contest, Lopez left the game with an apparent foot injury, and the team later announced that the center would miss the remainder of the season with a fractured fifth metatarsal in his right foot. Kidd had to figure out a way to replace his most dominant offensive player on a team already struggling to produce points.

The Nets dropped 4 of the final 5 games before the New Year; their record sank to 10-21. On January 2, Kidd sent out a small-ball lineup with Garnett manning the middle, Pierce slotted as power forward and Joe Johnson as small forward to face a Thunder team with a 25-6 record led by Kevin Durant and Serge Ibaka. Williams outdueled Durant, with the Nets' point guard going for 29 points on 6 of 9 from 3-point range. The contest was knotted at 93 after an Ibaka layup with just six seconds remaining. Even on a team featuring two first-ballot Hall of Famers, the ball found the Nets' most clutch performer, Joe Johnson, who splashed in a jumper as time expired to complete the dramatic road upset. The win unleashed a passion and fervor that had been absent from the team's play since the home-opening win over Miami, and "Iso Joe's" bucket sparked a 5-game winning streak capped by another rousing defeat of Miami, this time in double overtime. Brooklyn continued its steady climb toward the .500 mark as it compiled another 5-game surge after a loss to Toronto on January 11. Johnson represented the Nets in the 2014 All-Star Game. Brooklyn continued its upward momentum in the second half of the schedule. Kidd shuffled through multiple starting lineups, including inserting rookie big man Plumlee in place of Garnett, as well as three guard lineups with Livingston starting alongside Williams and Johnson. After the All-Star break, the Nets traded Jason Terry and Reggie Evans to the Kings for Marcus Thornton, but Terry never reported to the Kings due to lingering knee issues that had hampered his production in his short time in Brooklyn.

The Nets were finally stabilizing after a turbulent first half of the season and for the first time improved to over the .500 mark during a 4-game win streak, capped by a March 5, 103–94 win over Memphis. Brooklyn secured the no. 6 seed in the East with a 44-38 record and, perhaps more importantly, defeated the two-time defending champion Heat in all four regular-season matchups, three times by 1 point and once by 9 in double overtime. Before the Nets could turn their attention to a potential collision course with Miami, the Raptors would give Brooklyn a less than polite welcome to Air Canada Centre in the opening round. Toronto General Manager Masai Ujiri uttered, "f--- Brooklyn" to the crowd during a fan event in Maple Leaf Square prior to the series opener. The NBA fined the Raptors executive $25,000 for his profane remarks, but Kidd's Nets dealt an even more stern punishment in Game 1. Brooklyn's backcourt combined for 48 points while forcing Toronto into 17 turnovers on its way to stealing Game 1, 94–87. The Raptors protected home court in Game 2. In Game 3 back at Barclays Center, the Nets nearly squandered a 15-point lead with four minutes left, but Brooklyn sealed it at the line late. Toronto put the defensive clamps down in Game 4 by prevailing, 87–79, and in Game 5 back in Toronto, it was the Raptors who nearly blew a late advantage. Johnson scored 8 of his team-high 32 points in the fourth as the isolation specialist drained a 3-pointer to turn a 91–69 disparity after the third into a deadlocked contest at 101 with 3:19 left. Toronto regained the fourth-quarter edge at 115–112 and fouled Blatche with five seconds left to avoid the Nets attempting a game-tying 3-pointer. Despite outscoring the Raptors 44–24 in the final frame, Brooklyn came up short and had its back against the wall, down 3–2 in the series.

In Game 6, the Nets raced out to a 34–19 first-quarter lead and never looked back. Back in Canada for Game 7, the Nets built a 10-point fourth-quarter cushion and were just twelve minutes from advancing, but Kyle Lowry dumped in 13 of his game-high 28, and Terrence Ross converted a layup with nine seconds left to close the gap to 104–103. On the Nets' ensuing offensive possession, Ross stole Livingston's inbound pass to Pierce and spiked it off Brooklyn's forward before he teetered out of bounds. After a Toronto timeout, Lowry split a double team from Garnett and Williams and darted into the paint but was met at the rim by Pierce, who rejected his running layup attempt to give the Nets their first Game 7 win in the franchise's NBA history. In a near-identical playoff path to the one they took in 2007 with Kidd as the team's captain, the sixth-seeded Nets upset the third-seeded Raptors, with late-game heroics carrying them through the series.

The Heat patiently awaited Brooklyn's arrival in South Beach for a semifinal matchup, with Garnett, Pierce and company suffering lopsided losses in Games 1 and 2. The Nets responded in Game 3 to stabilize the series, as six players reached double figures in scoring and the team shot a blistering 52.8 percent from the field. Despite Brooklyn fashioning the third-best home record in the Eastern Conference (28-13), LeBron James' brilliance was too much to overcome in Game 4 at Barclays Center, as his whopping 49 points powered the Heat to within one game of advancing. The Nets showed grit and resolve back in Miami, carrying a 9-point lead into the fourth quarter with Johnson going off for 34 in the contest on a wildly efficient 15 of 23 from the field. The rest of the Nets' supporting cast shot just 22 of 55. Pierce's 19 and Williams' 17 were among the few offensive contributions. Brooklyn held a 91–83 lead with 2:58 left, but Wade and James were unstoppable down the stretch. The Heat went on an extended 13–3 run to close out the series. A Nets squad with sky-high expectations set by an unreasonably ambitious owner suffered another early playoff exit. Garnett showed his age during the playoffs by scoring just 24 points total in the 5-game series against Miami. Billy King had the unenviable task of determining how to proceed with the league's oldest and most expensive roster falling short of its lofty goals.

15

BLOCKBUSTER TRADE HANGOVER

2014–15 through 2015–16

After leaving his future draft capital unprotected in the wake of unrealistic directives from ownership, Billy King was without a 2014 draft choice. The Nets' GM traded cash to Toronto for its second-round pick, Xavier Thames, and sent cash to Minnesota for its second-round pick, Markel Brown, along with cash to San Antonio for its second-rounder, Cory Jefferson.

Following the playoff run, Kidd initiated a meeting with the Nets' brass to request final say over the team's future personnel decisions, recognizing that the shortsighted philosophy responsible for assembling the team's current collection of talent was not sustainable. The Nets' brain trust rebuffed Kidd's wishes to supersede King's control of the front office and granted their coach permission to explore a trade to another club. Marc Lasry, Co-owner of the Milwaukee Bucks, who previously owned shares of the Nets, served as Kidd's financial advisor and convinced fellow Co-owner in Milwaukee Wes Edens to fire Larry Drew and replace him with Kidd. With King in desperate need of draft picks, Brooklyn agreed to trade Kidd to the Bucks for second-round draft choices in 2015 and in 2019. Just like that, Kidd departed on an unceremonious note, as his power-play move saw each side go its separate ways. Two days later, the Nets swiftly reach a four-year, $20 million agreement with former Grizzlies coach Lionel Hollins to succeed Kidd in Brooklyn. Hollins had a lengthy assistant-coaching career, having spent seven seasons as a Suns assistant as well as seventeen total seasons spanning the Grizzlies' relocation from Vancouver to Memphis as an assistant and then eventually head coach for seven of those years. The Grizzlies turned the corner under Hollins' guidance, clinching the playoffs in his final three seasons, including 18 playoff wins and a 214-201 regular-season record. The Grizzlies opted not to renew Hollins' contract following a Western Conference Finals berth, and King swooped in to hire him.

The first domino to fall on the Nets' roster came when Pierce left during free agency to sign a two-year contract in Washington. After his departure, Pierce's assessment of his time with the Nets was far from glowing. He publicly questioned the toughness and commitment of all his former teammates not named Garnett. One of the centerpieces of the blockbuster trade amounted to a glorified rental, with a singular seminal playoff series moment to his credit along the way. The further dismantling of the roster and attempted undoing of prior missteps became a theme of that off-season. King executed a three-team trade involving Boston and Cleveland, but this transaction centered on young reserve players with potential as well as draft picks. Brooklyn netted veteran point guard Jarrett Jack and Sergey Karasev from the Cavaliers in exchange for Edin Bavcic and Ilkan Karaman, and Brooklyn shipped out Thornton to the Celtics.

Back during the 2013–14 off-season, King and Rasmunov engaged with representatives for Bosnia and Herzegovina sharpshooter Bojan Bogdanović to buy out his contract with the Turkish club that held his rights at that time, Fenerbahçe Ulker. Nearly one year later, Bogdonović agreed to a three-year, $10 million deal to come to Brooklyn to replace Pierce in the starting lineup. The Nets re-signed Anderson to fortify the bench, and Hollins added Tony Brown and Paul Westphal as his lead assistants.

On June 26, the team announced a naming-rights partnership with Hospital for Special Surgery (HSS) for its planned seventy-thousand-square-foot training center located just one subway stop away from Barclays Center in Industry City. The HSS Training Center intended to open its doors in time for the start of the 2015–16 NBA season—although that timeline was shifted back slightly. The complex planned to feature an industrial façade to match the vibe of the Sunset Park neighborhood it would be situated in and, like Barclays Center, pay homage to the borough's manufacturing history. The top-notch facility's plans included a panoramic view of New York Harbor, two practice courts, an expansive weight room, a training pool, two hydro pools, a rooftop entertainment space, an eighteen-seat multimedia theater, a three-thousand-square-foot player's lounge and a media workroom. With the project already in the works, the Nets were fulfilling their plans to officially relocate all team operations to Brooklyn and away from New Jersey.

Left: Kevin Garnett showcasing his signature stare down. *Photo by Dexter Henry.*

Right: Bojan Bogdanović interviewed by a pool of reporters. *Photo by Dexter Henry.*

While the privately funded, world-class practice facility would be a major selling point to marquee free agents in the years to come, the team was currently mired in salary-cap hell with an underachieving roster. On December 22, Prokhorov bought out Ratner's remaining stake in the Nets for $285 million in cash and notes.

Brooklyn reloaded its roster with new pieces, creating some early growing pains. The Nets sputtered to a 4-7 record after a deflating triple-overtime loss to Kidd's Bucks on November 19 for a fifth consecutive loss. The Nets' backcourt of Joe Johnson and Deron Williams regressed in the scoring department during the campaign, just when the onus was back on them to pick up the slack. Williams averaged a near-career low 13 points per game and Johnson a near-career low 14.4. Lopez poured in 17.2 per contest to go along with 7.4 rebounds, yet the Nets' big man needed several months to regain his pre-injury form. The team's big-ticket backcourt was not delivering, and in December, Hollins replaced Williams, who had suffered a calf injury earlier in the month, with Jack in the starting lineup. Jack played splendidly, averaging 12 points and 4.7 assists, but the wins did not follow. The Nets were heading nowhere fast at 21-31 entering the All-Star break. Garnett still had a powerful voice in the locker room and a commanding presence on the floor, but the thirty-eight-year-old was showing his age, and injuries took a toll on him. King executed a key trade that shifted the trajectory of the season, sending Garnett back to the team that drafted him, Minnesota, for Thaddeus Young. The young power forward made an immense impact, averaging 13.8 points and 5.9 rebounds in 28 games. Brooklyn went 15-13 after acquiring him.

On the final night of the regular season, the Nets needed a win over Orlando and for Hollins' former club, the Grizzlies, to defeat the Pacers to secure the eighth seed. The Nets and Magic were tied at 75 heading into the fourth quarter with Brooklyn searching for a way to keep the dynamic duo of Nikola Vučević and Victor Oladipo at bay. Hollins' crew put on their best defensive performance of the season, outscoring Orlando, 26–13, in the fourth, with Bogdanović going for a game-high 28. Johnson and Young added 16 apiece in the 101–88 win. Memphis held up its end of the bargain, knocking off the Pacers, 95–83, to officially punch the Nets' ticket to the playoffs, their third consecutive trip.

Mike Budenholzer's 60-win Hawks team secured the top spot in the East and took the first two games of the series in Atlanta, with Williams missing a potential game-tying jumper in the closing seconds of Game 2. Williams scored just 2 points in Game 2 on 1-of-7 shooting from the field. Even though the Nets bounced back at home to win Game 3, 91–83, Williams had another dismal performance, shooting 1 of 8 for just 3 points. Heading into Game 4, fans at Barclays Center called out the former superstar point guard, with his face superimposed on posters and milk cartons with the words "missing" or "finder's fee" for his disappearing act.

Williams answered the bell with 35 points on 7 of 11 from deep to go

Nets warming up prior to Game 4 of the first round in the 2015 NBA Playoffs. *Rick Laughland/NetsInsider.com.*

along with 5 rebounds and 7 assists as the once-bitter home crowd turned jubilant. The series was now even after a classic 120–115 overtime bout. Shockingly, the Nets were 1 win away from pushing the team with the NBA's second-best regular-season record to the precipice of elimination. Brooklyn needed its star floor general to play at his Game 4 level, but instead he reverted to his early-series form by yielding just 5 points on 2-for-8 shooting in Game 5. Williams produced a mediocre 13-point output in Game 6 as the Nets dropped the final 2 games and were eliminated.

Deron Williams drew the ire of Nets fans prior to Game 4 against the Hawks during the 2015 NBA playoffs. *Author collection / NetsInsider.com.*

Williams' playoff-round performance was among the most futile for a former All-Star and certainly the worst for a Nets' star in franchise history. Outside of his 35-point outburst in Game 4, he converted 14 of 44 field-goal attempts for 36 total points in the other 5 games. Williams' acquisition on February 23, 2011, had all the makings of a franchise cornerstone piece capable of filling the void left behind by Kidd. However, two straight disappointing regular seasons and a miserable playoff performance later, and the honeymoon period was officially over. Even after the team doled out a $100 million contract during the summer of 2012 to re-sign him and hired close friend, mentor and former Team USA teammate Kidd to maximize his potential, the point guard's production, motivation and passion for the game were all in steady decline. So, while the Nets' late-season push to the playoffs and feistiness against the top-seeded Hawks were pleasant surprises, the more pressing concerns came regarding the tenuous future of Brooklyn's overpriced backcourt.

2015–16

Billy King selected Syracuse product Chris McCullough with the no. 29 overall pick in the 2015 NBA Draft and Pat Connaughton in the second round at no. 41 overall, with Connaughton immediately sent to Portland along with Plumlee for veteran Steve Blake and its 2015 first-round pick, Rondae Hollis-Jefferson. King was starved for draft picks and strapped for cash space, but the Nets' GM parted ways with two picks, a 2018 second-rounder and a 2019 second-rounder, along with $880,000 in cash for the Hornets' 2015 second-round pick, Argentinian guard Juan Pablo Vaulet. The Nets signed Young and Lopez to multiyear contract extensions, along with free agents Shane Larkin, Thomas Robinson and Wayne Ellington.

After four-plus seasons with the Nets, Billy King announced on July 11 that the team was requesting waivers on Deron Williams. The thirty-one-year-old played in 277 total games with the Nets and posted averages of 16.6 points, 7.5 assists and 3.2 rebounds while ranking fourth in franchise history in assists with 2,078 and sixth in 3-pointers made at 485. All told, Williams' run in New Jersey and Brooklyn never realized its potential, and he never appeared to embrace the role bestowed upon him as the face of the franchise. Under Williams, the Nets were a perennial playoff team, but King mortgaged the future on unprotected picks, while Williams and Johnson refused to leave any cash on the table negotiating their free-agent deals. After five playoff-less campaigns to round out the franchise's run in New Jersey, the Nets paid a hefty price to enjoy moderate success during three consecutive playoff runs in Brooklyn. Now it was time for the organization to pay the piper after trying to fast-track its success. Meanwhile, Prokhorov reneged on his facetious promise to get engaged if the team failed to deliver a title within the five-year window dating back to May 2010. The championship-starved fan base was less than thrilled with an owner setting the bar so incredibly high and coming up laughably short.

Unlike his cost-prohibitive and splashy moves during the last few off-seasons, Billy King focused on quality, team-friendly veteran deals, signing the no. 1 pick in the 2006 NBA Draft, center Andrea Bargnani, and veteran point guard Donald Sloan.

The Nets' attendance figures were underwhelming the first few seasons in their stunning new arena. During the Brooklyn Nets' inaugural year at Barclays Center, they finished sixteenth in the NBA in reported average attendance (17,188), compared to their dead-last ranking in their final year in New Jersey (15,868). Even after trades galore and free-agent spending sprees in the previous few off-seasons, attendance was trending in the wrong direction. The Nets dropped into the bottom third in fan interest by their third season in the borough. Brooklyn's regular-season win total, playoff success and attendance were all slipping, with King and Hollins left holding the bag. This correlated with several creative marketing efforts and promising trades failing to pan out. On November 5, 2015, the Nets announced the purchase of a D-League Affiliate (since referred to as G-League), naming them the

Long Island Nets and intending for them to play at the newly renovated Nassau Veterans Memorial Coliseum. The renovations to the arena were not completed in time for the 2016–17 season, so the Long Island Nets played at Barclays Center their first season before being stationed at Nassau Coliseum starting in 2017–18.

Brooklyn opened the 2015–16 campaign 0-7, with Joe Johnson's scoring plunging to uncharted depths at just 11.8 per game, while Lopez and Young became lone bright spots for a team that started 10-27 under Hollins. On January 10, the Nets officially relieved Hollins of his coaching duties with still nearly two years left on his contract and reassigned King within the organization. King was in the final year of his contract with the team. Lead assistant Tony Brown was named the interim coach, and Brooklyn compiled a list of candidates for the potential head-coaching vacancy.

The final 45 games of the regular season were not friendly to Tony Brown and the Nets. They went 11-34, including losing the final 10 contests of the year to bookend a dismal season filled with prolonged losing streaks.

16

REBUILDING THE RIGHT WAY

2016–17 through 2018–19

On February 17, 2016, the Nets officially unveiled the HSS Training Center to complete their integration with the Brooklyn community. In that same frenzied period, the Nets conducted an exhaustive search for a new General Manager to replace King, with the vetting process led by Rasmunov, who reported to Prokhorov. Just one day after opening the HSS Training Center, Brooklyn agreed to terms with Sean Marks, who had spent five seasons with the Spurs in roles ranging from Assistant Coach, Assistant of Basketball Operations, Director of Basketball Operations and General Manager of the Spurs' then D-League affiliate and Assistant General Manager under R.C. Buford for two years. Marks was five years removed from his eleven-year NBA playing career after originally being selected out of Cal in the second round of the 1998 draft by the Knicks. The New Zealand native represented his country at the 2000 and 2004 Olympic Games, yet his 2.8 points and 2.2 rebounds per contest NBA career averages don't tell the full story of his playing days as a glue guy on several title-contending clubs, including the 2005 NBA champion Spurs. Marks inherited a dreadful Nets roster devoid of draft picks or franchise-caliber talent outside of Lopez and with money tied up in all the wrong places.

The Nets had become the laughingstock of the league and fodder for critics—a case study on how to run a basketball team into the ground as quickly as possible. The Celtics were reaping the benefits of King's missteps and absurd directives from ownership to win at all costs. The Nets were

A glimpse inside the Brooklyn Nets HSS Training Center. *Rick Laughland/NetsInsider.com.*

headed for the NBA Draft Lottery for the foreseeable future, and all the draft capital that should have been retained to put the team back on course was left unprotected and sent away to Boston.

Marks' first order of business was mitigating the team's losses by waiving Joe Johnson on February 25, 2016, who agreed to a buyout in the final year of the six-year, $124 million contract. When Johnson signed his contract in 2010, it was the NBA's most lucrative contract at the time. The Nets' GM successfully negotiated the buyout of the thirty-four-year-old's $24.9 million salary for that season, with the Heat signing the veteran after he cleared waivers. Johnson's legacy in Brooklyn was mixed, as he emerged as one of the NBA's top clutch scorers and most-feared players in isolation, but like Williams, his game-in and game-out production failed to match up to his record-setting free-agent contract. In 288 games with the Nets, "Iso Joe" averaged 14.7 points, 3.4 assists and 3.8 rebounds, but unlike Williams, he elevated his games during the playoffs, averaging 18.3 points, 3.3 assists and 4.6 rebounds in 25 games with Brooklyn. The second poster child of the "Hello Brooklyn" backcourt marketing campaign was now elsewhere, and Marks wasted little time in undoing some of the damage from the prior regime. He honed his craft in San Antonio and adapted the template used for its championship teams, tailoring it to form a better culture in Brooklyn. The Nets' front office put added emphasis on advanced scouting, analytics and uncovering talent other teams may have overlooked both domestically and overseas.

There is no better example of Marks' keen eye for talent than his signing of NBA then D-League standout and nearby Yonkers, New York native Sean Kilpatrick. The Nets signed Kilpatrick to a series of ten-day contracts before inking him to a multiyear deal before the 2015–16 season concluded. The former Cincinnati Bearcats star flourished in Brooklyn, averaging 13.8 points in twenty-three minutes, an exponential leap from the mere 12 total games he had played in his NBA career to that point. Marks' thriftiness in finding diamonds in the rough would be a theme his next few seasons, as the Nets' key executive was a major impetus in what ultimately redefined the team's trajectory.

Marks' nuanced and resourceful roster maneuvering helped expedite the tedious process of pulling the franchise out of NBA purgatory. The Nets' executive took the lead in the quest to fill the team's coaching vacancy and exercised a patient and measured approach by not jumping at the hottest retread on the coaching market but instead sought after a coach with a penchant for developing young players to unlock untapped potential.

Looking no further than the Popovich coaching tree, Marks uncovered another hidden gem, Kenny Atkinson, who worked under former Spurs assistant–turned–Hawks head coach Mike Budenholzer in Atlanta. Prior to his three years with the Hawks, Atkinson was hired by D'Antoni to join his staff with the Knicks for four seasons starting in 2008–09. Atkinson received ringing endorsements from his former coaches and players alike as a tireless worker who was a stickler for fundamental play and demanded accountability from all his players. The Long Island native was an overlooked candidate for several head-coaching openings over the years, but Marks was resolute in leaving no stone unturned by appointing Atkinson as the right man for the job.

Among Atkinson's notable assistant-coach appointments, former Nets' backup point guard Jacque Vaughn joined the staff along with development coach Adam Harrington. Brooklyn completed its coaching search, and

Marks painfully watched his team draw the no. 3 overall selection in the 2016 NBA Draft Lottery, only to see that pick fly out the door to the Celtics as part of the infamous 2013 trade, with Boston selecting Jaylen Brown out of Georgia. The Nets were without a first-round draft pick, and Sean Marks acted swiftly to acquire whatever draft capital he could get his hands on by shopping the team's short list of assets. To that end, Marks sent Young to the Pacers for their first-round pick, Michigan phenom Caris LeVert, along with acquiring a conditional 2021 second-round pick.

A series of leg and foot injuries throughout LeVert's college career saw his draft stock take a major hit, and the top-tier talent fell to the second half of the first round and into the Nets' lap via the trade with the Pacers. At just twenty-eight, Young was the team's second-oldest player behind Lopez and, coincidentally, the team's second-most-productive scorer. During 2016 free agency, Marks extended qualifying offers to Portland's Allen Crabbe and Miami's Tyler Johnson, with both franchises matching the Nets' offer sheet, yet both players would ultimately land on Brooklyn's roster in the seasons ahead. On 2016 NBA Draft Day, Marks sent his second-round selection, Marcus Paige out of the University of North Carolina, and cash, to Utah in exchange for Seton Hall's prolific scorer Isaiah Whitehead. The Nets had a glaring hole at the point guard position, and they set their sights on Jeremy Lin, whose improbable rise with the Knicks during the 2011–12 campaign earned him the nickname "Linsanity." Lin accepted a three-year, $36 million contract to join Brooklyn. Marks dedicated the rest of free agency to inking unheralded veterans to team-friendly deals, including Trevor Booker, Randy Foye and Luis Scola, and he signed seldom-used 3-point specialist Joe Harris, who spent two years riding the bench with the Cavaliers after they drafted him in the second round in 2014. Harris would personify the kind of culture that Marks and Atkinson were trying to build in Brooklyn: a selfless player who was highly coachable and solely focused on honing his craft. The Washington State native developed a reputation as a fundamentally sound player when he was recruited by several college coaches, including Tony Bennett, who was at Washington State and then accepted a job at Virginia, with Harris agreeing to follow Bennett there. Harris enjoyed a wildly successful four-year run with Virginia, being named First-Team All-ACC during his junior year while leading the Cavaliers to a regular-season ACC title, ACC Tournament title, ACC Tournament MVP and an NCAA Sweet 16 berth in his senior season. Harris would not disappoint at his second stop in the NBA, with Atkinson's system and Marks' scouting creating the perfect situation for the young shooting guard.

To start the regular season, wins were hard to come by, but Atkinson had his team playing at a breakneck pace—in fact, the fastest in the NBA—as he adopted many of the principles of D'Antoni's "7-seconds or less" offense that he made famous during his run as head coach with the Suns in the mid-2000s. Brooklyn played unselfishly on offense, pushing the ball with pace up the court and shooting 3-pointers in bunches to stretch the defense. The Nets surrounded Lopez with perimeter snipers. Even Lopez, whose shooting range barely extended into the midrange, began expanding beyond the arc so that the Nets could create bettering spacing and therein driving lanes. On the defensive side, the Nets were the second-worst defense in the league; opponents averaged 112.5 points per contest, due in part to the team's hurried offensive pace and extra possessions it afforded its opponents. Atkinson and crew were just 6-15 in the early season. On December 8, they signed Detroit's former second-round draft pick from 2014, Spencer Dinwiddie. The Los Angeles native was a highly coveted prospect coming out of Colorado, earning First-Team All-Pac 12 honors during his sophomore season as the team reached the NCAA Tournament for the second year in a row. During his junior season, Dinwiddie suffered an ACL injury on January 12, 2014, against Washington, casting doubt on his playing future.

Dinwiddie's parents made education a main priority. His dad worked as real estate agent, and his mom owned a preschool after earning her PhD from USC. When still in high school, Dinwiddie's top two choices were Colorado and Harvard; many close to him nudged him in the direction of the Ivy League school to put him on the fast track to a high-earning job after graduation from a prestigious institution. Dinwiddie ultimately chose Colorado, due to the increased visibility and possibility of the basketball program to get noticed by NBA scouts and to fulfill his dream of playing in the league. Despite having one year left of college eligibility and falling down the projected draft board due to his serious injury, Dinwiddie opted to enter the 2014 NBA Draft pool. In his first two-plus years in the NBA, he proved that he had fully recovered from the setback to his knee, but he was barely afforded playing time, averaging barely over 13 minutes per game in Detroit.

Marks and the scouting department were able to identify the untapped potential in the lanky six-foot, six-inch ball-handler and locked him up to a three-year deal. Dinwiddie's play earned him 18 starts, and he averaged 7.3 points and 3.1 assists in 59 total games with a quick first step and straight-line rim attacks, creating a nightmare for opponents. Bogdanović emerged as the team's second-leading scorer behind Lopez at 14.2 per contest and was utilized as the valuable centerpiece in a trade that Marks initiated with Washington for Andrew Nicholson, its protected 2017 first-round pick, and Thornton, in exchange for the Bosnian swingman and McCullough. The Nets' GM turned his second-most-valued asset into the precious draft asset he so desperately needed. Following the trade, Brooklyn turned a 9-49 mark following a February 25 loss to Golden State into an 11-13 stretch to round out the year at 20-62. The Nets' young nucleus of LeVert, Dinwiddie, Harris and Hollis-Jefferson was coming into its own in Atkinson's greenlight offense, while veterans Booker, Lin and Lopez carried most of the scoring

Spencer Dinwiddie became a fan favorite during his time in Brooklyn. *Rick Laughland/NetsInsider.com.*

load. In fact, on April 10, Lopez passed Buck Williams as the team's all-time leading scorer at 10,444 points with a 25-point effort against Boston, which, ironically, wound up being his final game in a Nets' uniform.

Kilpatrick continued his ascent by dropping 13.1 points per game to finish third in team scoring after Bogdanović was traded. Under Atkinson, Brooklyn developed a leaguewide reputation as competing with exceptional effort to make up for its talent deficit and mental mistakes by inexperienced players. This work ethic and passion became ingrained in the team's DNA and represented a culture-changing moment under Atkinson's tutelage.

2017–18

In the 2017 NBA Draft, the Nets held three total picks by way of Marks maximizing a barren roster's trade assets. Brooklyn selected Texas big man Jarrett Allen at no. 22, Utah's power forward Kyle Kuzma at no. 27 and Sasha Vezenkov of Bulgaria at no. 57. As part of a draft-day trade, Marks dealt his lone blue-chip commodity in the twenty-nine-year-old, seven-footer, Lopez, along with Kuzma to the Lakers for Timofey Mozgov and D'Angelo Russell. All told, Lopez played nine total seasons in three different arenas, including the final two years at the Izod Center, the two-year interim move at Prudential Center and five years at Barclays Center. Lopez left as the franchise leader in several statistical categories: field goals attempted (7,998), 2-point field goals attempted (7,580), field goals missed (3,954, tied with Kidd), blocks (972), points scored (10,444) and offensive win shares, (33.8).

Through it all, Lopez maintained an even-keel demeanor and exhibited a constant sense of professionalism, even with his name rumored to be on the trading block the previous two seasons. The former Stanford star expanded his shooting range to attempt a then-career high 5.2 3-pointers per game in 2016–17, compared to his minuscule .01, .01 and .02 attempts per game the prior three seasons. Lopez only attempted 31 3-pointers in his first eight seasons with the Nets combined.

Throughout franchise history, the Nets had a lengthy list of All-Star point guards and wing players, but as far as true centers are concerned, Lopez left the organization as its unquestioned premier player. The player Brooklyn netted by turning the page from the face of the franchise was a superbly talented twenty-one-year-old point guard who Los Angeles made the second overall pick in the 2015 NBA Draft out of Ohio State. Russell's first year in the NBA happened to overlap with Bryant's swan song in the legend's twentieth and final season in the league. The Lakers' championship window was closed, and drafting Russell signaled the changing of the guard. But while his production for the first two years proved to be impressive, former legend–turned–team executive Magic Johnson was critical of Russell's leadership skills and ability to make players around him better. The young star reportedly did not see eye to eye with ex-Nets coach and then Lakers coach Byron Scott during his rookie year, in addition to other locker room issues in Los Angeles. The public critiques by his former club served as the fire and motivation that the potential franchise point guard needed to make the Brooklyn Nets chapter of his NBA career a success story.

Russell and Allen joined LeVert, Harris and Dinwiddie as the Nets' building blocks for the future. They would be integral parts for the team in the seasons to follow. Marks immediately signed Allen to a multiyear contract. The one-and-done starter at Texas tallied 12 double-doubles in 33 collegiate games, leading the team as a freshman in rebounds and blocked shots while scoring 13.4 points per game. The seven-foot rim protector was just nineteen when he joined the Nets and played in 72 games during the 2017–18 season while starting in 31 of them. Marks then dealt a throw-in from the Bogdonović trade to Washington, Nicholson, to acquire Allen Crabbe, who signed an offer sheet with the team the prior off-season. The

Nets completed another shrewd trade with Toronto by finagling veteran shooter DeMarre Carroll, a 2018 first-round pick, and a 2018 second-round pick for Justin Hamilton.

On the Nets' ownership front, during the summer of 2017, Prokhorov went public with his desire to sell a minority interest in the team. The Russian billionaire turned the $223 million investment he made in the team back in 2010 into an exponential growth opportunity in just seven years, to the tune of a $2.3 billion valuation in October 2017. To that end, Alibaba Group cofounder and chairman Joseph Tsai agreed to purchase 49 percent of the team, while Prokhorov maintained controlling interest in basketball and business operations for the next few years. The agreement included an option for Tsai to buy the remaining 51 percent of the team, but the parameters did not include ownership of Barclays Center, which Prokhorov retained.

Tsai was born in Taipei, Taiwan, and came to the United States when he was thirteen to be educated at Lawrenceville School in New Jersey. Upon graduation, Tsai was accepted to his father's alma mater, Yale, where he earned an undergraduate degree in East Asian studies as well as a law degree while playing on the school's varsity lacrosse team. Tsai spent the early years of his professional career at various New York law firms in roles ranging from tax associate to attorney before changing tracks and entering the private equity field as a general counsel at Rosecliff Inc. in New York. In 1995, he relocated to Hong Kong with the private equity firm Investor AB. It was there that he met future cofounder of Allibaba, Jack Ma. The two took the vision of creating an international importing and exporting marketplace and brought it to life. Tsai was among Alibaba's eighteen cofounders and was principally responsible for creating the financial and legal structure of the company. Ma and Tsai eventually became the two leading shareholders, and the Nets' new minority owner brought with him international business savvy and a prestigious Ivy League education to go along with venture capital and legal experience. Tsai's minority ownership role along with the emergence of Asian American NBA star Jeremy Lin gave the Nets' brand appeal in Asia and across the globe. Prokhorov remained front and center, but it would not be long before Tsai would succeed the Russian oligarch as the team's principal owner and operator.

Marks busily loaded up Brooklyn's offensive talent that summer, but once again the team's defensive deficiency reared its ugly head, as the Nets allowed at least 120 points on eighteen different occasions throughout the 2017–18 season, including a whopping 140 points in a 9-point opening-night loss to the Pacers. In that loss, Lin suffered a ruptured patellar tendon in his right knee after landing awkwardly on a layup attempt. The veteran was sidelined for the rest of the season. It was a cruel twist of fate for Lin, who was finally rekindling the magic he had discovered a few seasons earlier with the Knicks. Russell slid over to point guard in Lin's absence but played in just 13 games before undergoing arthroscopic surgery to his left knee. He did not return to the court until January 19. Russell led the team in scoring average at 15.5, while, remarkably, the Nets had eight players average double digits in scoring that season to illustrate the squad's unprecedented balanced-scoring punch and selfless play. Brooklyn was scuffling at a 19-40 mark by the All-Star break, but Atkinson's spread system made every player a threat, and his deep rotations gave the opportunity for Marks to evaluate the roster top to bottom. During All-Star weekend in Los Angeles, Dinwiddie won the Skills Competition by defeating Bulls' big man Lauri Markkanen in the final round.

Marks kept his eyes on the future by sending Booker to Philadelphia for Jahlil Okafor, Nik Stauskas and a 2019 second-round draft pick. He made a separate deal with Milwaukee to acquire a 2018 second-round choice. The Nets' brass was working on two tracks, building a strong future by acquiring draft assets and developing its core of young talent.

Russell flourished in his first season with Brooklyn, as Atkinson refused to treat the floor general with kid gloves, not hesitating to pull him from the game for repeated mistakes and even relegating him to sixth-man duties. Not a single Net was named to the 2018 All-Star Game, nor did any player on the roster have a single All-Star appearance to their name prior to joining Brooklyn. The Nets were a collection of hardworking, unheralded veterans mixed with hungry young players who earned leaguewide respect and admiration for executing their coaching staff's game plan. Brooklyn's 28-54 record was an 8-game improvement from the season before, with Harris, Hollis-Jefferson, LeVert and Dinwiddie all seeing their scoring averages jump precipitously to reach career highs. The encouraging trend for Marks and Atkinson was that the young core was just beginning to scratch the surface. The upcoming 2018–19 campaign would finally bear fruit for the new regime in the form of the franchise's first winning campaign since the 2013–14 season.

2018–19

Sean Marks scoured the international basketball landscape in the 2018 NBA Draft, nabbing Džanan Musa from Bosnia and Herzegovina in the first round, Latvia's Rodions Kurucs in the second round and Kentucky product Hamidou Diallo with his final pick in the second round. Free agency was set to open, and the Nets' courtship of Dwight Howard dated back to 2011. Seven years later, the organization finally agreed to a trade for "Superman." Marks sent Diallo, Mozgov, cash and a 2021 second-round pick to the Hornets for Howard. The Dwightmare was finally over, but as it turns out, Howard never wore a Nets uniform. The superhuman center wanted the opportunity to choose his own team during free agency, and Marks agreed to Howard's request for a contract buyout. While Nets fans felt immediate disappointment, Marks was acquiring Howard largely for his $23.8 million expiring contract to create salary-cap space heading into the following year's free-agency period. As part of the trade, Marks was able to wash away the $16.7 million salary-cap hit from Mozgov to clear the way for two max-salary spots for the 2019 free-agent class. Brooklyn was working every angle, building a widely admired culture, developing young players, compiling draft assets and clearing cap space to create roster flexibility for a supremely talented pool of free agents ahead of the 2019 summer. The long-term outlook for the Nets was rosy, but fans seeking instant gratification desperately wanted to snap a four-year playoff drought and see a difference in the win-loss column to validate the team's progress. Atkinson and Marks were ready to hand Russell the keys to the offense as the full-time point guard and elected to deal Lin and second-rounders in 2023 and 2025 to Atlanta for Isaïa Cordinier and a 2020 second-rounder. Lin's short run in Brooklyn ended, but the organization sent a clear message to its twenty-two-year-old point guard that Russell would be first in command piloting the offense. Marks continued piling up assets by shipping out Whitehead to Denver for Darrell Arthur, Kenneth Faried a 2019 first round pick and 2020 second round pick.

To start the regular season, Atkinson tinkered with starting lineups shuffling the core of Allen, Harris, LeVert and Russell, along with veteran journeyman Jared Dudley in and out for the first 13 games of the year. The team went 6-7 before LeVert suffered what appeared to be a catastrophic injury in the second quarter of the team's eventual 112–102 loss to the Timberwolves on November 12. The budding star landed awkwardly after a block attempt, and replays showed what appeared to be a gruesome right ankle fracture. With a history of leg and foot injuries dating back to his college days at Michigan, LeVert was stretchered off the court.

Luck was on LeVert's side. The team issued an update the next day revealing that he did not suffer any fractures but, instead, moderate ligament damage and a subtalar dislocation of his right foot that would not require surgery. Brooklyn's guard escaped a worst-case scenario, but the rest of the team floundered in his absence, going 2-11 over their next 13-games—including the remainder of the game LeVert left after being injured in Minnesota. Brooklyn lost 8 consecutive games to spiral to an 8-18 mark. The campaign that was billed as the Nets' potential breakout season was in serious peril of snowballing into yet another lottery-bound season. Atkinson's group strung together 7 consecutive wins after the 8-game slide with Hollis-Jefferson and Kurucs as new additions to the starting lineup, bringing energy and hustle. Russell played at an elite level, averaging 21.1 points and 7 assists, while Dinwiddie's game was on the rise at 16.8 points and 4.6 assists in a sixth-man role. On January 26, Dinwiddie opted for surgery to repair torn ligaments in his right thumb and was sidelined for five weeks, just when he was emerging as the favorite to win the league's Sixth Man of the Year Award. Even with their super-sub on the shelf, the Nets were finding their way with Allen's interior presence fortifying the previously porous resistance in the paint. He was blocking 1.5 shots per game to go along with 10.9 points and 8.4 rebounds. LeVert returned just before the All-Star break on February 8 and tallied 11 points, 5 steals and 4 assists in just under fifteen minutes of action. The Nets' bench was bubbling with enthusiasm as it featured unrivaled team chemistry and unity.

By the All-Star break, Brooklyn's record had climbed to 30-29 following an epic 148–139 triple overtime triumph over Cleveland on February 13. Russell was named a first-time All-Star, and Harris participated in the All-Star Saturday night's 3-point challenge. Harris became the first Net to win the 3-point challenge, making 26 treys, including hitting his entire money rack for 9 straight shots in the final round to outduel Steph Curry's 24 and Buddy Hield's 19. Brooklyn's dead-eye shooter proved that the contest outcome against a field of the league's premier snipers was not merely a fluke, as he went on to lead the entire NBA in 3-point shooting for the 2018–19 campaign at 47.4 percent. Dinwiddie was unable to defend his Skill Competition title due to ongoing recovery from thumb surgery. Russell scored 6 points and dished out 3 assists for "Team Giannis" while representing the Nets in the All-Star Game. The franchise had a representative for first time since the 2013–14 season. Dinwiddie returned to the lineup on March 1 for the playoff push. On March 19, Russell tallied a career-high 44 points as the Nets became the third team in league history to overcome a 25-point fourth-quarter deficit, besting Sacramento. Brooklyn snapped its playoff drought and clinched a spot with a 108–96 win over Indiana on April 7.

The Nets fashioned a 42-40 record to secure the sixth spot in the East and set up an opening-round matchup with Philadelphia. Marks and Atkinson boasted the franchise's first winning season since 2013–14 by systematically reshaping the roster, even with a problematic salary-cap situation, to finally produce winning basketball. Brooklyn split its four regular-season meetings with Philadelphia, but the Nets had no answer for Joel Embiid's dominance inside, as he averaged 30 points and 14.3 rebounds during those clashes, while All-Star Jimmy Butler, acquired in a four-team trade in the offseason to lift the Sixers into championship contention, burned the Nets throughout the regular season and in Game 1 of the series with 36 points.

Despite a lopsided matchup on paper, the Nets came out like gangbusters in the series opener, sinking 11 3-pointers on 26 attempts and making 24 of 26 free throws on their way to a 111–102 upset win. Russell and LeVert led the way in scoring with 26 and 23, respectively, while Embiid was held to 22 points on just 5 of 15 from the field. In Game 2, Philadelphia erupted for a 145–123 win as its former top overall pick in the 2016 NBA Draft, Ben Simmons, notched a triple-double with 18 points, 12 assists and 10 rebounds. During the first half of the contest, Embiid was whistled for a Flagrant 1 foul for elbowing Allen in the face during a post move. The Nets hardly appreciated the Sixers center's antics and their point guard chuckling about the play postgame. The seeds of anger and revenge were planted within the Nets' leadership. Brooklyn's veteran journeyman, Dudley, who scored 4 points total in the first 2 games of the series, provided bulletin board material for Simmons' side by calling the budding star's halfcourt game "average" heading into a pivotal Game 3 back in Brooklyn. Embiid sat out with lingering knee soreness; the crowd back at Barclays tormented Simmons with posters that featured his image with the word "missing" to reference his shooting deficiencies.

The Australian-born baller wasted no time in making Brooklyn regret its trash talking, as Simmons converted 11 of 13 field-goal attempts and 9 of 11 free throws on his way to 31 points with Dudley as his primary defender. Russell and LeVert again carried the scoring load for the Nets with 26 apiece in the loss, while Dudley failed to score in Game 3 but provided added fuel and motivation to the opposing side. Looking to even the series in Game 4, Brooklyn raced out to a 63–57 halftime lead even with Embiid back in the

Nets warming up prior to Game 3 of the first round in the 2019 NBA Playoffs. *Rick Laughland/NetsInsider.com.*

fold. With under eight minutes left in the third quarter of Game 4, Embiid took a hard foul on Allen that Dudley took exception to; he stood chest-to-chest with the Sixers' big man to chase off the bully. A scuffle ensued, with Dudley and Butler getting tangled, while Simmons shoved Dudley into the baseline courtside seats. Dudley and Butler were immediately ejected from the game, and the officials issued Embiid a Flagrant 1 foul. The riled-up Nets' faithful cheered on the literal fight its team was showing. After the dust-up, the Nets carried a 101–94 advantage to the 5:20 mark of the fourth quarter before Embiid splashed through 8 straight points on his way to 31 points and 16 rebounds. The lead changed hands seven times over the final three minutes with Mike Scott's 3-pointer with 19 seconds left putting Philadelphia ahead to stay in an eventual 112–108 final. LeVert dropped 25 and Russell 21, while Allen added 21 points and 8 rebounds in the losing effort. Philadelphia finished off Brooklyn back in the City of Brotherly Love, 122–100, as they led by as many as 37 points in the second half. The Nets came into the series like a lion but went out like a lamb. The exuberant young core got its first taste of heated NBA playoff basketball. The experience that Atkinson and his crew collected was immeasurable, but the upcoming off-season was filled with shocking developments in the form of superstar talent joining the team.

17

NBA BUBBLE-PANDEMIC SUSPENSION

2019–20

The summer of 2019 marked a seminal period in the history of the Nets, as Sean Marks' years of compiling draft assets and carefully crafting the roster to free up salary space culminated in undoubtedly the most exciting and, to many, the most unexpected free-agency signings to date. Historically speaking, the Nets were an organization that did not spend on or attract premier free-agent talent. Whether it was the acquisitions of Julius Erving, Jason Kidd, Vince Carter, Rick Barry or Dražen Petrović via the trade route, or drafting and developing Bernard King, Buck Williams, Kenyon Martin, Brook Lopez, Derrick Coleman and Kenny Anderson, among others, the franchise's legendary players seldom joined the team via free agency. John Williamson and Bill Melchionni were among the few exceptions to that rule, as they flourished with the team after signing as free agents. But while both players were terrific, they were not nearly the highly touted players with championship experience as the dynamic duo who joined Brooklyn that summer.

Marks held three total picks in the 2019 NBA Draft, with his lone selection in the second round at no. 31 overall, Nicolas Claxton out of Georgia, making the greatest impact in the seasons ahead. Claxton spent two collegiate seasons with the Bulldogs and was named Second-Team All-SEC in his sophomore year before declaring for the NBA Draft. Brooklyn traded its 2019 no. 27 overall pick to the Clippers for their second-round selection, UCLA guard Jaylen Hands, as well as a 2020 first-round pick. As is often the case when unforeseen blessings rain down from above, the stars aligned for Marks and the Nets to successfully recruit and ultimately sign game-changing talent that not only created a seismic shift for the team but also changed the landscape of the NBA for the foreseeable future. On July 1, 2019, the Nets signed Kevin Durant to a four-year, $164 million deal and Kyrie Irving to a four-year, $141 million contract, making the two max players and former NBA champions the new faces of the franchise. Along with signing the wildly talented duo, the Nets inked big man DeAndre Jordan to a four-year, $40 million deal on the opening day of free agency. Marks had an agreement in place but had to make some additional roster manipulation to free up two max salary roster spots by sending its no. 17 overall pick in the 2019 NBA Draft, Nickeil Alexander-Walker, Crabbe and a 2020 first-rounder to Atlanta for Taurean Prince and a 2021 second-round draft choice. Brooklyn's GM executed a three-team trade with the Spurs and Wizards that netted Marks Aaron White from Washington and Nemanja Dangubić from San Antonio, with the Nets sending the Spurs DeMarre Carroll. Marks' wheeling and dealing was not quite done. He then formalized the Durant move by agreeing to a sign-and-trade scenario with Golden State by signing restricted free agent point guard Russell and sending him, along with Treveon Graham and Shabazz Napier, to the Warriors for Durant and a top-twenty protected 2020 first-round draft choice.

The Nets were moving on from their twenty-three-year-old primary ball-handler coming off his first All-Star selection in Russell. His brief but powerful meteoric rise with the Nets saw him become a fan favorite in his two seasons with the team. As for Irving, the godson of former NBA great Rod Strickland, he grew up watching the New Jersey Nets as the West Orange, New Jersey native marveled at Kidd's teams' back-to-back NBA Finals runs. The chance for Irving to come home to the franchise he grew up rooting for was too much for him to pass up. Irving's father, Drederick, played under coach Rick Pitino at Boston University and played professionally in the Southeast Australian Basketball League, on the continent where Irving spent the first two years of his life before moving to New Jersey. Irving's high school basketball career blossomed at Montclair Kimberley Academy in the Garden State, where he led the program to its first Prep B state title before transferring to powerhouse St. Patrick High School in Elizabeth under coach Kevin Boyle and with future NBA player Michael Kidd-Gilchrist alongside him.

During his junior year, Irving led St. Patrick to a conquest of New Jersey's Tournament of Champions, but Boyle's program was barred from the state tournament in Irving's senior year due to holding practices prior to

Kyrie Irving at the Nets' Media Day in 2019. *Rick Laughland/NetsInsider.com.*

the start of the winter basketball season. Irving committed to Duke in October 2009 and played just one season with the Blue Devils under Mike Krzyzewski and suffered a toe injury 9 games into his stellar freshman year. Irving eventually returned to the court and led Duke to the NCAA Tournament's Sweet Sixteen round. He declared for the 2011 NBA Draft and was the consensus no. 1 pick by the Cavaliers as the organization was still reeling from LeBron James having left his hometown team during the 2010 summer free-agency period for South Beach. Irving earned Rookie of the Year honors and was named the All-Star Game MVP in the 2013–14 campaign. James returned to Cleveland in 2014–15 for his second stint with the team that drafted him. James, Irving and the Cavaliers clinched four straight NBA Finals berths and won the 2016 Larry O'Brien Trophy over the record-setting 73-win Warriors after overcoming a 3–1 series deficit.

The hometown title held extra significance for James, and now Irving was returning to the New York metropolitan area to try to replicate that feat with his own childhood team, the Nets. The newly signed point guard carefully selected a running mate to try to deliver on that championship promise.

Irving's partner in crime, Durant, served as the blockade to a trophy during Irving's and James' final two seasons together in Cleveland. The smooth-shooting seven-footer joined the 73-win Warriors, the same team his then-Thunder franchise held a 3–1 series lead over in the 2016 Western Conference Finals only to lose that series. Durant's decision to leave the Thunder—where he had spent seven seasons after being drafted no. 2 overall in 2007 by the then–Seattle Supersonics—was met with frustration from fans. The perennial All-Star joined forces with an already dominant Warriors team after he spearheaded the Thunder to four Western Conference Finals appearances and one NBA Finals berth, in 2012, when they lost in 5 games to the Heat.

After Durant captured his first two rings over Irving and James in relatively carefree fashion, his impending free agency was the talk of the league heading into the summer of 2019. The power forward's final year in the Bay Area was nightmarish. He left Game 5 of the 2019 Western Semifinals against the Rockets with a calf injury. Golden State advanced to its fifth straight NBA Finals round even with Durant sidelined. He made his return in Game 5 of the NBA Finals with 11 points in under twelve minutes, but as he attempted to dribble around Toronto's Serge Ibaka, he pulled up lame and sat on the hardwood clutching his right foot. A subsequent MRI revealed a ruptured Achilles; doctors anticipated he would miss the majority, if not the entirety, of the 2019–20 campaign. Durant's dogged work ethic and passion for the game garnered the respect and admiration of fans. But as an unrestricted free agent, the track record for athletes returning to full strength and regaining explosiveness following an Achilles tear was not all that encouraging. Golden State held out hope that Durant would re-sign with the club, but the writing was on the wall that he had one foot in the door and one foot out.

In anticipation of the 2019 free-agency period, it was the Knicks that were often mentioned as the landing spot for Irving and Durant among NBA pundits, yet the Nets were lurking and on the duo's radar throughout the entire process. Despite playing on opposite sides during their NBA Finals clashes while in Golden State and Cleveland, Durant and Irving had a kinship and mutual respect for one another, culminating in them agreeing to team up in the point guard's home market. Irving's brilliance was often overshadowed by James' larger-than-life persona in Cleveland, while Durant received more backlash than praise for lifting an already loaded Warriors squad to unprecedented heights.

In a league driven by star power and with a penchant for premier players teaming up to form super teams, Marks and company established the Nets as a free-agent destination. Through team building and developing a winning culture, Brooklyn finally turned the corner and made a quantum leap into the upper echelon of the NBA's power rankings. Durant and Irving coalescing their powers with the Nets sent shockwaves throughout the basketball world. However, attention quickly turned to Durant's Achilles rehab, his potential playing status for the upcoming season and whether he could regain the prime form he exhibited as the NBA's most lethal scorer prior to the injury. Marks fortified the supporting cast around the two superstars by inking Wilson Chandler and Garrett Temple as well as agreeing with LeVert on a multiyear extension. The 2019 media day was held at the HSS Training Center, headlined by Durant, Irving and Jordan holding press conferences and praising the Nets organization from top to bottom. One of the key question marks heading into the regular season was if Atkinson would adjust his coaching style to resonate with superstar-level talent. The Nets' head man already established a leaguewide reputation as a developmental coach who pushed young players to get better. Coexisting with and acquiescing to two players with otherworldly talents and supersized egos to match was a balancing act that Atkinson needed to delicately manage. On August 19, Prokhorov agreed to sell his remaining 51 percent ownership stake in the Nets for $1.35 billion and nearly $1 billion for full ownership of Barclays Center to Tsai. The Russian oligarch turned a $223 million investment in 2010 into a $2.35 billion team valuation, but to Nets' fans, his mouth wrote checks his backside couldn't cash with regards to his championship promise.

Kevin Durant and Džanan Musa (*left to right*) posing at the 2019 Nets' Media Day. *Rick Laughland/NetsInsider.com.*

Sans Durant, the Nets hosted the Timberwolves on October 23 in the season opener. Irving dazzled in his team debut, scoring a whopping 50 points. But he missed a potential game-winning jumper in overtime. Brooklyn dropped the contest, 127–126.

Through the first 11 games, the Nets managed just 4 wins even with Irving not just putting up career-high numbers but garnering recognition as a legitimate league MVP candidate. The Nets point guard's star power was undeniable, and his motivation level was high in his homecoming season, but the team's continuity was hardly at an optimal level. The supporting cast was guilty of simply watching Irving's heroics, outside of Dinwiddie's exceptional play as the team's sixth man. To make matters worse, Irving was diagnosed with a right shoulder impingement, which sidelined him for the next 26 games.

Dinwiddie gladly took on the scoring and playmaking load, while Harris, LeVert and Allen raised their level of play to secure a 13-13 mark without the newly minted point guard in the lineup. After a win in Irving's return on January 12, the Nets dropped 6 of the next 7 contests, with Atkinson's group not settling into clearly defined roles. It was somewhat baffling that the Nets were 7 games below .500, and speculation grew that Atkinson's job could be in peril if he did not right the ship in a hurry. Irving did his part. His 45-point, 6-rebound and 7-assist showing against the Pistons on January 25 came just one day before a tragedy struck one of the NBA's most legendary players. An eighteen-time All-Star and almost a Net savior, Kobe Bryant was killed in a helicopter crash in Calabasas, California, along with his thirteen-year-daughter, Gianna, and seven others flying to a youth basketball tournament. Reduced visibility and minimal cloud clearance resulted in the aircraft slamming into a mountainside in the early morning hours of January 26. Just weeks earlier, on December 21, Bryant had attended the Nets' and Hawks' contest at Barclays Center. He gleefully sat courtside with Gianna taking in the action and bonding over the game he loved.

Leaguewide, teams honored Bryant's memory, along with the other victims, by taking a twenty-four-second shot-clock violation in remembrance of his jersey number in the first games played after the accident. The NBA rallied together to mourn the loss of all the innocent lives lost that day. Irving, who was close with Bryant, left MSG before the Nets and Knicks were set to tipoff on January 26, clearly distraught in the immediate aftermath of a friend and mentor being taken away far too soon. Irving missed just 1 game and, on January 31 against Chicago, went off for a season-high 54 points on 19 of 23 from the field, citing Bryant's influence as the inspiration for what amounted to a tribute game to the fallen Hall of Famer. A California native and Bryant superfan, Dinwiddie changed his no. 8 to no. 26 out of respect for the former Laker as the league and its players paid homage to Kobe's legacy in similar fashion.

The NBA was shaken up by the tragic events, but in true "Mamba Mentality," the games went on as scheduled, with Brooklyn still underachieving and bad injury news pertaining to Irving coming down. He was sidelined from February 3 through the All-Star break with lingering shoulder discomfort. On February 20, the Nets announced that Irving would undergo surgery to relieve the impingement in his shoulder through an arthroscopic procedure that ended his campaign after just 20 games.

On March 4, LeVert dropped a career-high 51, with 37 coming in the fourth quarter and overtime to shock Boston in TD Garden, 129–120. He became the ninth player in franchise history to reach the 50-point plateau.

Three days after LeVert's monumental performance, the Nets were still sputtering along well below .500. On March 7, the team issued a surprising press release that Atkinson and the organization had mutually agreed to part ways. This was not the outcome Marks nor Atkinson envisioned when they laid the blueprint and foundation for a winning culture that brought them two of the league's elite stars during a historic free-agency period. After four seasons with the team, Atkinson amassed a 118–190 regular-season record, but the team's marked development and improvement from year to year was a signature of his impact on the team. For a multitude of reasons, that progression stagnated during the 2019–20 campaign, as Atkinson was unable to integrate the pieces around a score-first, dynamic All-Star in Irving. Vaughn was designated the interim head coach, with Nets' fans less than thrilled with the decision to move on from Atkinson. Clearly, irreconcilable philosophical differences in handling the team's lineup combination and roles brought about the divorce, but without their leader on the court and along the sidelines, the Nets had to find a way to fight back into the playoff picture. Brooklyn played 2 games with Vaughn at the helm with wins over the Lakers and Bulls before a macro-development interrupted the NBA season and changed the entire world as we knew it.

The Oklahoma City Thunder were hosting the Utah Jazz on Wednesday, March 11, 2020, in what turned out to be the most consequential night of the NBA season. Prior to tipoff, Jazz center Rudy Gobert tested positive for the coronavirus. Little was known about the virus at the time, other than that it was rapidly spreading to all corners of the globe. With fans packing the Chesapeake Energy Arena (later renamed Paycom Center) anxiously anticipating a compelling midweek matchup, Gobert's positive test result prompted NBA Commissioner Adam Silver to suspend the game and later the season, with thousands of perplexed fans instructed by the PA announcer to head to the exits. In the days and weeks ahead, the COVID-19 pandemic led to worldwide lockdowns. The Centers for Disease Control (CDC) issued requirements for face coverings and masks in all public places, effectively restricting and prohibiting mass gatherings of any kind. Over the next year, over 161 million people across the globe contracted the virus, which claimed the lives of nearly 3.5 million. Economic, social and political unrest unfolded across the world, most prominently in the United States, with citizens taking to the streets to protest social injustices and inequities. Without the distraction of attending sporting events in person or consuming them at home, the physical, psychological and mental impact of the coronavirus was felt by virtually everyone. For almost five months, the NBA went on hiatus, during which time the virus wreaked havoc on the world.

In a sign of the times, Durant, Dinwiddie, Prince and Jordan all tested positive for the virus and would not rejoin the team even when the NBA schedule restarted. Chandler opted out over virus concerns, while Sean

Marks signed veterans Jamal Crawford and Michael Beasley to fill the void left behind by the opt-outs. Crawford opted out just one week after signing with the team, and Beasley tested positive and was unable to rejoin the team after signing. Brooklyn was playing with a skeleton crew when the season picked up at ESPN's Wide World of Sports Complex in Walt Disney World Resort on July 31 with no fans permitted to attend the games. As part of the NBA restart, only teams within 6 games of the eighth seed in each respective conference or already holding a playoff spot were invited to play, making for twenty-two teams qualifying.

LeVert, Harris and Allen headlined the key players carrying the Nets through the restart. They would propel the team to a 5-3 record to capture the seventh seed and a playoff matchup with the defending champion Raptors, who featured a robust collection of talent even without 2019 NBA Finals MVP Kawhi Leonard. They included Lowry, Ibaka, Pascal Siakam, Fred VanVleet, OG Anunoby and Marc Gasol. The Nets played well under Vaughn, clinching a 7-3 regular-season record, but Nick Nurse lived up to his reputation as one of the league's elite coaches by capitalizing on the Nets' defensive deficiencies. Brooklyn was swept in 4 straight games, with Game 2 the only contest decided by single digits at 104–99 in Toronto's favor. The Nets were simply outgunned, outclassed and outcoached by the reigning champs. While a playoff sweep at the hands of an Atlantic Division foe didn't sit well with Brooklyn, Vaughn's crew had no reason to hang their heads during a tumultuous season.

18

CHAMPIONSHIP DREAMS

2020–21 to the Present

The 2020–21 season marked the franchise's ninth since moving to Brooklyn, its second-longest stay within the same host city and arena, trailing only the twenty-nine seasons the Nets spent at the Meadowlands. With the league calendar pushed back by over four months due to the pandemic-related suspension, the 2020 NBA Finals ran until October 11, the NBA Draft was held on November 18 and the league year was set to begin on November 20 for a shortened 72-game regular season. Teams accustomed to a lengthy off-season were expected to report back just weeks after the playoff bubble let out in Orlando.

The Nets had a coaching hire to make and explored several options, including retaining Vaughn and checking in about Popovich's availability. Even Kidd's name was floated as a potential candidate. Sean Marks shocked the NBA world when the team announced it was hiring former eight-time All-Star point guard and two-time league MVP Steve Nash to be the next coach. The former Santa Clara standout was six years removed from his Hall of Fame playing career but had no coaching experience prior to his appointment. Nash had served as a part-time consultant to the Warriors, and it was there he formed a bond with Durant. Marks spent two seasons playing with Nash under D'Antoni in Phoenix, when the point guard was taking the league by storm. Nash was inducted into the Naismith Basketball Hall of Fame in 2018 alongside contemporaries Kidd, Grant Hill, Ray Allen and nine others, including Nets' former GM Rod Thorn.

Right: Naismith Memorial Basketball Hall of Fame 2018 class promotion. Rick Laughland/*NetsInsider.com*.

Below. Steve Nash (*fifth from left*) of the 2018 Basketball Hall of Fame class. Rick Laughland/ *NetsInsider.com*.

Nash assembled his coaching staff in Brooklyn, with D'Antoni as his lead assistant and Stoudemire along the bench.

Brooklyn held claim to two picks in the 2020 NBA Draft and took Saddiq Bey, a six-foot, seven-inch small forward out of Villanova in the first round and Kentucky product Jay Scrubb in the second round. Both Scrubb and Bey were immediately traded in a three-team deal between the Nets, Clippers and Pistons. Detroit received Bey, Jaylen Hands, Džanan Musa and a 2021 second-rounder via Brooklyn in exchange for Bruce Brown. Scrubb was sent to Los Angeles for the 2020 NBA Draft's no. 57 overall pick, Reggie Perry, along with veteran shooting guard Landry Shamet among other moving parts between the three teams. Brown established a reputation as a hard-nosed defender and energy force off the bench, while Shamet's knockdown shooting was regarded as nothing short of elite.

Marks then inked a valuable veteran rotation player in Jeff Green to a one-year, $2.56 million deal. He had played with LeBron James in Cleveland during its finals run in 2018. Green was drafted three picks after Durant by the Celtics in the 2007 draft class and subsequently traded to the then-Supersonics to join Durant. Green spent parts of four seasons alongside Durant, one in Seattle and three in Oklahoma City, before being dealt back to Boston in 2011.

The Nets' GM had a convoy of reinforcements and healthy bodies expected back after injuries and opt-outs of the NBA's Bubble in Orlando. Irving, Durant, Jordan and Dinwiddie were back in the fold as the Nets geared up for the most highly anticipated season in franchise history.

Kevin Durant in his 2007–08 rookie season with the Seattle Supersonics. *Photo by Andrew Bernstein.*

Simply put, the Nets' championship hopes hinged on Durant regaining his pre–Achilles injury form and Irving staying off the injured list, along with Brooklyn's dynamic duo coexisting with a new coaching staff. Nash had a great rapport with both superstars having played against him during his playing career and then mentoring each after his retirement from the NBA. Irving always had an up-and-down relationship with the media, and after he refused to take part in virtual interview sessions, instead opting to write statements without taking questions, the league fined him and the team $25,000 each. Marks and Nash were able to work with the misunderstood player to sort

Kyrie Irving maintains a hot-and-cold relationship with the media. *Rick Laughland/ NetsInsider.com.*

through the issue in the best interest of the team. The Nets put out an early fire, but there were many more obstacles to come.

With the NBA season start date bumped to December 22, the Nets played host to Steph Curry and the Warriors on opening night. The contest would be Durant's first action since Game 5 of the 2019 NBA Finals, with fans anxiously awaiting his Nets' debut. Against his former club, Durant poured in 22 points in just under twenty-five minutes, while Irving led the way with 26 points in twenty-five minutes. Brooklyn dismantled Golden State without Klay Thompson and Draymond Green, 125–99. Durant enjoyed redemption against his ex-teammates in the opener, and on Christmas Day, it was Irving who tangled with Boston at TD Garden. He led all scorers with 37 points on 13-of-21 shooting and 8 assists as Durant chipped in 29 in the 123–95 shellacking of the Celtics. During a preseason meeting between the two clubs, Irving captured fans' attention when he was seen burning sage during pregame warmups in an apparent effort to cleanse any bad energy in the arena and bring his team luck. Clearly, the ancient Native American ritual, with which Irving was honoring his heritage, worked wonders. The Nets improved to 2-0 and had the league buzzing.

Just two days later, the first major injury hit Brooklyn, as sixth-man extraordinaire Dinwiddie suffered a partially torn ACL in his right knee in the third quarter against Charlotte. The backup point guard was sidelined indefinitely, but he left the door slightly ajar for a potential return in the playoffs.

The Nets held their first two opponents to under 100 points, a feat they accomplished only nine times throughout the remaining 70 games of the 2020–21 campaign. Critics poked holes in the Nets' defensive flaws, as not a single player outside of Durant, Jordan or Brown was known as an above-average defender.

Within the first month, Irving missed 7 games due to personal reasons, and the team put up little resistance on the defensive end. Nash's challenge was mixing between small-ball lineups and balancing the minutes between the veteran Jordan and the up-and-coming Allen at the center position. The

HSS Training Center poster features Kyrie Irving, Kevin Durant and their supporting cast. *Rick Laughland/NetsInsider.com.*

NBA, out of an abundance of caution, put Durant in virus protocol dating back to his positive test from March 2020 and listing him as inactive for 3 games starting January 5 in Utah.

Throughout Nets' history, virtually nothing was linear. The team had taken a circuitous route from Teaneck before landing in Brooklyn some forty-five years later. Nets' fans were accustomed to lady luck not being on their side more times than not. Dating back to early December, rumors were circulating that nine-time All-Star and three-time scoring champion James Harden was disenchanted with the direction of the Houston Rockets and made a formal request to be traded. The Nets were supposedly his preferred destination; he could reunite with Durant, with whom he played three seasons in Oklahoma City and clinched an NBA Finals berth in 2012. Harden's former coach in Houston, D'Antoni, joined Nash's staff in

Brooklyn, and Houston's former General Manager, Daryl Morey, stepped down on October 15 and was named President of Basketball Operations for the Sixers just eighteen days later. Morey orchestrated Harden's trade from the Thunder to the Rockets. The 2012 Sixth Man of the Year transformed into arguably the NBA's most lethal scoring option in nine seasons with Houston. With Harden as the team's centerpiece, the Rockets clinched four division titles, eight straight playoff appearances and amassed a 7-8 playoff series mark, with two Western Conference Finals appearances. Harden's teams were close to climbing to the NBA mountaintop, but after repeated playoff runs fell short, Houston cleaned house and turned the page by hiring former legendary NBA coach Paul Silas' son Stephen.

That franchise's cornerstone piece initiated a trade request in the off-season and did not report to the team's first two days of training camp before showing up on December 8 visibly disgruntled and out of shape. Harden appeared in just eight games with the rebuilding Rockets squad. Following a 117–100 shellacking by the Lakers on January 12, he put the team on blast in his postgame press conference, essentially intimating that his supporting cast was not good enough to compete in the league. To that point, the Rockets held firm on their intentions to hold on to their premier player, who was under contract through 2022–23, but Harden's brutally honest assessment of his teammates and organization in the public light forced Houston's hand. On January 13, the trade changed the tenor of the season for the star-studded Nets and rocked the foundation of the league. Brooklyn acquired "The Beard"; sent Allen and Prince to Cleveland; sent Kurucs, three first-round draft picks (2022, 2024 and 2026) and four first-round pick swaps (2021, 2023, 2025 and 2027) to Houston; and sent LeVert to Indiana. As part of the trade, the Cavaliers sent a 2024 second-rounder to the Nets, and the Cavaliers traded Dante Exum and a 2022 first-rounder to Houston. To complete the four-team monster transaction, the Pacers shipped Victor Oladipo back to the Rockets. LeVert's physical with Indiana to complete the trade was a hidden blessing for him, as it uncovered a cancerous mass in his left kidney. The mass was successfully removed, allowing him to return to the court on March 13 and quite possibly saving his life.

As for Harden, he reported to Brooklyn overweight. The Nets had parted ways with significant draft capital along with a young core of LeVert and Allen to bring him in the fold. Detractors pointed to Harden's defensive shortcomings and overdribbling as a recipe for disaster to pair with a score-first point guard in Irving and Durant's shooter's mentality. Nonetheless,

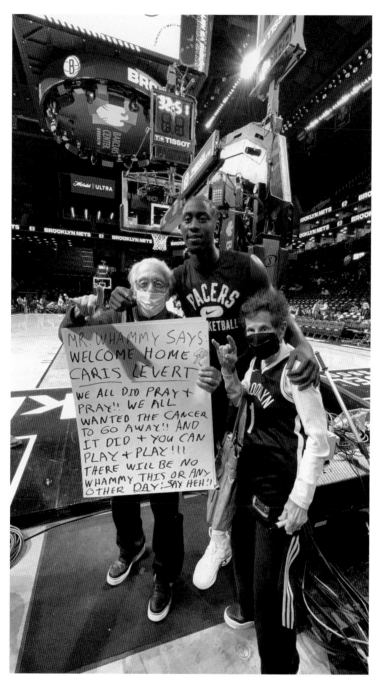

Caris LeVert greeted by a heartwarming message from "Mr. Whammy" at Barclays Center. *Photo by Doug Bearak.*

Harden's Net debut came on January 16 against Orlando, and he put on a mesmerizing performance at Barclays Center, tallying 32 points, 14 assists and 12 rebounds while committing 9 costly turnovers. Harden's outing was historic, as he became the first player in NBA history to post a 30-point triple-double in a team debut. With Harden in the fold, the Nets' newly formed big three looked to have a world of potential but needed game experience to develop a rapport and chemistry. Musical chairs with each of the big three in and out of the lineup made it doubly difficult in the weeks and months ahead.

The Nets were trending as one of—if not the—worst defensive teams in the NBA, and even after Irving's return to action following what he classified as a family matter, Brooklyn dropped back-to-back games to Cleveland to fall to 9-8.

From that point, the Nets improved with 4 straight wins and 5 out of 6 overall before hosting Toronto on February 5, looking to continue their forward momentum. It was announced shortly before tipoff of that game that Durant would not be permitted to start due to contract tracing regarding the coronavirus. Midway through the first quarter, the Nets' sharpshooter was then allowed to check in to the game after producing three negative COVID-19 tests within a twenty-four-hour period. After scoring 8 points, snatching 6 rebounds and putting up 5 assists in just over nineteen minutes of action, the four-time scoring champion was removed from the contest due to contact tracing. This was the second such virus-related disruption to impact Durant's season. He was placed on the inactive list and missed 3 games. Brooklyn's megastar returned to action against Golden State on February 13; he dumped in 20 points in a 134–117 season sweep of his former club. During that game, Durant suffered a left hamstring injury that was originally diagnosed as a Grade 1 sprain, but further imaging and MRI results indicated it was more severe than originally thought. All told, Durant missed the next 23 games. The Harden-led Nets went 19-4 over that span, including 12 victories in 13 tries.

Harden's signature performance came on February 16 against the Suns, as he helped the Nets erase a 21-point third-quarter deficit. Without Irving or Durant, Harden was masterful, splashing through 38 points, doling out 11 assists and ripping down 7 rebounds in the 128–124 victory. For the first time in franchise history, the Nets swept a West Coast road trip, with wins over the Warriors, Kings, Suns, Lakers and Clippers. On March 1, the Nets earned their first win in San Antonio since Game 2 of the 2003 NBA Finals, with Harden's 30 points, 15 assists and 14 rebounds spurring Brooklyn on to a 124–113 overtime triumph

Fans flock to the Nets Team Store during the record-setting 2020–21 season. *Rick Laughland/ NetsInsider.com.*

The Harden trade was already paying huge dividends, but despite a roster overflowing with talent, the Nets' big three could not seem to stay on the court together due to injuries, virus-related disruptions and personal issues. The Nets' frontcourt was the team's weakest link, and Sean Marks scoured the trade and buyout markets, looking to add savvy veterans to bolster the lineup. Luckily for Brooklyn, the Pistons bought out six-time All-Star and 2011 NBA Slam Dunk champion Blake Griffin. The former no. 1 overall pick in the 2009 NBA Draft, Griffin spent eight seasons with the Clippers and four with Detroit before signing with Brooklyn. He reunited with former Clippers teammate DeAndre Jordan. Both had been part of the "Lob City" era, with Chris Paul serving up alley-oops to the highflying big men with the Clippers. Age and leg injuries took their toll; after a stellar first season in Detroit, Griffin's numbers hit career lows.

Remarkably, one of the game's most electrifying leapers did not have an in-game dunk from 2019 until his Nets' debut on March 21 in a 113–106 win over the Wizards. Griffin's athleticism was clearly diminished, but his sharp outside shooting, tough-nosed defense and scrappy play made a major impact during the team's playoff push. Brooklyn's inside presence got another jolt when it signed the former no. 2 overall pick in the 2006 NBA Draft, LaMarcus Aldridge, who made seven All-Star appearances in sixteen seasons in the league. Unfortunately, the thirty-five-year-old played in just 5 games for the Nets before electing to retire due an irregular heartbeat that he was first diagnosed with back in college at Texas. Aldridge's abrupt retirement forced Marks to replace his production in the lineup; he inked former castoff-turned-Raptors G-league standout Alize Johnson to a contract after giving him a series of ten-days beginning on March 22. Johnson's season highlight came when he recorded 23 points and 15 rebounds on March 24 in a blowout loss to Utah.

On March 31 against Houston, Harden aggravated his hamstring and was sidelined for the team's next two games. Brooklyn's prized trade acquisition returned for a cross-town battle with the Knicks on April 5, but four minutes into the game he exited with tightness in his right hamstring. An MRI revealed a strain, and the team ruled him out for at least ten days; he would ultimately miss the next 18 games. Ironically, Durant made his return from injury on April 7 against New Orleans and for the second time in his career came off the bench on a minutes-restriction, with Nash backloading his minutes. On April 13, with Harden out and Dinwiddie sidelined indefinitely with a torn ACL, Marks inked thirty-one-year-old point guard Mike James to a ten-day contract. He had spent nine seasons playing professionally overseas, most recently with the EuroLeague's top team, CSK Moscow.

Brooklyn went 10-8 in Harden's absence, with a tangible asset of on-court leadership and playmaking missing. The Nets lost 4 straight games (April 30–May 6) for the first time all season, including back-to-

Blake Griffin and Kevin Durant during a stoppage in play against the Hawks. *Rick Laughland/ NetsInsider.com.*

back games against the Bucks to bump them behind Philadelphia for the top seed in the East and precariously close to falling into third, with Milwaukee hot on their tail. Brooklyn's training staff refused to rush any of its players back from injury. Harden finally returned on May 12 in a win over the Spurs. One game later against the Bulls marked just the eighth time all season the trio of Nets stars were on the court together. Brooklyn needed wins in its final 2 games to secure the no. 2 spot in the East. While Harden's shooting was noticeably rusty in his return from injury, his playmaking and scoring threat alone paved the way for 48 bench points by opening the floor for his supporting cast to propel the Nets to a 105–91 win in Chicago.

With Harden resting in the season finale, the Nets bested Cleveland, 123–109, to clinch the second seed and set up a playoff matchup with the Boston Celtics. Marks did not assemble a roster with Irving, Harden and Durant just to gloat about regular-season accomplishments. The new big three rewrote the team's record books. Irving became the first Net to join the 50/40/90 club, meaning he shot at least 50 percent from the field, 40 percent from 3-point range and 90 percent from the line. Brooklyn's big three played in just 8 games together and compiled a 6-2 record in those contests. Durant appeared in just 35 games, Harden 36 and Irving 54 in the shortened 72-game season, yet somehow the Nets finished with the most efficient offense in NBA history at 118.3 points scored per 100 possessions. Steve Nash was forced to assemble thirty-eight different starting lineups, a franchise record, while Harden tied Kidd's single-season mark for triple-doubles with 12 in just 36 games played. Irving's 92.2 free-throw percentage during the regular season topped Newlin's 88.6 for the best in Nets' history. The Nets locked up the no. 2 seed at 48-24 to secure the best winning percentage in the franchise's NBA history. While the Durant and Irving signings in the off-season catapulted the Nets into the championship conversation, the acquisition of Harden made the team the oddsmakers' favorites to win the title for the first time ever.

Fittingly, Brooklyn matched up with a Celtics squad that had stockpiled the Nets' draft picks over the previous six seasons. The Nets steamrolled Boston by double digits in Games 1 and 2, with Durant, Irving and Harden combining for 82 and 61, respectively. The Celtics salvaged Game 3 by way of Jayson Tatum's 50-point Herculean effort. Brooklyn's big three combined for 104 points in a 141–126 Game 4 win, with Irving stomping the Lucky Leprechaun midcourt logo as unruly Boston fans tossed water bottles in his direction. Brooklyn made sure there was no return trip to

Kevin Durant refining his shooting touch during the 2021 NBA playoffs. *Rick Laughland/ NetsInsider.com.*

Beantown, with the Nets' trio combining for 83 in Game 5 to advance to the semifinals against the Bucks.

Brooklyn had lost two of three regular-season meetings with Milwaukee, including in a back-to-back scenario on May 2 through May 4 opposing a cast of Giannis Antetokounmpo, Khris Middleton and Jrue Holiday with championship aspirations. Merely forty-three seconds into Game 1, Harden tweaked the same hamstring that had sidelined him during the season to mark an inauspicious start to the playoff round. Sans Harden,

James Harden during pregame warmups of Game 5 of the 2021 playoffs against the Bucks. *Rick Laughland/NetsInsider.com.*

who wouldn't return until Game 5, Brooklyn still prevailed by 8 in Game 1 and 39 in Game 2, a contest they led by as many as 49. Budenholzer went back to the drawing board, with the Bucks winning Game 3, 86–83. Bruce Brown missed a potential go-ahead layup with six seconds left, and after a pair of Middleton free throws, Durant misfired on a game-tying 3-pointer as time expired. In Game 4, Irving suffered a season-ending ankle injury as he was undercut by Antetokounmpo in the second quarter as Milwaukee triumphed, 107–96. Irving's injury was another devastating blow, yet the Nets got an emotional lift when Harden returned for Game 5 in Brooklyn. The Nets trailed by 17 points with under eight minutes left in the third quarter before a hobbled Harden scored his first points of the game to help ignite a 27–16 spurt to close the quarter down only 6. From there, Durant went off for 20 fourth-quarter points, including a dazzling shot from beyond the arc with fifty seconds remaining to extend to a 4-point cushion on his way to a colossal 49-point game. Durant's greatness helped swing the series' pendulum back in Brooklyn's favor. Aside from Green's 27 points and 7 3-pointers in Game 5, the Nets were living and dying with Durant's heroics. That show did not travel well on the road in Game 6, with the Bucks winning handily and forcing a do-or-die Game 7.

Just as he was in Game 5, Durant was magnificent in the series' final contest, splashing in 48 points, while Harden's mobility improved by adding 22. The decisive game came down to the final moments with the

Nets trailing, 109–107, and six seconds left. Everyone in the building knew whose hands the ball would find, and in true storybook fashion, Durant pivoted at the 3-point line, elevated and sank a cold-blooded jumper. Upon replay review, the tip of Durant's shoe touched the top of the arc, turning a potential game-winning 3 into a game-tying 2. Inches away from advancing on the back of their superstar player, the Nets had nothing left in the tank. Down 113–111 in overtime, Durant's potential game-winning jumper failed to hit iron in the closing seconds.

As stinging and painful as the loss was, Brooklyn saw its team fight through significant injuries, with Harden gutting out a Grade 2 hamstring strain and Irving's severely sprained ankle sidelining him the final fourteen quarters in the playoff round. Unfortunately, health, luck and the basketball gods were not on the Nets' side. Brooklyn's star power proved to be unrivaled, with Durant cementing himself as the NBA's premier player on the heels of his legendary playoff performance.

The Nets are still chasing that elusive Larry O'Brien Trophy, but with the wealth of basketball talent residing in Brooklyn, the brightest and most prodigious moments appear to be fast approaching for this once-nomadic franchise.

2021–22

The 2021–22 campaign, like so many in franchise history, was filled with dysfunction and self-inflicted wounds. Before drama engulfed the team in the regular season, Sean Marks pulled off another heist in the 2021 NBA Draft by selecting LSU's lethal scorer Cameron Thomas no. 27 overall at the urging of Nets' superstar Kevin Durant. The Nets then took swingman Kessler Edwards in the second round out of Pepperdine University along with signing undrafted rookie David Duke Jr. out of Providence later that summer. The trio of rookies developed into key contributors in the team's rotation during a tumultuous regular season that was nearly derailed by an injury to its top superstar, a disgruntled secondary star asking out and another costar unable to play full-time due to his unvaccinated status. Brooklyn selected Marcus Zegarowski with the no. 49 pick and forward RaiQuan Gray with the no. 59 pick to wrap up draft night. On August 6, Brooklyn completed a convoluted sign-and-trade to send Dinwiddie to Washington. The deal expanded to include five total teams and saw the

Nets receive second-round picks in 2024 and 2025, among other moving parts. Brooklyn then traded Landry Shamet to Phoenix for Jevon Carter and Day'Ron Sharpe, the no. 29 overall pick in the 2021 NBA Draft. Free agents Patty Mills, Paul Millsap, James Johnson, Bruce Brown, DeAndre' Bembry, LaMarcus Aldridge—who was medically cleared to return after his heart condition flared up in April 2021—along with Blake Griffin, rounded out a group of veteran reinforcements on the roster. On August 6, Durant led the 2020 U.S. Olympic Men's Basketball Team (delayed until 2021 due to COVID-19) to a gold-medal win over France, 87–82. In so doing, he became Team USA's all-time leader in points scored (435) for his international career. Hours before winning the gold in Tokyo, Durant agreed to a four-year, $198 million contract extension with the Nets. Kyrie Irving was eligible for a four-year, $181.6 million extension and James Harden for a three-year, $161.1 million extension. Marks insisted publicly that all three of his superstars would be locked up long-term by training camp.

When 2021 Nets' Media Day arrived on September 27, Irving and Harden had yet to ink extensions, and the media's attention turned to the cliffhanging contract status for the two basketball savants. To make matters worse, reports and speculation were mounting that Irving was unvaccinated, thereby making him ineligible to play in any games held in New York City or Canada. Irving joined Media Day via teleconference, refusing to address his vaccination status, while Harden told reporters he planned to re-sign with the Nets but wanted the opportunity to test free agency for the first time in his career. On October 12, Marks issued a statement on behalf of the entire organization that it would not allow Irving to play or practice with the team until he complied with local vaccine mandates. Irving remained unvaccinated and forfeited over $381,000 for every game he missed. Trouble was brewing right from the onset of the Nets' season, and now the prospect of Irving being eligible for most road games was out the window. On October 19, Brooklyn opened the regular season in Milwaukee, with the Bucks receiving their 2021 NBA championship rings. The defending champs cruised to a 127–104 landslide win over Brooklyn. The Nets jumped out to a 21-8 record, with Durant playing at an MVP level. But Harden struggled to regain the explosiveness he showed before his hamstring injury and failed to adapt to NBA rule changes that aimed to curtail his trips to the free-throw line. Record-wise, the Nets were sitting atop the Eastern Conference, but they weren't passing the eye test. The majority of the team's wins came against weaker opponents, while they lost the vast majority of games to upper-echelon clubs. On November 14, during a win over the Thunder, Joe Harris severely sprained his left ankle, which required surgery and a four- to six-week recovery period.

Durant logged the most minutes per game (37.0) since his 2013–14 season with Oklahoma City, due in large part to a slew of injuries to his supporting cast and with Irving ineligible to play. In light of these developments, along with Harden's balky hamstring flaring up throughout the season, the Nets' brass reversed course and allowed Irving to return in a part-time capacity. After missing 35 games, Brooklyn's point guard made his season debut on January 5, scoring 22 points in a 129–121 win over Indiana. Just ten days after the "Scary Hours" lineup was reunited for road games only (outside of New York and Canada), Durant suffered an MCL sprain in his left knee when teammate Bruce Brown tumbled into him against the Pelicans on January 15. At the exact instant when the Nets' stars were aligning, Durant missed the next 21 games with the setback. In its first 8 games without Durant's leadership, Brooklyn went 2-6, and the locker room started fracturing from within. Harden privately expressed frustration to his confidants about Irving's refusal to get vaccinated and reportedly did not see eye-to-eye with head coach Steve Nash regarding offensive philosophy. Mike D'Antoni, who served as the architect of Brooklyn's offense in Harden's first year there, left after the 2020–21 campaign to be an advisor with New Orleans.

Despite public comments to the media made by Harden, Nash and Marks refuting any acrimony in the group dynamic or any potential roster shakeup, reports began to surface about "The Beard" being discontented with the overall situation in Brooklyn and how he preferred to sign a long-term contract with Philadelphia following the season. There was growing belief in league circles that Sixers' GM Daryl Morey, who had served in that same role in Houston with Harden as his star player, would make a major push to sign and trade for the slashing two-guard come free agency. On February 2, the Nets fell, 112–101, to lowly Sacramento; an uninspired Harden scored 4 points and turned the ball over 6 times in what wound up being his final game in a Nets' uniform. On February 10, the Nets and Sixers agreed to a blockbuster deal just hours before the NBA trade deadline, with Harden and Millsap going to Philadelphia and Ben Simmons, Seth Curry, Andre Drummond and a first-round pick in 2022 and 2027 coming to Brooklyn. It was a stunning move, but one that made sense for both clubs. The Nets had a disgruntled player eager to play elsewhere in Harden, as was the case for the Sixers with Simmons. All told, the Durant-

Irving-Harden combination played in only 16 games together and went 13-3 in those games (8-2 in the regular season and 5-1 in the playoffs). The trio of stars formed an all-time superteam on paper, but a combination of injuries, inflated egos and vaccine compliance issues ultimately led to Harden going his separate way. Once the dust settled from the mega-deal, it became clear that the Nets addressed several key weaknesses on the team, including defense, rebounding and perimeter shooting, while the Sixers went all-in for a title, teaming Harden up with big man Joel Embiid. Brooklyn's title hopes were still realistic, but they hinged on Irving returning full-time, Durant regaining pre-injury swagger and Simmons returning to the court for the first time since Game 7 of the 2021 Eastern Conference Semifinals against the Hawks. Simmons was essentially banished from Philadelphia for his brutal offensive performance in that series, when he was reluctant to attack the rim and shot a woeful 33.3 percent from the free-throw line. The Australian-born point guard reported to Sixers' training camp for one day only before citing mental health reasons for not reporting back to the team. Simmons was the centerpiece of the trade for the Nets, and the twenty-five-year-old's lockdown defense, playmaking ability and knack for pushing the pace in the open court looked to pair well with lethal scorers in Irving and Durant. At the time of the trade, Drummond ranked no. 11 all-time in rebounds per game (13.3) and Curry no. 3 all-time in 3-point percentage (.440) to fill major needs for Brooklyn. During the 2022 NBA All-Star break, an injured Durant served as captain for "Team Durant," and with his final selection in the televised draft, he took Rudy Gobert over Harden to snub his former teammate. Patty Mills participated in the 3-point contest, but his 21 points wasn't enough to advance past the first round. During Durant's 21-game absence, the team lost 6 games in a row including Harden's final game as a Net and 5 thereafter. Mired in an 11-game losing skid, the Nets were spiraling into utter tailspin mode. One game after snapping the skid, Brooklyn completed the largest comeback in franchise history by overcoming a 28-point deficit against the Knicks with rookie Cam Thomas scoring 16 of his 21 in the fourth quarter. On February 22, Brooklyn signed veteran point guard Goran Dragić after waiving Bembry ten days earlier and with Irving still ineligible for home games. On March 3, the same day Durant returned from his injury to drop 31 against Miami, the team announced that Joe Harris would undergo a second ankle surgery, effectively ending his season. Another bump in the road didn't bother Durant, as he wasted little time in regaining MVP form and, alongside Irving, dismantled Harden's Sixers, 129–100, at Wells Fargo Center on March 10.

Brooklyn went 6-4 in Durant's first 10 games back, but the biggest news came on March 24, when Mayor Eric Adams reversed New York City's private-sector vaccine mandate for performers and athletes, making Irving eligible for all home games. That same week, Simmons received an epidural for a herniated disc but only resumed light shooting in the final week of the regular season, leaving the door open for his Nets debut in the playoffs. Astonishingly, by March 29, Nash had used an NBA record forty-one different starting lineups. Durant tallied three 50-plus point games, including 55 against Atlanta on April 2. Irving amassed two 50-point plus nights, most notably setting a new franchise record with 60 on March 15 versus Orlando. Brooklyn concluded the regular season winners of four straight to clinch the no. 7 seed in the East at a record of 44-38. The Nets became the first team in NBA history to secure a losing record at home, a winning record on the road and finish the regular season with an overall winning record. On April 7, the Nets waived James Johnson and converted Edwards to a standard contract, making him eligible to play in the playoffs.

The stage was set for a play-in game against the Cavaliers, with the winner facing the Celtics. At Barclays Center, Irving dazzled with 34 points on 12 of 15 from the field along with 12 assists, while Durant added 25 points and 11 assists to power Brooklyn to a 115–108 victory. Awaiting the Nets was a healthy Celtics team that played its best basketball of the season in the second half. Prior to the series, it was reported that Ben Simmons might be available to play starting as early as Game 3 at Barclays Center.

In Game 1, Brooklyn fell behind by 15 points at TD Bank Garden, only to claw back for a 2-point lead with just over 8 minutes left. With 45 seconds left, Irving drained a 3-pointer to provide Brooklyn with a 114–111 edge as he registered 39 points in the contest. Boston responded on its next two offensive possessions with Jaylen Brown attacking the rim for a quick 2 points and Jayson Tatum's spinning layup at the buzzer stunning the Nets, 115–114. Brooklyn almost stole Game 1 and was in the driver's seat to take Game 2 with a 17-point second quarter lead. From there, the Nets' offense was stagnant as Irving tallied just 10 total points and Durant 27 on just 4-of-17 shooting along with 6 turnovers to give Boston a second half lead it wouldn't relinquish. Celtics head coach Ime Udoka, Nash's former assistant, was familiar with what made Brooklyn's offense tick and threw multiple bodies at Durant to force him into tough shots and costly mistakes throughout the series. In Game 3, Irving and Durant combined to go 12 of 28 from the field for 32 points, 17 assists and 7 turnovers. Bruce Brown led all Nets scorers with 26, while Tatum's 39 propelled Boston to a commanding 3-0 series lead. Simmons was expected to make his season debut in Game 4, but he was held out, much to the chagrin of Nets fans. While Durant's scoring and playmaking got back on track with 39 points in Game 4, the Nets never led as Seth Curry added 23 and Irving 20 in the losing effort. LaMarcus Aldridge never saw the floor, while Blake Griffin played just 26 minutes the entire series as fans harshly questioned Nash's rotations. The disjointed nature of the regular season, including 43 different starting lineups, Irving's part-time eligibility, Harden's trade, Durant's MCL injury followed by him logging heavy minutes just to make a playoff push, became too much for Brooklyn to overcome that playoff run. Once the dust settled on a chaotic and drama-filled campaign, the organization remained unwavering in its commitment to deliver a title to Nets fans in New Jersey, Long Island, Brooklyn and around the globe. With Durant, Irving and Simmons in Brooklyn's arsenal, the Nets are well positioned to compete for multiple championships in the seasons ahead.

BY THE NUMBERS

COACHES

Max Zaslofsky	1967–69
York Larese	1969–70
Lou Carnesecca	1970–73
Kevin Loughery	1973–80
Bob MacKinnon	1980–81
Larry Brown	1981–83
Bill Blair	1983
Stan Albeck	1983–85
Dave Wohl	1985–87
Bob MacKinnon	1987–88
Willis Reed	1988–89
Bill Fitch	1989–92
Chuck Daly	1992–94
Butch Beard	1994–96
John Calipari	1996–99
Don Casey	1999–00
Byron Scott	2000–04
Lawrence Frank	2004–09
Tom Barrise	2009

Kiki VanDeWeghe   2009–10
Avery Johnson   2010–12
P.J. Carlesimo   2012–13
Jason Kidd   2013–14
Lionel Hollins   2014–16
Tony Brown   2016
Kenny Atkinson   2016–20
Jacque Vaughn   2020
Steve Nash   2020–present

RETIRED JERSEYS

Jersey Number	Player	Position	Years with Nets
25	Bill Melchionni	PG	1969–76
32	Julius Erving	SF	1973–76
23	John Williamson	SG	1973–77, 1978–80
52	Buck Williams	PF	1981–89
3	Dražen Petrović	SG	1991–93
5	Jason Kidd	PG	2001–08

FRANCHISE LEADERS

Games Played	Buck Williams (635)
Minutes Played	Buck Williams (23,100)
Field Goals Made	Brook Lopez (4,044)
Field Goals Attempted	Brook Lopez (7,998)
Three-Point Field Goals Made	Joe Harris (842)*
Three-Point Field Goals Attempted	Jason Kidd (2,377)
Free Throws Made	Buck Williams (2,476)
Free Throws Attempted	Buck Williams (3,818)
Offensive Rebounds	Buck Williams (2,588)
Defensive Rebounds	Buck Williams (4,988)
Total Rebounds	Buck Williams (7,576)

Assists	Jason Kidd (4,620)
Steals	Jason Kidd (950)
Blocks	Brook Lopez (972)
Points	Brook Lopez (10,444)
Triple-Doubles	Jason Kidd (61)

REFERENCES

Alibaba Group. www.alibabagroup.com.
Architectural Record. www.architecturalrecord.com.
Associated Press. www.ap.com.
Association of Luxury Suite Directors. www.alsd.com.
Atlantic Athletic Conference. www.theacc.com.
Back Sports Page. www.backsportspage.com.
Barclays Center. www.barclayscenter.com.
Baseball Almanac. www.baseball-almanac.com.
Basketball Ballparks. www.basketballballparks.com.
Basketball Hall of Fame. www.hoophall.com.
Basketball Reference. www.basketball-reference.com.
BBC. www.bbc.com.
Biography.com. www.biography.com.
Bloomberg. www.bloomberg.com.
Boston.com. www.boston.com.
Boston Globe. www.bostonglobe.com.
Britannica. www.britannica.com.
The Brooklyn Game. www.thebrooklyngame.com.
Brooklyn Nets. www.brooklynnets.com.
Chicago Tribune. www.chicagotribune.com.
CNBC. www.cnbc.com.
Dropping Dimes Foundation. www.droppingdimes.org.
Entrepreneur.com. www.entrepreneur.com.

ESPN. www.espn.com.

Fansided. www.fansided.com.

Five-Thirty Eight. www.fivethirtyeight.com

Forbes. www.forbes.com.

Forest City. www.forestcity.net.

History.com. www.history.com.

Inside Hoops. www.insidehoops.com.

Internet Archive. www.archive.org.

Island Garden Basketball. www.islandgarden.com.

Jewish Sports.org. www.jewishsports.org.

Kyrie Irving. www.kyrieirving.com.

Land of Basketball. www.landofbasketball.com.

LinkedIn. www.linkedin.com.

Long Island.com. www.longisland.com.

Los Angeles Times. www.latimes.com.

Main Line Times and Suburban (Philadelphia, PA). www.mainlinemedianews.com.

Major League Baseball. www.mlb.com.

Michael Hammel. www.michaelhammel.net.

National Basketball Association. www.nba.com.

NBA G League. www.gleague.nba.com.

NBC Sports. www.nbcsports.com.

Nets Insider. www.netsinsider.com.

New Jersey.com. www.nj.com.

New Jersey.gov. www.nj.gov.

New York Knicks. www.nyknicks.com.

New York Times. www.nytimes.com.

North Jersey.com. www.northjersey.com.

Patch.com. www.patch.com.

Pluto, Terry. *Loose Balls*. New York: Simon and Schuster, 2011.

Postive Impact. www.positiveimpact.net.

Prudential Center. www.prucenter.com.

Real GM. www.realgm.com.

Remember the ABA. www.remembertheaba.com.

Rutgers University. www.rutgers.edu.

Rutgers University Athletics. www.scarlettknights.com.

San Antonio Express-News. www.expressnews.com.

SB Nation. www.sbnation.com.

Spencer Dinwiddie. www.spencerdinwiddie.com.

Sporting News. www.sportingnews.com.

Sports Team History. www.sportsteamhistory.com.

Spotrac. www.spotrac.com.

Teaneck Library. www.teanecklibrary.org.

USA Basketball. www.usabasketball.com.

USA Today. www.usatoday.com.

Washington Post. www.washingtonpost.com.

Wikipedia. www.wikipedia.com.

Yahoo. www.yahoo.com.

Yes Network. www.yesnetwork.com.

ABOUT THE AUTHOR

Rick Laughland has been front and center in the New York sports scene, covering the Brooklyn Nets, New York Jets, New York Mets and New York Giants as a beat reporter for various media outlets over the past decade. Laughland's work has been featured online via FOXSports and CBS Sports, along with broadcast appearances on FOX 5 TV in New York, Sirius XM Radio, FOXSports National Radio and FOXSports Radio New Jersey. Laughland currently operates an independent Brooklyn Nets blog at NetsInsider.com, with syndication on Bleacher Report, Hoopshype and Yardbarker. Laughland currently serves as an adjunct professor of marketing at his alma mater, Fairleigh Dickinson University. He enjoys spending time with his family, including traveling with his wife, Kristen, and playing catch with his dog, Theo. In his free time, Rick can be found playing and watching the sport he loves most, basketball. You can reach Rick at Rick.Laughland@gmail.com for any comments or inquiries.

Visit us at
www.historypress.com